THE SISTER KNOT

THE
SISTER KNOT

WHY WE FIGHT,

WHY WE'RE JEALOUS,

AND WHY

WE'LL LOVE EACH OTHER

NO MATTER WHAT

TERRI APTER

W. W. NORTON & COMPANY   NEW YORK LONDON

For information about permission to reproduce selections from this book, write to
Permissions, W. W. Norton & Company, Inc., 500 Fifth Avenue, New York, NY 10110

Manufacturing by Courier Westford
Book design by Brooke Koven
Production manager: Julia Druskin

Library of Congress Cataloging-in-Publication Data

Apter, T. E.
Sister knot : why we fight, why we're jealous, and why we'll love
each other no matter what / Terri Apter. — 1st ed.
p. cm.
Includes bibliographical references and index.
ISBN-13: 978-0-393-06058-4 (hardcover)
ISBN-10: 0-393-06058-6 (hardcover)
1. Sisters.   I. Title.
BF723.S43A67 2007
306.875'4—dc22

2006024657

W. W. Norton & Company, Inc., 500 Fifth Avenue, New York, N.Y. 10110
www.wwnorton.com

W. W. Norton & Company Ltd., Castle House, 75/76 Wells Street, London W1T 3QT

1 2 3 4 5 6 7 8 9 0

To my sister, Marion,
and my favorite sister pair,
Miranda and Julia

CONTENTS

Contents

ACKNOWLEDGMENTS

This book is rooted in the idea that close relationships develop throughout our lifetimes. Any exploration of these patterns of development requires generous participation of people whose relationships are being recorded. Hence my first and greatest debt is to the girls and women who spoke to me about their sisters, who accommodated me in their sister groups, who ferreted out old diaries and memories, who revealed the complicated feelings that drove them apart and bound them together.

Intellectually, I owe a great deal to Juliet Mitchell, whose vision of siblings' role in the formation of the psyche has influenced my management of material. I have also been encouraged by her warm response to the use I have made of her groundbreaking work. Carol Gilligan helped me think through the ramifications of the sister knot in the complicated sphere of female friendships. Rebecca Kilner introduced me to fascinating studies of sibling behavior from a zoologist's perspective, including her own creative readings of sibling rivalry and cooperation in cowbirds. Helaine Blumenfeld highlighted the ways that having or not having a sister could lead to different friendship glitches. Anna Baldwin was always an active listener, careful to ensure that I combined theory and example. Colleagues at Newnham, in particular Liba Taub and Claire Hughes, guided me to examples and theories I would otherwise have missed. Michelle Spring and Daphne Wright, with their distinctive slants as thriller writers, each highlighted the warmth and the terror of these bonds. Soulla Pourgourides' generous excitement about the topic also helped to nudge a musing into a project.

My editor, Jill Bialosky, and my agent, Meg Ruley, have for many years been encouraging forces behind this book, so I feel that what developed is a team effort.

THE SISTER KNOT

INTRODUCTION

Why Sisters?

WHEN I WAS a child I was burdened by a secret that seemed to me at once strange and normal. The secret consisted of two parts: First, there were times when I loved my sister more than anyone else, even more than I did my parents. Though the bond had both a ferocity and a comfort I found nowhere else, it had no place in the familiar language about family attachment. The link I forged with my sister made me feel off center, even guilty, because it was outside all we had been taught about the pecking order of love. Honoring, respecting, and obeying parents were high on the list of moral injunctions, but bonding with, caring for, and appreciating one's sister were never cited in the rule book. Yet I thought about these issues daily, as my sister comforted me, rebuffed me, and presented herself as both an ally and a competitor.

Second, I knew that I often felt toward my sister something very different from love. It was overpowering, and it was awful. I eventually learned to give it the name "envy," but it was different from the portrayal of envy in TV soaps and in children's stories, in which envy was felt by nasty girls toward nice ones. The envy I experienced consisted of panic and of emptiness. My sister's virtues and talents called up love and admiration; they also slapped me hard, left me stunned, my head buzzing within a vast emptiness. This added to my guilt, because in its grip I felt capable of destroying the person I felt I loved most.

The special nature of sisterhood, and of others' apparent ignorance of what being a sister meant to me, dawned on me at the age of five. For some reason my sister, aged eight, was having a blood test. We sat side by side, the only two people in a row of plastic chairs that formed a formidable line against the corridor wall. It must have been summer, because I was wearing shorts, and the backs of my legs stuck to the seat. I kept shifting my weight in the chair, releasing with little "pops" the constantly forming films of sweat and skin. Eventually a nurse emerged from a room at the far end of the hall. Equipped with a tray, she marched toward us. On the tray a pipette and slides were laid out on a white mat as if they were valuable silver. Some awful medical-style banter followed: "Which one of you is the lucky girl getting the blood test?" She seemed distracted, eager to get this finished and move on to something else, something worthier or more pressing. Yet it took an inordinately long time for her to swab my sister's middle finger. "Why are *your* hands shaking?" she demanded of me. "Your sister's the one who's getting her finger pricked."

I froze and suddenly noticed that my hands were suspended in midair. I'd been shaking them frantically to ward off the oncoming pain. They now dangled in front of me like limp paws.

Ashamed, I tucked my hands between my sweaty legs and the sticky chair. The blood oozed out of my sister's finger and was drawn onto a series of glass slides. When a Band-Aid was placed over the puncture, I felt a rush of relief (no more blood), but I also felt dizzy and weak. When my sister stood up a chill went through me, and I burst into tears. The nurse's professional sympathy battled valiantly with her impatience: "Don't worry; we're letting you off the hook today," she assured me. My tears then were fueled by anger and confusion: What difference did it make whether the target of her needle was me or my sister?

I took away from that medical center the knowledge that what I felt for my sister was not part of every person's ordinary world. Weird, I thought, what some people just didn't get.

But there is another side to the empathy and identification I have with my sister. From the birth of my consciousness, she was a presence in my life, a superior being who laughed with good-natured condescension at my compulsive efforts to challenge her. In early childhood my greatest pleasure was to be in her company, but her capacity to entertain and delight others aroused my profound anxiety. Even today, whether she is telling a joke, decorating a house, or performing surgery, I find I am partly admiring her wit, her creativity, or her skill; but I am also locked in a room whose features I wish to ignore. Its walls are charged with the meanness and rage of envy. In that room I breath a soulless air that smothers any assurance as to my own abilities, connections, and status. The feeling is primitive and terrifying, and, while I contain it with increasing success as I grow older, it casts a long shadow. I felt it in school, among my classmates, whose various qualities were apt to attack me with surgical precision. Even among my closest friends, for whom I had genuine affection, envy sliced into me, striking where it hurt most. It had immense strength but could not be justified by the context in which I experienced it. An ancient battle was being fought, and at stake was my very existence.

For most of my life I assumed I was alone when I stood in this terrible place that was devoid of good feelings. But when I began interviewing women about their sisters, I learned that others, as children, had shared this room with me. Looking back on her childhood with two younger sisters, Jane, now in her thirties, says, "I would lie in bed and hear her breathing, and be terrified that in my sleep I would get up and kill her. I tried to stay awake to prevent this." And Elsa, thinking about the impact that having a second child might have on her first daughter, explains the dichotomy of delight and envy. "My life expanded like a rubber band when I was in the same room with her. She always looked at things in a way that made them more significant. The world was just a busier place with her around. I'd look at the cat and see my little sister watching the cat, and suddenly the cat was more interesting. She'd look at it with that shivering concentration, and it came to life in ways I'd never see by myself. But my delight in her ate me up inside. So there was this oddity—everything was bigger, but I had no room to breathe."

With sisters we learn one of the most disturbing lessons about human connection—that we can love and hate the same person. This amalgam of feelings, apparently so good and apparently so bad, has been noted in the combined dependence and love, rage and resentment we may feel, particularly in infancy,[1] toward a parent. The combination of dependence and the rage at what a parent might withhold does indeed make a mark on our interpersonal responses, but there is a range of other lifelong concerns that child-to-parent attachments do not explain. The power of our mixed feelings toward other women, the unease about our own status and achievement that so many of us experience in the presence of our sisters, and in the presence of our more extended sisterhood of female friends—even when we are wise enough and old enough to know better—casts a mysterious shadow over all theories of psychological development, particularly as they apply to women. Recently this shadow has been lifted by Juliet Mitchell's presentation and analysis of the sibling trauma, wherein she reveals the abiding psychological impact of our multiple feelings toward siblings.[2]

Sibling relations, Mitchell explains, prioritize experiences that are more salient in women, such as fear of the loss of love, and fear of annihilation through personal rejection.[3] Uncovering the power of sibling relationships provides new explanations of female connection, identity, and conflict.

*   *   *

My approach as a psychologist rests on a continuing effort to explore how we come to understand ourselves, including our deepest attachments and anxieties. The methods I have used to gather the data on sisters are varied, but they rest on the premise that the best sources of information about the impact and nature of sister relationships are sisters themselves. I interviewed seventy-six sisters, ranging in age from five to seventy-one. The sisters came from thirty-seven family groups; in twelve of these families there were also brothers.[4] In addition I asked the participating girls and women for written or recorded reflections on their experiences of being a sister and having a sister. At some points I referred to material from previous work I had done on girls' friendships and cliques,[5] and I drew on my own experience. I build on new theories of sibling relationships that change forever assumptions about the development of our understanding and emotions.

I begin at what seems like the beginning: a girl's awareness that she has a sister. This experience will be very different for an older and for a younger sister, but basic and significant similarities emerge. The powerful realization that I am not unique of my kind is experienced within the context of many other relationships. In the first three chapters I present new psychoanalytic theories of the sibling trauma, and explain its special impact on girls and women.

Having shown that sibling rivalry, in its most primitive form, is experienced as a threat to one's self, I follow, in the fourth chapter, the birth of human understanding, and present research on the role siblings (often still in a triangular relationship with a parent) take in expanding our awareness of others' thoughts and feelings. Self-awareness then refines distinctions between self and other, me and my sister; the "borderwork"[6] we do to discover and maintain these distinctions is explored in the fifth chapter, " 'Just Like' and 'Completely Different.' "

However strategic girls are in differentiating themselves from a sister, there remains a ferocious impulse to protect. This is perhaps the most striking omission in psychological theory about sibling relationships. The tug to protect a sister—because we empathize with her, because we take on roles as ally and carer, because she belongs to us and is like us—is on the same rope that jerks us into resentment that someone so like us, a peer, should have more than, or something different from, us. So, in chapter 6, I explore the themes of protectiveness and resentment, ranging from daily dangers and defenses to those special circumstances when one sister's condition demands more family resources. An autistic sister, an anorexic sister, a sister suffering from cancer—such conditions throw family dynamics into a spin. Here, too, sisters' jealousy collides with protectiveness. In this context sisters describe a bewildering vacillation between love and resentment.

In the seventh chapter, "Sisters and Friends," I explore the frequent and telling cross-references between sister ties and girls' friendships. I explain why "sisterhood" and "sister" are apt metaphors for a whole range of female friendships, and why the dynamics of sistering can easily be shared by girls and women who have never had a sister. But I also distinguish between the actual sister bond and the sister associations of female friendships. Girls' friendships do not quite parallel sister relationships. At different phases of childhood and adolescence, girls act out different aspects of the sibling trauma. Sisterhood is also a productive metaphor for a social and political movement, but at times the motive to valorize relationships between women for social or political ends has increased the unease surrounding familiar bitter rivalries and resentments. Romantic visions of an all-embracing sisterhood neglect the complex frictions and uneven love among biological sisters. When these are ignored and remain unexplained, they become sources of guilt instead of real points we can manage in our real attachments.

All relationships are influenced by the human environment in which they are developed and enacted, and in chapter 8 I look at sistering as a subgroup that functions within the larger family group, sometimes by enforcing the more dominant family dynamics and sometimes by lodging an effective resistance. Often, even before they have the ability to describe the uncomfortable patterns they see enacted in their families, sisters act together to interrupt family patterns that constrain or harm them. I discovered that sisters, in adolescence and adulthood, cross-check their family stories: "Did that really happen?" and "Why did she do that?" and "Who really was to blame?" In chapter 9 I look at how sisters sometimes collaborate over family stories. However, given the intimate link between our sense of self and our family stories, sisters are sometimes divided by their different accounts of family histories and motives.

In chapter 10, I turn to long-standing and disturbing questions about our ability to enjoy the success of someone close to us, and take readings of these in the context of the sister knot. The discomfort girls and women often feel in dealing with a highly successful sister illuminates problems familiar to many women as they negotiate status with other women. In exploring the complex and powerful relationship between sisters, we can understand the basis of common tensions between women as remnants of the sister knot that are caught up in contemporary puzzles about our own status within the family and in the wider social worlds.

The sister bond is negotiated throughout one's life, and in the final chapter, "Sistering: A Lifelong Tie," I examine the positive force of this bond in the later stages of life, and the lingering effects of grief at a sister's death. The voices of older women confirm that sisters root us in our past and enliven our old age.

WHY ONLY SISTERS?

AN OBVIOUS QUESTION that arises from my approach is, Why are you looking only at sisters? Where are the brothers in this?

My answer is threefold.

First, while the long-established habit of leaving girls and women out of broad-brush psychological theories has been shaken and shamed in the past few decades,[7] it is still possible to present brand-new theories of sibling effects and peer influence on human development with reference to brothers and to men, while noting in passing that girls and women are "an anomaly,"[8] or that one's conclusions could never be supported by studying girls.[9] An obvious retort by any psychologist is that we have to study girls and women to see what general theories of development might then emerge.

Second, as well as refining new research and theory to highlight the special features of sistering, the aim of this book is to challenge some common assumptions in the psychology of women. Once fresh and revelatory, some tenets of female psychology have become worn smooth with repetition and simplification.

During the past three decades, as awareness of girls' and women's special developmental patterns has grown, attention has focused on girls' sense of self as connected and similar to others. So, too, attention has been drawn to girls' capacity for interpersonal skills, including their ability to empathize and to cooperate with others. What has often been ignored, however, is girls' and women's strategic resistance to identification with others and their persistence in defining themselves as different from others. When we bring sistering into the framework of female psychology, we can see that girls and women are eager to establish themselves as different and special.

We can also see, as we look at the sister knot, that while girls and women are primed to care for others, they are also primed to assess the cost of such care to themselves and to look out for themselves. In this way pallid assumptions about girls' and women's empathizing skills take on a new dimension, with the consequence that the polarity so often presented between men's and women's psychological leanings shifts to a more subtle position. The sister knot reveals empathy as a complex device used for control and denigration as often as for care and protection. In this light skills that may be more easily acquired by women, and preferences that may be more often demonstrated by women, lead to multiple behaviors with multiple ends.

Third, an important consequence of revising psychological theory with reference to the sister knot is the integration of opposing views on bonds between women. During the past decade, there have been best-selling books extolling the endurance of female bonds;[10] these have been followed by best-selling books uncovering the cruelties expressed in those same attachments.[11] The passionate bonds between girls and women are either idealized or demonized. On the one hand girls together or women together are described as intimate, consoling, supportive; on the other hand the bonds that hold girls and women together are seen as weapons in disguise. A hidden culture of aggression has been revealed in the life of "mean girls," whether in the primary school playground as they tease and taunt, or in the high school lunchroom as they gossip and condemn, or in the corporate boardroom as they judge and exclude.[12] Transfixed by this subtext of apparently friendly societies, female solidarity appears as a social veneer or a disguise of a base backstabbing relationship. The split perspective—loving versus destructive, nice versus nasty—signals a broken vision. Nothing marks more clearly our failure to understand something as does this either/or approach, this wonderful/terrible debate. And we have got it wrong because we have left the sister story out of the picture.

What we see changes when we bring in the story of sistering.[13] What we feel as sisters and how we manage these feelings allow us to see simultaneously the love and envy inherent in female connection. Sistering, as Melanie Mauthner reflects, "is as fundamental as mothering and daughtering in the construction of feminine subjectivity."[14] Girls' experiences of connection with other girls inform their sense of identity as girls and as women, as people with the power to care for and love others, as people who have to defend their own desires and pursue their own goals.

In unraveling love and rivalry between sisters, we take a new look at all strong attachments among women; we take note of the abiding conflict and ambivalence in all human attachments; and we bring into women's psychology a much-needed multidimensionality.

1

The Power of
Complicated Feelings

"WHY HAVE YOU ruined my life?" is a question familiar to anyone who has witnessed a first-born's outrage and bewilderment during the process of accommodating a newborn into the family.[1] It is not that the new baby is unloved or unappreciated. Most children are baby-loving creatures. They are fascinated by an infant's intensely purposeful movements. They are delighted when they themselves elicit a response from that sensitive creature. Older children tend to be protective and proud of their new sibling; they exhibit concern and offer comfort when "their" baby cries. Yet there is also something profoundly unsettling in an older child's response: A sense of displacement and rage accompanies the new attachment. The older child experiences a kind of grief but is unable to understand it. A primitive fear of being replaced, usurped, and annihilated stands at its center, forming a template for subsequent anxieties and doubt about one's status in the human world, the safety of relationships, and the stability of one's self.

When my younger daughter was born, her older sister was filled with pride. Grave and self-important, she greeted the visitors who arrived to view the baby. She provided them with up-to-the-minute reports on the baby's age as of today, and what she had eaten or expelled during the past hour. She cast aside her playmates to make herself available as the watchful big sister. She joined me as an intense admirer of this new child, and was engrossed by questions neither of us could yet answer: "Does she know I'm her sister?" "Does she know you're her mother?" and "Does she know we love her?" I was as soothed by her fluttering presence as by the minute movements of the baby I held. Each child, in her different way, constantly broadcast her contented vitality. Yes, this is right. This is easy, I thought. Though it had taken my own big sister a fair while (so my mother had told me) to accept a little sister, my own splendid daughter would be quicker to learn.

I was wrong. Within two weeks the still-loving sister hung her head in abject misery as gift after gift was presented to the baby: "These are too good for her" she wailed. "She'll get it dirty. She'll ruin the bow. She's too little to appreciate it. Why is everyone giving her everything?" And when her best friend had a new sister, too, she challenged his delight: "How can you love her? Can't you *see*? She'll ruin your life!"

The initial attachment was still there, clear and present in the whirlwind of her distress. But there was also a rage against her sister, against me, against the betrayal by her entire family. She was now the second little person to be greeted when her grandparents arrived. "They only came to see the baby," she sulked. Her playroom was now crowded with useless baby stuff. "I hate this crib. It takes up all the room. It smells. It's stupid." Even her simplest requests to family members were now routinely met with, "Just a minute. I have to see to the baby first." When she expressed her displeasure, she was reprimanded. So she vented her frustration at the baby, and then the reprimands got worse.

Yet the younger child appeared to have no trouble loving *her* older sister! As a baby she watched her older sister with an intensity that would have softened the most indifferent heart. In her eyes this older child was a source of wonder. She could tie her own shoes, shout at her mother, skip rope with her friends. When the younger sister was old enough to play, it was always the big sister who decided what the game would be, and who would take which role. Any routines initiated by the younger sister were defined by the older sister's undeniable instructions: "You're just the lookout," and "*I'm* the one driving this spaceship." The older sister's bossiness and superiority were conditions for joining the fun. When the younger girl did come up with an idea or demand of her own, it was judged to be "stupid," "silly," "babyish," or "dumb." She received these judgments stoically, comforted by a thumb plugged into her mouth, until her older sister derided her as a "thumb-sucking idiot." This was likely to drive her to tears, and the odds were then even as to whether the older sister would console her or taunt her.

It was not that the older child did not have any positive or protective feelings toward her little sister. The younger sib's distress would trigger overpowering empathy, if anyone other than she were the cause. Nothing pitched her anxiety higher than her sister's obliviousness of the dangers of cars on the street or heights in the playground. The younger girl's delight in a rabbit, a cartoon, or a shoe buckle splashed color onto the big sister's world. The little sister's body was delicious—fun to hug, squeeze, and bite. But her significant place within the home and the admiration and interest she aroused in parents, grandparents, and visitors were annoying. The older girl wanted her sister to be cut down to size, to be declared little, not large in significance, and to maintain her status as a sidekick, not a centerpiece. When the younger girl reached the age of drawing, she composed a wonderful picture of her cat, with soft tufts of fur in its ears, and black spots carefully recorded, just as they appeared on the real cat's pink nose. Proud of her work, she announced that she would show her artwork to her sister. "It's lovely, whatever she says," I assured her. She caught my gaze and held it solemnly as she explained, "I want to hear her say it's *dumb*."

This sign that she accepted, and was even entertained by her sister's compulsive denigration, was a relief. However exhausted I was by their endless battles over the head versus the body of the gingerbread man, over the second versus the third cushion of the sofa, over *Scooby-Doo* versus *Buffy* on TV, I was glad that each girl was willing to challenge the other's claim to "come first." I wanted feisty girls, but I did not want mean ones. So it was disturbing to witness the daily fights, in which they slid back and forth across the border between horseplay and abuse with disconcerting ease. It was unsettling to see them tease and ridicule each other, to see one suffer from the other's successes, and to witness their pleasure in undermining each other.

Why, I wondered, was such fighting necessary? For, like most parents, I believed that the fights were not really about the minuscule differences of material things or the idiosyncratic, ridiculous meaning they read into who said what or, indeed, any of the terms they appeared to be fighting over. Like most parents, and like most psychologists at that time, I assumed that sibling rivalry was triggered by the fear that one would lose out on a parent's love and attention. Yet did I and their father and grandparents not love them both, equally, in perfectly fair-size portions? Was I not careful to give each the same, and enough, attention? Did I not praise each equally, and show even-handedness in the distribution of necessities and treats? Given that there was nothing of substance to fight over, why did they fight? What was the source of that powerful irritation one felt at the mere existence of the other? Moreover, how did this constant display of hostility make sense within the framework of their good feelings? Why did they seem prepped to attack each other when each girl would clearly give her life for the other?

THE BEGINNING OF RIVALRY

SIBLING LOVE AND sibling rivalry have long been recognized as staple features of the human world. The easy slide from hugging to strangling, the blurred distinctions between a playful pat and an aggressive push, are familiar to all who have witnessed children growing up together. The very word "horseplay" to indicate activities that combine friendliness and hostility marks the familiar territory in which affection and aggression coincide.

The sibling relationship is distinctive in its emotional power and intimacy, and in its heady mix of competitiveness, protectiveness, antagonism, and affection. When children speak about their siblings, they talk about loving, comforting, and helping; they also talk about antagonism and quarreling.[2] These vastly different features of the relationship are not linked in any obvious way. Children who describe their relationship with their brother or sister as very warm, close, and affectionate are not necessarily the children who experience less conflict with the sibling or who express less rivalry with each other. And children who fight a great deal with their siblings are not necessarily the children who report much jealousy over parents' love and attention. Jealousy cuts across, and does not necessarily blend with, other aspects of a relationship: A pair of siblings who rarely fight and who also frequently share may be very jealous of each other's relationship with their parents. Another pair of siblings who are always fighting are not jealous of their parents' affection and attention.[3]

While some siblings exhibit more and some less affection, while some siblings exhibit more and some less hostility, most sisters and brothers are both friendly and aggressive toward one another. The *mix* of behavior patterns signals a need to move away from the single dimensions of warmth/hostility, or love/hate. In short, most sisters and brothers display ambivalence.[4] When we are able to separate the different strands in this powerful bond, we come closer to recognizing the mixed and varied nature of all human attachment.

THE SHAPE OF AMBIVALENCE

THE SIBLING WORLD allows us to view the primitive elements of attachment and envy. The role siblings play in the development of human understanding has, over the past two decades, been meticulously observed and recorded. Judy Dunn shows that siblings learn about other people's minds through their interest in each other. They monitor each other closely and note the other's personal likes and dislikes. They learn what frightens, comforts, or delights the other. Understanding is developed partly through love and concern, and partly through hostile and machiavellian intents to disturb, annoy, and even terrify. There is no doubt that siblings both love and hate each other.

Until recently it seemed enough simply to accept that siblings were ambivalent about one another without considering the complex nature of this ambivalence and its impact. Most parents simply wanted tips to contain the jealousy, to manage the quarrels without favoring one child over another, and to allow acceptable expression of the full range of feelings. The mind- and heart-shaping tensions that underlie these quarrels were, with a few exceptions,[5] ignored.

Instead psychologists focused on how the child-parent relationship underlay future attachments. In the love, power, and dependence of this bond, psychologists were fascinated by the impact of an infant's ambivalence toward a mother or mother figure. When an infant's needs and wishes are not immediately and totally fulfilled, the infant experiences disappointment and rage. Dependence and love, combined with anger and hatred, issue in a powerful ambivalence. Integrating the "good" and the "bad" aspects of one's mother into one single person, whom one can love, is both difficult and necessary to human attachment. This integration involves acceptance that someone can be frustrating or disappointing without being hateful. It involves the ability to experience gratitude and love toward people who only imperfectly meet one's needs. It involves acceptance that we have to preserve and value relationships even when they have limits and rough edges. At the heart of this task is the ability to relinquish the primitive illusion that others exist solely for one's own gratification.

The emotional cauldron of sibling attachments, however, was brushed aside as a minor subplot to the parent-child story. Freud judged that a child's initial hatred and resentment of a new infant were based on the older child's shrewd measure of the threat a newborn sibling posed to his status. Love for a sibling was something you should have if you were going to be acceptable to your family. Furthermore, love was something you could see was right and appropriate, because the person you really wanted to be, and wanted to imitate, such as your parent, loved the baby.[6] In Freud's highly influential view, love was an emotion foisted on an older sibling by the parents' example and morality. It was only by loving the new child that an older child could remain acceptable to his family. Love for a sibling might be genuine, but this love was derived from one's attachment to a parent: The older child saw that the parent loved the baby, the older child identified with the parent, and therefore the older child came to love his sibling.

But what so many of us know from our own experience, whether as siblings or as parents of siblings, is that the love and delight are as primary as the rivalry and resentment. There is little doubt that an older child's relationship with parents changes sharply when a new sibling arrives. Older children become more aggressive and "naughty";[7] yet most children are interested in and affectionate toward the baby, and almost all children are extremely eager to help with caring for the baby.[8]

It is the primacy of both types of feelings—care and rivalry—that has now been brought within the central framework of the psyche. While Judy Dunn records the pervasiveness of sibling love and protectiveness, new theories in psychoanalysis underscore her observations of rivalry and distress. "I believe we have minimized or overlooked entirely the threat to our existence as small children that is posed by the new baby who stands in our place or the older sibling who was there before we existed," Juliet Mitchell writes in her groundbreaking book on siblings. It is the initial presence of siblings that produces what she calls "a catastrophic psychosocial situation of displacement"[9] as one realizes one is not uniquely secured in one's relationships.

This new model extends our understanding of the challenges presented by love and attachment, and brings siblings into the center of psychological development. Sibling relationships generate, no less than parent-child relationships, experiences of a near-intolerable ambivalence, wherein love resides alongside hatred. "Thinking siblings"—that is, noting the significance of the sibling trauma on development—oriented Juliet Mitchell toward fresh analysis of clinical material. Mitchell goes beyond traditional psychoanalysis, dominated by parent-child relationships, to present a new vision of primary ambivalence and its associated patterns of development. In this context we can now understand the terror of losing love, the intense anxiety aroused by competition, and the disturbing shape of envy. These features of the psyche are often relegated to female weakness, but in the sibling perspective they emerge as part of a common human condition.

THE SIBLING TRAUMA RESOLVED

THE FEARS WE confront in the sibling trauma play a crucial role in our development as individuals living alongside other individuals. In most contexts there is the possibility of being replaced—more so, perhaps, in our crowded contemporary society than at any other time. The shock of displacement plays a crucial role in our development of self. It also has, ultimately, a positive role. It allows us to replace an unreflecting narcissism (a pure sense of oneself as the center of the world) with a more complex sense of identity. We note that we can be excluded from positions we value, that our sense of belonging is something we have to share with others, and that we cannot always be assured of our supreme or even unique value. In this trauma, Mitchell concludes, lies the birth of self-esteem; for it is when we understand that who and what we are must be achieved, defined, and redefined that we forgo a primitive belief in a narcissistic self who needs to consider only oneself. We can see that we are a person among many people. To accommodate this human reality, we differentiate and define ourselves as an individual cooperating with, supporting, and sometimes competing with others. A sister negotiates her unique identity within an interpersonal context through awareness of her common measure of humanity.

Acceptance of our shared place is never complete. Throughout our lives we encounter events that reawaken this early trauma. A friend suddenly leaves us behind as she gains popularity; we lose our position in the workplace; our talents are outstripped by someone else; a romantic partner shows preference and love to someone else: Any of these familiar experiences can trigger our terror of displacement. In our social environment there are constant shifts that dislodge us from who and where we thought we were. We all struggle to manage this process. We can now use the discovery of the sibling trauma to understand it.

2

Younger Sisters and Other Variations: Why the Sibling Trauma Is Universal

THE NEGLECTED STORY OF THE YOUNGER SISTER

THE MOST FAMILIAR model of sibling trauma is that of an older child, accustomed to being the only child, confronted with a brutal adjustment. The family in which she or he held a unique position suddenly has to be shared. Yet a trauma of displacement is experienced by most siblings, regardless of birth order. Even twins tell stories of feeling ousted by the other. In Jincy Willett's novel about sororal twins, Dorcas describes her birth as a struggle for air and light in the face of Abigail's attempts, even in the process of birth, to usurp her. "My sister mooned in the world for two hours, while behind her, I choked for air and sustenance. . . . All I wanted was to breathe and see." [1] The prototype of twins is sameness and parity, but the experience Jincy Willett delicately unravels is of one twin seeing herself as the real child and the other fearing she is an afterthought. Each fights the other to remain whole, only to discover that each needs the other to *be* whole.

While a younger sibling may not point to one specific memory jolt, the way older siblings often report memories of the sudden arrival of a new baby and the consequent distress, younger children, too, face the trauma of displacement. Awareness that someone else can threaten one's status as a unique person in one's most significant, immediate world, may be both gradual and traumatic. A continuing, mundane fear can be as powerful as a single acute episode. In fact, a central feature of psychological trauma is that it represents something that on some level goes on happening, endlessly. [2] The sibling trauma is often described as a sudden realization that one is no longer unique within one's family configuration; but its true impact is layered by ordinary experiences, repeated in daily life, in our dreams and in our fears.

As a younger sister myself, I am frustrated by the way rivalry is presented as a disruption to the firstborn. [3] Whether the threats are sudden and final or come in installments, children in any birth order see one sibling as interrupting their claim to unique status in the family. The full force of the meaning of having a sibling does not come at once for either a younger or an older sibling. The introduction of a new infant to a firstborn is simply a useful image of a sustained process.

The younger sibling not only comes to realize that the powerful bond she experiences as binary (between her and her parents) is something that is shared, she also has to deal with the older sibling's hostility. My first experience of being the victim in a sibling attack has been relegated to family myth, and I have no memory of the episode. According to my mother, when I sat in my playpen, the minute my mother turned her head away, my older sister bashed me over the head with an egg beater. Whether or not this event occurred (my sister tells a very different story), I knew my sister was capable, sometimes, of doing me damage. That my mother shared this knowledge was a perk when she refereed our quarrels. But this knowledge also set up an exciting framework in which I would test my sister's patience, and her aggression, by touching her, tickling her, engaging in a series of physical intrusions we referred to as "bothering." ("Stop bothering me!" and "Mommy, she's bothering me!") I was eager to see how far her anger might drive her. I am not sure whether I tested this from the vantage point of safety or foolhardy curiosity.

In addition to the physical threat my sister posed, I remember the exclusion I felt when my sister and mother got together. One of my early memories is of watching my mother and my sister embrace. My mother bent low, into my sister's hug, and I seemed to be an awfully long way from them. In a flash I set up a scenario that offered what seemed like a perfectly reasonable excuse to separate them: We were in a crowd, and I had to move from my perch on the stairs to a place just beyond the embracing pair. The space around my mother and sister was impossibly crowded in this scenario, and the only way through was between the two of them. "Excuse me," I said as I pushed between my mother and sister. This sudden intrusion so startled my mother that she pushed me aside. I felt my shoulder hit the wall, but I was more stunned by her fury than the physical impact. She accused me of being "petty and jealous." I immediately identified these feelings, but I was confounded by her ability to see them so clearly, when, in my view, I had disguised my intent so well with my imaginary scenario. "We were in a crowded place—" I explained, but to no avail. Her lightning-quick understanding inflamed my shame. It never occurred to me that my feelings were common, and it never occurred to me that anyone could at once see them and not cast me out of her life.

Even when my sister was as young as eight, I sensed some woman-to-woman understanding between her and my mother from which I was excluded. It filled me with irritation, which I expressed as disgust. "You always have to do what mommy says," I whined; then, sometime later, when I was more adept at taunting her, I would say, "You're Mommy's pet," and, "You have no mind of your own."

Later I was to find that the larger world of fiction all too often was in collusion against younger sisters. The second-born Elizabeth Bennet might be the star of *Pride and Prejudice*, but this could not compensate for the group of younger sisters who were always lacking in one area or another, such as the airheaded Lydia and Kitty or the dull Mary. In Jane Austen's *Sense and Sensibility* the youngest sister was dismissed as silly and shallow. (This young girl, Margaret, was nicely resuscitated in Emma Thompson's 1996 screenplay as a perky observer of her older sisters' tragedies and idiocies, but that rewriting came too late to comfort me.) I loved Anne Frank's arch derision of her older sister, Margot, on the grounds that she appeared to be "Mama's good girl." I adored Laura Ingalls Wilder's books for having a younger sister as the main focus; Laura's irritation and frustration at her mother's sanctimonious and stupid preference for the older girl were just right, I thought; and while my mother read aloud what I called the "Laura and Mary" books, and I sat next to her, feeling her breath and hearing her voice, I waited for the light of my superiority over my older sister to dawn on her. But it never did.

The fantasy that we are the primary person in our world seems well established at birth—a human counterpart to the self-survival focus of any creature. As soon as a child becomes aware of siblings she is alert to the fact that the child-parent bond, which in so many ways reinforces the fantasy, has boundaries. She has to work out why *her* unique place is not recognized. She is puzzled that her anger is seen as the naughtiness of a little child rather than the sophisticated argument she believes it to be, though she cannot articulate it. So, while younger children are on the whole welcoming and warm to the family members that are lined up to greet them when they enter the world, and while younger children tend to express friendliness to older siblings, even when the older child rebuffs them,[4] younger children key into the hostility that greets them. Even before they have a clear sense of how their older siblings may threaten them in the family, they sense that the older sibling is willing to attack them. Younger children may be clingier because they need protection not only from predators in the wild but also from their siblings in the home. As Mitchell notes, "the wild things," for humans, reside not only in the forest: They are also found within the family.[5]

Since the beginning of human history siblings have represented potential threats to each other's claim on a unique position in the family. Sometimes the threat is to the material blessings of family inheritance, as it is for Esau vis-à-vis his brother, Jacob. Sometimes the threat is to a preferred place in a parent's, or parent figure's, esteem, as when Abel gains God's approval at Cain's expense. The outcome is not merely having to step down but being cast out. Someone takes one's place, and one then is adrift.[6] This is the crux of the sibling trauma.

SISTERS IN THE MIDDLE

FROM A VERY early age I had no doubt that having a sister and being a sister were central to my sense of who I was, and essential to any ability I had to find my way in the world. At the same time I was wary of allowing another child to join my sibling group. I worried about three things, in the following order. First, I worried that a new baby would take away my sister's very occasional and transient delight in me as a soft-skinned, cuddly, cute little sister. Second, I worried lest I hate a new baby, and that this hatred would confirm my low moral worth. Third, I worried that I would lose the status my sister and I now had in our family as a single and complete item. "The two of us" and "the pair of you" were satisfying designations. Giving them up would involve giving up my sense of place in the family. So, when my mother died, among a host of other feelings was a prominent anxiety: Would my father have more children? Whether or not he married was immaterial to me, but I anticipated that having another sibling would threaten everything I still had in the family.

The middle sisters in my sample of seventy-six sisters from thirty-seven family groups expressed unease at being "neither the oldest or the youngest." Two middle sisters, Jessie, twenty-one, and Sasha, twenty-three, both insist that the middle sister is the most displaced. Jessie said, "It was cool sometimes to slink into the background, especially when Mom was blowing off steam. But most of the time it was either, 'You're old enough to know better,' and I was blamed for what Adi did, or it was, 'You're not old enough to do that,' so I couldn't do what Libby was allowed to do." Sasha felt she was "saddled with having to look out for Meg, but I never got that sickly praise for being 'good' that Vicki always got." Sasha also recalls being expected, as a middle sister, to be good at sharing. "I felt I had no right to be as selfish as Vicki. But I knew I was. And it made me mad that no one saw I had a right to be as selfish as my big sister."

When Dalton Conley studied the allocation of family resources among siblings, he found that "middle borns experience the crunch of sibling competition for parental resources both coming and going."[7] The disgruntlement voiced by the sisters in my relatively small study is justified by a far more general assessment of parental attention and family resource allocation for middle siblings.[8] The middle sibling, who might be thought to hold the best position, is simply the sibling whose voice has not been heard.

STEPSISTERS AND THE SISTER KNOT

DURING THE PAST half century there have been many changes in family structures. The change most frequently highlighted is that of parental divorce. This disruptive process presents new renditions of siblings as usurpers, competitors, and allies. Siblings clearly provide mutual support during the process of divorce, but divorce also may lead to a new family formation, with a new range of step-siblings who change forever one's position within the new family.

The story of Cinderella has been used many times to explore themes about contemporary women's lives. It has been seen as a warning that women are likely, still, to lapse into dependency on others, that even as they act as independent, high-achieving agents, a wish for a male savior is shaped with each heartbeat.[9] It has been read as a story about mother-daughter conflict: The stepmother represents that dark side of the mother who demeans and denigrates the young, beautiful daughter.[10] Surprisingly, what has been ignored in this simple and rich story is the theme of the sister knot.

Cinderella's stepsisters work together with the stepmother to oust her from her position as the true daughter of the household, the one entitled to the father's love and the one in control of the family resources. The stepsisters are portrayed as ugly and mean to make them hateful and hence justify a desire to oust all other sisters from her father's heart and household. The "stepsisters," like the "stepmother," can be seen as the dark and hated side of a full-blooded sister; but this archaic tale is also a story about stepsisters, who share many dynamics with biological siblings.

Stepsiblings, too, have to vie for their position in the family. As families reconfigure themselves, some children have to confront a true displacement. "One day I discovered that my father wasn't living with me," Paula explains. "Instead he was living with two other girls. He's the father in my stepsisters' home but not in mine. When I'm in his house I'm an outsider, except I'm the one daughter who really belongs there. So I'm the outsider, but my stepsisters are taking my place."

The jealousy reported by some stepsisters was fierce, untempered by that broad range of sisterly attachment. Jenny, at fifteen, looks back to the time she was twelve and realized that her father, who had left her and her mother two years before, would not come back, and that her bond with him was changed forever.

"When my father left I kept thinking he was really going to come back. My mom said, 'But he's married to someone else now. He's not coming back.' How did that wash? He'd been married to her and left her. Why couldn't he leave this other wife and come back to us? Why did my mother keep emphasizing, 'He's married to someone else?' But then he had a new baby. A girl.

"I think that was the worst day of my life. Nothing changed. I woke up that morning, and I did all the usual things, and I stared at my room, and the wallpaper was just the same as it was yesterday. I looked in my closet, and my clothes were the same. The kitchen was the same, and I had the same things for breakfast. And I looked at my mother and I thought, Why aren't you screaming? I met my friend at the corner, and we went to school, and it was everything I did every day, and it wouldn't be different tomorrow. But something inside changed, and I felt things would never be the same again, and for the first time I realized what it meant to have a father leave you. All those fears that the grown-ups tell you are 'just nightmares.'. . . You know? They tell you not to worry because it's just your imagination? Well, the new baby girl was there. I wasn't imagining her, and I would never have my father like I once did, and my mother would never have him back. I still see him, pretty regularly, like before, but it will never be the same." Stepsiblings offer new sibling networks, but with these come new occasions for experiencing displacement.

TRAUMA WITHOUT SIBLINGS

AN OBVIOUS QUESTION that follows is: What about children who do not have siblings? Do children without siblings avoid that mind-shaping threat to their self-in-relationship? Does an "only child" have a different psychology?

Whether we have siblings or whether we are a singleton will have wide-ranging impact on an individual life. But whether or not we have a sibling, we come to realize that we are not unique of our kind, that others may eclipse us even in the most intimate settings, that our position with those we love and whose love we need can shift. This is what we confront in the sibling trauma, and we do not require a sibling to learn this. Adoring parents of an only child can focus on another child's talents and qualities; a cousin or even a friend can appear to threaten one's status within the family. In Amy Tan's *The Joy Luck Club*, Jing Mei-Woo's mother bridles at her friend's pride in her own daughter, Waverly, who is a child chess prodigy she labels a genius. The closeness of the two mothers is underlined by the title "Auntie" they bestow on each other. They compete as "sisters," and therefore compare their daughters, like for like, with differences highlighted as points of competition. The mothers' siblinglike rivalry is passed on to their daughters. The pride one mother takes in her own daughter is seen as an affront to the other mother. Jing's mother tries to make her own daughter into a prodigy, too, but her efforts fail. Jing is caught between a fierce spirit that informs her of her right to fall short of a mother's expectations, and her terror of losing a mother's love. Our struggle with the sibling trauma is not confined to our struggles among biological siblings.

The general models of human attachment that we draw upon are built up from many things. They are built from actual experiences of trust and betrayal, of safety and danger, of delight and disappointment. But, as we find our way in the complex human and social world, we draw on far more than our own actual experiences. We draw on possibilities conceived imaginatively, and on our empathy for others' experiences. We have a register of expectations, ready for use and refinement as we make sense of individual histories, responses, and personalities. Our sense of who we are, of what threatens us, of where our safety lies, of what marks us as good, or of what evil seeps into us does not derive from actual experiences alone.

As we negotiate the power of our individual feelings, we imbue attachments with associations and fantasies. We watch others and listen to stories and follow our own imaginations into human understanding. Common, well-established family configurations become both psychically and socially relevant. The configuration of two parents, a mother and a father, for example, remains a reference point even in families that function perfectly well in a variety of different patterns. Children who thrive within a single parent family, or in a family headed by a grandmother, or jointly by a grandparent and parent, or within any combination of a "blended family," still find the so-called nuclear family a point of reference. In a similar way siblings enter the imagining psyche of an only child. Throughout human history children have expected to have a sibling. Most children today still have siblings, so that a child without a sibling will understand the possibility of changing configurations. The sibling relationship is what Lévi-Strauss refers to as an "atom of kinship."[11] What is possible and familiar and also exciting and frightening is likely to take hold in the imaginative shaping of the psyche. This widely observed dynamic supplies the prototypical experience for the sibling trauma. It is experienced in a variety of contexts, with actual siblings, stand-in siblings, and transient sibling figures.

Hence the importance of the sibling trauma comes into play even when a girl doesn't have a sister. Eighty percent of children do have a sibling, and the arrival of a sibling is a common occurrence, and always a possible occurrence. *Possible* threats are active and powerful influences: Children are terrified of abandonment by their parents, and display this fear very clearly, in ways recognizable to all, and these fears persist and are understood even when a child has a parent who never has abandoned her and never would.

A child sees a sibling win special attention and praise, and panics lest her parents will forget about her. This is not a fear based on rational assessment of what a parent will do, but it is shaped by awareness of what in some circumstances is possible. A child sees a parent's brow furrow, and hears an angry voice, and thinks she has done something to make her parent stop loving her. This has never happened, and it is not likely to happen, but the fear snaps awake at the slightest alarm. The sibling trauma that is experienced by a child who does not have a sibling stems from a similarly imagined and deeply felt fear, based on primitive fantasy and observed possibility. The fear of losing a parent's approval and love, which chimes throughout our lives, is not more powerful than the fear of being displaced by someone a parent loves, possibly more than us or instead of us.

The identification of a "sibling trauma" is useful in explaining the depth of sibling attachments and antagonisms. It also allows us to see far more than that, providing a framework for understanding a range of relationships, particularly those shaped by both identification and envy, by identification and a craving for difference, by identification and a fear of displacement. It is both the syndrome we identify when we see siblings squabbling and the developmental starting point that explains the disturbing power of ambivalence and envy throughout our lives.

A girl or woman does not need to have a sister in order to have a strong sense of sisterly experiences of caring and pairing. The fascination of sisters in fiction, plays, films, and biography signals the multiple sister references we deal with, whatever our actual experience. Because sistering is fundamental to norms of female interaction, it shapes our psyche whether or not we actually have a sister. In her paper "Imagining Sisters," Pam Hirsch describes a singleton's fascination with the sister bond. As an only child living with two parents and two grandparents, she visited her friends' homes "in the spirit of an anthropologist gazing at the strange kinship behavior of these differently constructed families."[12] She delighted in novels with characters to whom she might imagine herself as sister, and gathered pride from her knowledge that she could be a good sister. Sistering is as much an imagined as an experienced relationship. Hence it has the power to take us into the heart of questions about who we are and where we stand among the people who matter most to us.

3

The Sister Knot

A NY CHILD RESENTS the shift from center stage when a new sibling joins the family, but the threat of displacement has a special impact on girls. Fear of losing love, anxiety about being ousted from a safe relationship, and guilt about aggression toward others are prominent themes in women's psychology. The salience of these themes in girls' and women's lives has been the subject of much attention but little helpful explanation. When we look at these through the lens of the sibling trauma, new patterns emerge wherein both the strengths and possible fault lines in women's psychology take on new subtleties and new dimensions.

We create our lives within a network of connection to others. The relational spaces between ourselves and the key people in our lives vary enormously in each individual; there are also broad differences between women and men: Girls develop a sense of themselves as essentially connected to others, whereas boys define themselves as more separate from others and at a greater emotional distance from others. The crucible for these differences is the traditional family structure and accompanying social norms. Because girls and boys are parented primarily by mothers, girls, as they grasp the importance of gender in their identity, maintain continuity between intense attachment and identity; whereas when boys grasp the importance of gender in their identity, they must define themselves as distinct from the person they first love and on whom they continue to depend. In this developmental context, intense love may threaten their sense of male self as it harks back to an earlier ungendered experience.[1]

While this model of connectedness provides girls with distinctive psychological robustness in early childhood,[2] it deepens the meanings in the sibling trauma. If girls indeed do identify closely with their mothers, and if they see connection to others generally as central to who they are, then being displaced as the only child will be mortifying. The question posed is, How can I maintain any sense of who I am, if that connection, which is basic to my sense of self, is threatened?

The ensuing hostility to the new, or other, sibling may also be more problematic for girls. Girls and women experience care and responsiveness as significant organizers of themselves;[3] and the quality of their feelings toward others is linked to self-esteem. When love and attachment are mixed with rivalry and envy, they often report feelings of guilt and low self-worth. The sibling trauma, then, presents a range of puzzles about the quality and shape of relationships.

INTERRUPTIONS IN MATERNAL LOVE AND NEW CONNECTIONS WITH A SISTER

PARENTS FREQUENTLY SAY, with total sincerity, that they love all their children "the same," and that a newborn does not take away any existing love for older children. However, a newborn does shift parental (and grandparental) focus. And while all children key in to minute variations in a mother's behavior, girls show particular sensitivity to modulations of mood and affect.[4] Glynis recalls the breach in her relationship with her older daughter, Vera, now aged nine, when the younger sister, now five, was born. "It was like some kind of wall was between us. She could irritate me just by asking for a drink. I felt so wrapped up—you know?—that one-to-one you have with your baby? And everything else was somewhere else. There were moments when I'd think: What is Vera doing hanging around me? And then I'd go cold, like, What's happened to me? But mostly I just turned a blind eye to my feelings. I'm so sorry now, when I look back, and I know it's changed her—changed us."

In Judy Dunn's studies of families with newborn second children, mothers reported feeling shut out from the easy closeness they had enjoyed with an older daughter when a second daughter was born.[5] The displacement that is so traumatic for the child has a concomitant effect on the mother, who finds it difficult to recapture a comfortable relationship with her older daughter.

Yet a sister also brings the promise of new connections. Sisters display their close identification with each other in many ways. As young children they are more likely to imitate each other than are either brothers or brother-sister pairs.[6] Imitation of a sibling is usually playful and blatantly enjoyable, but it also leads to uneasy questions: Do I really do that? and Do I look like that? Sisters' lifelong comparisons with each other are even more complicated: Am I leading the right life for me? and Should I be leading your life? are questions spiked by contemporary worries over the balance between love and ambition, between family and work. Am I the person I should be? and Should I be more like my sister? are underpinned by anxieties about personal worth.

As with all human relationships, the dynamics between sisters are informed by questions and conflicts that arise at a given time within a given society. The uneasy dialogue women conduct between actual paths taken and other possible life routes, occurs at a time in which the ideal of the "good woman" can shift from homemaker to superwoman and back again. Questions of who they should be often destablize women in a society in which familiar female roles are sometimes idealized and sometimes minimized: The mother who is the linchpin of a sacred marriage is, in another context, the woman who is "merely a housewife." As women accept the challenge to succeed in male corporate cultures, and then become figures of suspicion, they may feel "without a place." All these distortions about "place" and "status" and "value" are reflected in the dynamics of the sister knot. They are also played out among the women who come in some ways, at certain times, in certain lights, to represent a sister.

CHALLENGING CURRENT ASSUMPTIONS ABOUT WOMEN

THE SIBLING TRAUMA has been left out of mainstream psychological theories because male development has traditionally been studied with far more interest than that accorded female development. The fear we all share of losing our place on the relational map, and the fear of losing love, have been screened over by fears of threats to masculinity and fears about losing one's distinct and separate sense of self.[7] The threats that are prioritized in the sibling trauma—annihilation and losing another's love—are more closely associated with girls' development and women's psychology than with a male model of development. The blindness to the impact of siblings is therefore a legacy of psychology's previous blindness to women's experience.[8]

The lens of the sibling trauma also allows us to challenge many recurring themes about how girls and women differ from men. As a general (but by no means universal) rule, women give weight to personal obligations and others' needs as they make practical and moral decisions. In their daily lives they are more likely than men to set high standards for empathy and communication. In their conversation and management styles, women show sensitivity to others' voices and are more likely than men to aim for consensus and solidarity rather than status or control. But a close look at sistering shows that what women seek from love, what they are willing to offer to others, and how fully their sense of self is connected to others may differ from what many current models of women's emotional makeup would indicate.

Subtle, significant distinctions between female and male psychology have many sources. There are cultural factors that shape girls' and women's responsiveness to others' needs. Social roles and social exclusion influence the special value many women place on being loved, and the link they draw from being loved to having value. In a changing society, with expanding roles outside the home and a wider range of pressures to succeed, one's sense of place and position and status is more easily dislodged. At this time and in this place, the sibling trauma has a particular salience in women's experience.

When we look at girls' and women's experience of sistering, we have to question and revise many common assumptions about the psychology of women. Among sisters, girls and women take a shrewd measure of what is in their own interests and what is in another's. They prove their capacity to draw boundaries around themselves. They establish their difference and their separateness. They fight and jostle for status and demand things from one another. Girls are as good at fighting with a sibling as a boy is. Twice as many boys are involved in fights outside the family, but within the family girls are just as likely to come to blows.[9] Among siblings, girls and women display active concern about status; they prove themselves adept at direct confrontation; and they are emphatic about marking personal borders between self and other.

Sistering takes us several steps forward in catching sight of the many dimensions of female psychology. It highlights the difficulty of making those familiar distinctions between men and women, along the lines that "women seek connection, while men seek boundaries and separateness," or "women inhabit a world of love and men inhabit a world of aggression,"[10] or "women feel and men think."[11] What we learn from sistering is that capacity for aggression and concern about drawing self-boundaries and establishing status are as much a part of female as of male psychology. From a sistering perspective we can see the differences in female and male psychology and their implications, and the prevalence in girls and women of many traits previously labeled "male traits." The sister knot forces us to acknowledge that when we deal with psychological differences between men and women, we are dealing with subtle distinctions, not polarities.[12]

FROM SIMPLIFICATION TO TRUTHFULNESS

LISTENING TO SISTERS reminds us of the complexity of human connection. At the beginning of the interviews I held with sisters, I usually heard clear statements: "I'm very close to my sister," and "I love my sister to bits" or "I have very little to do with my sister," and "My sister and I hate each other's guts," "I trust my sister more than anyone else," or "My sister is out to get me. Her greatest worry is that I'll end up with a little more than she has. I would never trust her with anything."

But during the course of the interviews, a more complicated story emerged; in all cases the feelings were complicated. The most devoted sisters reported stories of resentment.

Jessica and her sisters speak on the phone every day. When one is in trouble, the others will do everything in their power to sort the matter out. They speak about love and connection and delight. But there are also themes of resentment, from the petty to the terrible. "As a middle sister," Jessica reflected, "I only had two new dresses, ever. The first one was a brown-and-yellow check with a square neckline, and Libby tore it when she was 'catching' me in a game of tag. The other was blue, with white flowers on it and a white collar, and Adi bit my shoulder when she was a baby and made a hole in the sleeve." She also remembers a time when her hot-tempered older sister was so furious with her that she feared for her life. "Our mother wasn't home, and I ran to the apartment upstairs and told the woman who lived there that I had to stay with her because my sister was going to kill me."

Usually there was a strong component of love; but even when love was buried by anger, there was a profound sense of identification, with the ensuing capacity for care and for either pride or shame. As women reflected on sistering, they moved from a straightforward position of a "good" or "bad" relationship to one that was "the most interesting and complicated of relationships" and "a bond that lies like a knot in my heart, which makes me wonder whether I know myself," and "something I dread looking at too closely, because I know I love her, but there's also something else."

In conjunction with love there ensues an emotional drama that is played and replayed throughout one's life. "The ecstasy of loving one who is like oneself is experienced at the same time as the trauma of being annihilated by one who stands in one's place,"[13] writes Mitchell. Seeing annihilation as a real threat, we try to protect ourselves. In this mind-set the best protection—the most efficient method that can be conceived by a primitive and impatient mind—would be to murder the other child. In other words, when we feel threatened, we want to annihilate the person who threatens us: "The normal reaction," writes Mitchell, "is to kill in order not thus to be obliterated."[14] But the wish to kill is mixed with the wish to protect and preserve someone who is one of us, someone who is like us, and someone we love. The consequent struggles to manage conflicting feelings and conflicting perspectives emerge at different points, in different relationships, throughout our lives.

ENVY, ANXIETY, AND THE DEATH WISH

THROUGH THE EXPERIENCE of having a sibling, a firstborn or a previous-born experiences an acute anxiety: Now I am not the unique child; now I am not the parents'/grandparents' favorite; I am not what I was, and I do not have the love I once had. In this conundrum envy emerges from anxiety over loss of love, and this anxiety is linked to loss of self. In this early dependent relationship love, identity, and existence are bound together.

We often think of envy as focusing on a single person: I envy Sue her looks, her charm, her talent. In the grip of envy I watch her and wonder about her; she becomes my obsession. But envy is triangular. The person suffering envy looks at someone and thinks, I want to have what she has. What she has (or is) should be what I have (or am). If I have what she has, if I became what she is, I would have the love I need.

What shapes a longing to have what someone else has is the assumption, If I have what I envy, or become who I envy, then I will be loved by the person or the people who matter to me most. If I do not have what I envy, or become who I envy, then the person I envy will take from me the love that I want. If I do not receive the love I long for and depend on, then I'll be obliterated: I will not have a place among the people I care for; I will not be protected; I will not have any place; I will not be who I want to be or think I should be; I will not know who I am; I will in fact be nothing. It is by this route that envy triggers the panic of annihilation.

The peculiar sense of "flooding" that often accompanies envy, which many women and men describe as "overwhelming" and "smothering," can be explained in the context of the sibling trauma. Feelings of envy and rivalry are quintessentially the terror of being excluded and abandoned. And the terror does not disappear when we grow old enough to know better. As the psychiatrist Dan Stern reflects: "I would say that the feeling—the fear of being abandoned—and the biological response to it changes very little from nine months until we die."[15]

The English language does not attribute gender to its nouns, but green-eyed envy is distinctly female, however often men experience it. In its starkest form envy is a sense that another person's qualities will not merely surpass but also sully one's own. The starkest statement of envy was made by a male character about another male character: Iago says of Cassio, "He hath a daily beauty in his life that makes me ugly."[16] A counterpart signaling experience more common among women might be, She has a daily beauty in her life that makes me *nothing*. Begrudging and destructive, envy signals doomed self-dissatisfaction; what others admire one dreads. What is admirable in another threatens to annihilate one. What is lovable in another leaves one loveless.

These strange conjunctions make sense when we look at envy from a sibling perspective. Psychologists have puzzled over why it is we do not envy someone simply because she has what we want. Instead we envy someone when what she has or is seems to diminish us, and when we fear that someone's good qualities will deprive us of love. It has often been observed that envy is not sharpest when the discrepancy between oneself and another is greatest, but when we are up close, standing side by side, and measuring small differences in a context of broad similarities. The rationale is clear when we look at envy and status anxiety within the sibling framework: It is similar status and common background and shared personal connections that make a sibling threatening.

Envy is sharpest when the qualities of someone close to us and very much like us are its focus. The sense of displacement is therefore played out in different ways between sister and brother. For brother and sister there is at least a clear difference to mark each from the other and sometimes this offers a buffer between them. Yet the subordination on the basis of gender may inflict a further wound: I thought I was loved, but that love does not give me protection because my brother is preferred as a male. The broader social canvas takes over. Envy in such cases is transformed into shame and defeat.

Throughout life it is the person who has been like us— who takes a step forward or makes a sudden gain—who triggers the poisonous anxiety of envy. When someone far above us ascends rapidly, we are more likely to be tolerant or even indifferent. Envy breeds when there are more similarities than differences, and when we can easily imagine ourselves in the place or position the person we envy now occupies.

This makes the viciousness in envy all the more terrifying. We wish to obliterate—or murder—the person we envy, but we are also close to her and admire her. In the sister knot we face the guilt of wanting to annihilate someone we love; but, perhaps even more important, there is the dread of harming someone we do love, someone with whom we identify. Without that primitive link of identification we would not have that primitive envy. So the wish to obliterate and the love are bound together.

This models a powerful and formative experience of sisters and brothers. But the model that fits this best is that of sisters who feel most like one another. In Western countries sisters are likely to be closer than any age combination of brother and sister, and closer, too, than brothers,[17] and therefore most confused by the usurpation of love, identity, and status. And while this particular developmental trauma can be seen as a formative experience for anyone, its themes are played out more commonly among women, between women.

GUILT ABOUT NORMAL SISTERLY FEELINGS

WHILE GIRLS FIGHT with their siblings as often and as viciously as boys do, the natural-born hostility they share with their brothers tends to haunt them. In *The Interpretation of Dreams*, Freud reported that he had never encountered a woman patient who had not dreamed of murdering her sibling. "In none of my women patients, to take an example, have I failed to come upon this dream of the death of a brother or sister, which tallies with an increase in hostility."[18] This was echoed by the women who spoke to me about their experiences of sistering. Jane, now thirty-two, described her fear that, as a sleepwalker, she would kill her sister by acting out, in her sleep, the aggression she could control when she was awake: "So much of my childhood—so often—I felt repulsed by her. I thought everyone around me must feel the same. It was so irritating that people pretended—consistently and convincingly—not to be repelled by her. They pretended to love her. When she sat in the backseat of the car with me I would look out of the window and turn my head so I couldn't see her at all, not even in the smallest part of my peripheral vision. But I still knew she was there. One sound of her breath, or that disgusting noise she made when she pulled her thumb out of her mouth and sighed, made me realize that she was there. She was close to me and she was next to me, and when she launched that breathy laugh she might as well have been inside me. That flame of annoyance—it was awful and I'd either kick her or just kick the backseat and someone would shout at me, and that would make my blood boil, and I'd really know what it's like to explode with anger."

When I interviewed girls and women whose ages ranged from five to seventy-one, I was likely to be told, within the first half hour of the interview, about a time they had been mean to a sister. They also said that this memory continued to haunt them: It was a knowledge, some indicated, of their capacity for evil, a breach between who they feared they were and who they wanted to be.

Meng, now twenty-seven, said that there had been a long hard struggle to become friends with her sister, who was three years younger. "My mother always says I adored her when she was a baby, but I don't remember that. I remember thinking she was often funny, and I liked showing her things, but I also remember being so annoyed because she was always there. I couldn't understand why she didn't go somewhere else or maybe just disappear. I'd come home from school, all happy and thinking about just ordinary things, and there she was. I don't know. . . . It's hard to explain, but I kept being surprised that she was still sharing my home. And then one day I discovered she was going to be going to the same school. *My* school. I couldn't believe it. I couldn't understand how my parents had let this happen. My mother laughed at my outrage, and that only made me angrier. And the day kept getting nearer, and no one was doing anything about it.

"I told her she couldn't speak to me at school, that she had to keep with kids her own age, and that if she came up to me at recess she'd get into trouble. Then, in a kind of blinding rage, I told her that anyone who went into the toilet during the break would never make any friends. And then I hated her for believing me. And I ran home after school. I knew in her state she couldn't run! And when she cried and when she wet her pants, I felt the most awful pleasure, and I was also furious.

"I sometimes forget about this, because there were so many meaner things I wanted to do. But when I remember that this was something I really did do, I feel sick. No—I still can't think about it without shame."

The older sister uses the trust her younger sister places in her superior knowledge to increase her vulnerability, embarrassment, and discomfort. Meng wanted to punish Lucy for infiltrating her world. She saw that her life was once again, in the social arena, threatened. "I worked so hard to present myself as someone different from my family, and she was going to pull me down. I hated being identified with her, but I also wanted her to be publicly humiliated."

I expected then to hear stories about how "my sister was mean to me," but the theme "I was mean to my sister" emerged far more clearly. There were boyfriends either "snatched" from a sister or "passed on, and known to be faulty, and then sometimes snatched back again." But the guilt or shame that one sister harbored for being mean was rarely mirrored by any lasting resentment in the victim. When women speak about girls' friendships, they are much quicker to talk about how mean other girls were to them; in the world of sisters the opposite is true.

Meng's sister, Lucy, for example, remembers her first awful day at school, but has a very different take on Meng's role in it. "I was scared of the toilets. I had a spider phobia, and I was afraid there would be spiders scuttling across the floor in those stalls. They were scary, and that's why I didn't want to use them. I loved being at the same school with Meng. I liked to watch her at recess. And we always walked home together. I was so proud that she was my sister. And she was usually nice to me."

It was sister guilt rather than one's own experience as a victim of a sister's meanness that was the more common theme. Girls and women feel guilty for fantasizing about harming a sister, but sisters who are the object of these fantasies are rarely really harmed. And when a sister does die, many surviving siblings assume that they had a hand in it. Trisha Goddard has spoken about her guilt at the suicide of her sister: "Why didn't I answer her last letter right away? Why didn't I tell her that I loved her?" Mary Hoffman is working on a novel that opens with the gripping sentence, "It is quite by chance that I find out I killed my sister." A sister is likely to think that her own hostility plays a part in her sister's death, whatever the actual cause. The guilt of wishing harm to someone who is also loved is one reason grief over the death of a sibling has such staying power.

GUILT FOR HATING SOMEONE WHO IS CLOSE TO US

"I HAVE SUCH a clear memory of those awful feelings, and how they were both directed at her and at everyone and everything," explains twenty-five-year-old Donna. "But however much I hated her, she was always there, right there with me. I wanted everyone else to see how hateful she was, but when she *did* get shouted at, I'd feel a different kind of terror and was always running to comfort her. She blubbered and sobbed, and put her disgusting hand, wet with all her slobber, into mine and I hugged her, and I felt this. . . . Oh, it was awful: I really wanted to comfort her, but I also wanted to punch her, so I started crying and that surprised her so she stopped crying and took the comforting role and started patting my head. I must have been stooping down in front of her—because there's four years between us—and there she was, looking at me with her wide eyes. The tears were still on her face, but her face wasn't a crying face at all now, and she was doing this funny patting gesture. It was such a serious imitation of a grown-up comforting her. I was so annoyed because—well, who was she to comfort me? But it was also cute and funny, and I realized how much I loved her, but how defeated I felt by this love. And for the longest time I thought I could never have children if this was how I was going to respond to them."

Donna's inability to accept her resentment leads to confusion and self-distrust. She is isolated from any social norm that integrates sibling love and rivalry. Donna recalls the painful ambivalence of feelings that seem connected but refused either to mix or to integrate. She was aware of her hatred and her love. She felt evil, and she believed her wish to hurt her sister signaled a deep failing: "It made me wonder whether I could be trusted, emotionally, to care for anyone. If I could have such feelings toward a sister, then what might I do to a child? How would I ever be a suitable mother? Who would ever be willing to be close to me?"

*   *   *

Some sisters in this study were able to combine in their fantasies both the wish to kill and the wish to protect. Jessica, now twenty-one, looks back on her childhood fantasies. Jessica explains that she "warmed her daydreams" with elaborate rescue scenarios. "My favorite was the first one, when Libby, who was four years older than me, and Adi, who was just a year older, were trapped in the back room, and I climbed up to break the window and get them out. I even did the practice climb a few times, and kept rehearsing it in my mind, until a neighbor complained to my mom. There were also shoot-out scenarios, when I pushed them to the ground just in time, and these complicated ones about fatal illness, but that was when I thought I might be a doctor. I always imagined my dad looking at me with enormous pride when he heard about my heroism.

"He'd say, 'Gosh, was I wrong about you, girl.' But don't think that was the main point. There was every bit as much pleasure in the visions of the dangers they faced as in my heroism. It was real comforting to think of all those dangers that they might face. I remember Libby coming home one day—it was when we were at different schools—and she gave me this bland "Hi" when she came in, and I wanted to shout at her. I couldn't see how she could get through the day and be oblivious of all those dangers I was imagining for her."

Jessica wants to be "tested"—to see whether she can both indulge her wish to destroy her sisters and to make them safe. "I can't imagine being able to survive without my sisters. Getting through a bad breakup, or one of those low points when everything that happens tells you your life isn't going to amount to much. That's when I need my sister. Or having a success and not being able to gloat in a silly sisterly way— I couldn't face it. But I also have to live with this really wicked urge to imagine that their lives are messed up."

As women look back on the early ambivalence of sistering, they wonder what it says about their value, their worth, their capacity to love and to be loved. They are dealing with problems that may be as old as human reflection and attachment, but they are also dealing with questions that arise in a particular culture at a particular time. The animosity felt by a woman toward another defies the ideal of sisterhood. Resentment is seen as something that should be suppressed, rather than as an inevitable adjustment to sharing our world. The peculiar shape that sister rivalry takes is linked to powerlessness: We envy when we do not see a way to gain the things we want for ourselves. We envy when the resources we need seem scarce. We envy, and feel the consequent hostility, when the love and admiration of others is something we both see as essential to our survival and believe ourselves unworthy of. At this point in the cultural and historical shift in women's lives, when they are gaining power to claim the good things they want, when women's place in the wider world is less restricted, envy is less rampant and therefore easier to confront. At this point in women's history, naming that envy, and facing it, may be feasible.

CULTURAL TEMPLATES

ANY PATTERN OF experience that is now being addressed by psychologists will previously have been noticed by creative storytellers, whether the stories are based on religious truths or come in the form of novels, plays, or films. Creative writers are always ahead of the psychologists, and their work should be a touchstone for academic theories. Having articulated the sibling trauma and the sister knot, we can look at how it has already been developed in a range of literature.

The threat siblings pose as usurpers of one's social position and as thieves of identity is stamped on Western culture. In the Bible, Jacob appears to his father disguised as the older brother, Esau, to receive both his father's blessing and the good life that goes with it. The underlying charges of the sibling, "You took my life" and "You are leading the life that should have been mine," continue as a theme today. In Annabel Dilke's *The Inheritance*, a sister poised to embark on a life liberated by education is entrapped by the sister who has been marked as the inheritor of the family class and feminine role. The traditional sister dupes the radical one into helping her and brings shame upon her. The sisters remain bound to each other, resentful and conflicted, neither free to be who she wants to be, each usurping the other's place.

But a wicked intent is not necessarily part of this universal query of sister to sister: "Whose life are you living?" In Judith Michael's novel *Deception*, identical twins play with the notion of replacement. Bored by their own lives, curious about the other's life, they engage in what they suppose to be a harmless deception. Instead they find themselves in a real replacement, all too easily taking over the partners and children who belong to the other. They displace each other while still loving and caring for each other. Judith Michael explores the way replacement themes do not need to be motivated by ill feeling to have devastating effects. The possibility of replacement is intriguing and releasing, but it is also confusing and entrapping.

It is in *Drowning Ruth* that we find one of the most powerful renditions of sister themes. When Amanda's sister is born the grown-ups expect that she will be jealous "to have such a pretty little sister." Amanda is amazed by this expectation. Being the beautiful baby's sister means that the beautiful baby belongs to her: "The baby that everyone wanted for herself belonged to me," Amanda explains. Sistering means loving and caring for and belonging to: Why should she be jealous?

Yet Amanda's life is disrupted by her sister. The baby's wailing rages like a storm through her dreams. Their mother is now so focused on the baby that she appears, at times, to hate her older daughter. When Amanda touches Mattie, her mother explodes with rage: "Don't touch her! Get out of here." What Amanda experiences as rejection, however, is simply the mother's protective panic: The baby is ill; they are worried she will die, and they do not want the older girl to be infected, too.

The love among the women of the family becomes a puzzle about attachment, and attachments change shape and purpose in different contexts. Amanda, as older sister, feels that she has the baby, in the way one speaks of a mother having a baby. Then their mother dies, and Amanda takes on the maternal role; the older sister becomes mother to the younger. Later it is the younger sister who cares for Amanda, when she is seduced, impregnated, and abandoned.

In this novel Christina Schwartz brings together the two different meanings in "replacing" someone. A girl fears her sister will replace her in the family in the sense of displacing her. But there is another meaning to replacing someone: a sister can replace a mother who is dead; a sister who loses a sister seeks someone to replace her. The prospect of being replaced by another person, in the sense of being "usurped," has another side; for in taking someone's place there is also the potential to compensate for the loss of another person.

When Amanda's illegitimate child is born, she carries the baby across the ice to take her to a surrogate mother. The younger sister, Mattie, with her own child, Ruth, in tow, tries to stop Amanda. As Mattie follows her sister, she and Ruth fall through the ice. In the frozen waters there is a second struggle: Amanda tries to save her sister, but Mattie tries to save her own daughter, Ruth. When Amanda grabs hold of Mattie to pull her out of the water, Mattie bites Amanda's hand. Mattie wants Amanda to let go of her so that Amanda can tend to Ruth. Mattie, as mother, forces her sister, Amanda, to save her own child. Amanda then carries the guilt of having drowned her little sister.

With Mattie dead, Amanda becomes mother again, this time to her sister's daughter, while she gives away her own daughter to a childless, child-hungry woman. In time the daughter she gave away and the niece she raised as a daughter become best friends. Unaware of their blood-link as cousins, they express their sisterlike affinity through friendship.

The great originality of Schwartz's novel lies in the transformation of the sister knot. One sister unwittingly causes the death of the other; but their death struggle is bonded and loving: Mattie runs onto the ice to protect Amanda, and Amanda is furious with her for endangering herself. First Amanda's role as older sister is transformed to mother; then the younger sister reciprocates by mothering the older sister. The theme of replacement, which in the most primitive version of the sister knot is a theme of annihilation, is transformed, in *Drowning Ruth*, into a theme of reparation. Each sister stands in for the other as a means of carrying on another's life.

The novel presents, from various angles, sisters' familiar guilt about complicated feelings. Without suppressing the theme of sisterly aggression, it shows the breadth and mutability of sister bonds. The intricate plot provides a framework in which we see that though tragedies may emerge from the forces and counterforces between sisters, this bond provides a lifeline of support and continuity. This promise is the theme of my book. The sister knot leads us to confront the deepest questions about the need for love, the persistence of self-doubt, the envy we may suffer in our pursuit of both love and security. It also shows the strengths of love, protection, and attachment among sisters, and, by extension, it clarifies the strengths and the pressure points in our attachment to the women with whom we learn to stand as sisters.

4

Shared Minds: Empathy and Identity Between Sisters

" KNOW JUST WHAT she's feeling," "I know just how she thinks," "I can imagine exactly what she'd say," are common responses to the question, "How well do you know your sister?" The easy access siblings, in particular sisters, have to one another's mind, mood, and emotions creates a distinctive bond. A shared sense of what is significant, what is interesting, and what is absurd or amusing is played out daily. Sisters quickly pick up on the real meaning and matter of a conversation or game; they grasp what to say and when to say it in order to get the effect they are after. Normally we have high access to a sibling, and particularly high access to one of the same gender, and one who is relatively close to us in age.[1]

Sisters' fast track to understanding contains all the good feelings ordinarily associated with empathy, including the urge to comfort and console; but it can also include a wish to disrupt, confuse, and terrify. In this chapter I look at the way empathy between sisters arises in childhood, as girls monitor and observe one another. But observing empathy among sisters forces us to reassess the basic elements of empathy. Empathy's usual guise of care and comfort has to be shed. For empathy has hard edges. Knowledge of others' minds involves shrewd calculation and sophisticated skills that are not always used to comfort and protect. And this brings us to a more robust understanding of female bonding and female responsiveness, so often linked to empathy.[2]

FANTASY AND EMPATHY

SISTER CLOSENESS EMERGES in mutual understanding and childhood play. The women I interviewed about sister relationships recalled elaborate and rewarding games that went on for days or months, filled with secret codes and references. Their engrossing fantasies often irritated others: The grown-ups found such nonsense tedious and boring; other children were bemused or excluded; but for the sisters themselves the play had a clarity and excitement they found nowhere else. "We were stars in our own world," Jessica explained. "Libby really was, for me, everything she declared she was in our games. She was the ruler, the wizard, the mother, the teacher. Playing with her always had a special excitement."

Imaginative play in childhood is a sophisticated form of learning. Through play, children process their observations; they explore relationships and social interactions; they enact and reenact events that have particularly pleased or disturbed them. They pick a single incident that made a special impact and link it to other events, elaborating wider meanings of any single experience through theme and variation. In play, children practice social roles and consider their power to influence their environment; they explore their hopes and fears, in both their present and their future lives. Their first and longest-term playmates are siblings.

When Simone de Beauvoir wrote about her sister, she described her as the perfect playmate. Together the girls brought imaginary stories to life. The most ordinary games, when shared with her sister, became marvelous adventures. Only her sister's imagination could resonate so clearly with her own. The two having shared a family environment, having spent so much time together, the ideas of one set those of the other in motion. Each found multiple shortcuts to the other's thoughts, so that even the briefest comment was sufficient to summon up complex understanding. Apparently banal games drew on "something secret and intimate within us which would not bear the searching light of adult gazes."[3] As in Louisa May Alcott's classic about sisters, *Little Women*, extended and mutually created dramas provide a basis for lifelong intimacy.

In the sister groups that spoke to me, play and fantasy, private and shared, remained a prominent theme. For Jessica, on the cusp of adulthood and far from the childhood games that so excited her, shared fantasies leave a powerful legacy. "Libby understands me better than anyone. We grew up together. There's this background knowledge, that means you don't have to explain stuff. So when I complain about my boss, and what he's said to me, she has this immediate sense of the situation. She'll know it's awful because it's just like something our father would say. But sometimes she'll know something is awful because we were never treated like that at home. I was really upset the other day about something that happened at work, and she said I had to accept that I wouldn't always get a chance to explain myself, like I did at home. And suddenly we were staring at each other and she said, 'I guess things weren't that bad at home,' and we laughed, because complaining about Mom and Dad's ways is just one of the things we do."

Jessica is starting life in the "real world" of jobs and work colleagues and employers, and her sister Libby, twenty-five, understands precisely how a boss's impatience or criticism will pitch her little sister into a series of questions about whether she's messed up or whether the accusations are unfair. Libby picks up on implicit references to punishments at home, and knows Jessica will try to defend herself in her homespun style. She warns that the strategy of challenging criticisms that can be so effective at home may be counterproductive at work. Jessica then notes that this forces both of them to make a new assessment of their "impossible parents." It strikes her as amusing that the people she has been so used to complaining about are actually, in contrast to many others in her new adult world, fair and reasonable. Libby shares the comedy of this revelation, and the sisters see it as a growing-up station that they reach together.

Each sister has easy access to the other's viewpoint and response. Communication is light-footed, comforting, and profound. As Jessica says, her sister "knows her better than anyone else."

THE USES OF UNDERSTANDING

WE NORMALLY TALK about being understood in a positive way. Being understood is comforting and eases the pinch of loneliness. But being understood also makes us vulnerable. In fact, it is by looking at siblings that one can see most clearly the two faces of understanding: On one side someone's understanding of us can lead to support and sympathy; on the other side someone's understanding of us allows her to manipulate and wound us.

Jessica values her sister's shortcuts to understanding as she relates day-to-day stories, but she notes that there is another aspect to their connection. "When Libby wants to hurt me, she can strike right to the core. Even now, she'll say, 'Oh, Jessie, don't be such a twit,' just when I'm at my most insecure. The awful thing is that I see what she means, and it can push me into a pit, because I know she means I'm being like *that*. Like I am when I'm really difficult and awful. She knows just what she's doing, and she traps me in the most awful part of myself. When she wants, Libby can be meaner than anyone else."

Libby, aware of herself as "the older sister," explains her

occasional cruelty. "It can be great talking to Jessie. It's so much better now than it was when we were kids. Boy, was she a whiner! She would go into a funk and just stay there, moaning and complaining about herself and her life. We can really talk now, most of the time, but when she gets into that infantile state, I feel I'm being sucked into something. I'm being sucked into her dark mood, and I'm being sucked back into our childhood, and I get so annoyed! I just don't want to go back there!"

The process by which siblings get to know one another explains the resonance with a sibling's mood and mind. But that profound connection is not always welcome, and when one sister wants to reject or disturb that closeness, she is well placed to know how to do so. To appreciate the significance of the mutual understanding of siblings, we have to look back even further than the earliest childhood memories, to consider those tricky philosophical questions, How do we know other people have minds, since we cannot access them in the ways we access our own mental activity? and, How do we come to know that other people have those inner thoughts and feelings that we have? and, How do children learn that their perspective, which they experience as central, is not the only possible way of seeing things?

OTHER MINDS

TO FUNCTION IN our society, we need to mind read. Understanding language is not enough. Someone who understands only the meaning of language cannot sustain a conversation. Every conversation, however trivial, is shaped by context, gesture, and tone of voice. To get on in a conversation, we need to pick up on signals that what we are saying is either interesting or dull. We need to know when someone is "telling us," by movement and by intonation, when the conversation is coming to an end. To respond in a conversation, we need to know if someone is making a joke or a complaint.

Others' actions can only be understood in the context of feelings, motives, and intentions. When someone asks you if you want to come for a drink, you are misunderstanding the question, and in effect rebuffing the offer, if you reply simply in terms of whether you are thirsty. When someone slams a door, we misunderstand him if we think he is simply closing a door loudly. We need to watch and listen to others and get from their behavior a sense of their mood and emotion. We need some sense of how people will respond to our gestures and voice.

Someone who lacks all facility in mind reading does not know whether another person is angry or happy. People who lack these interpretative skills have a great deal of trouble functioning in the social world. Most children, fortunately, do develop a strong sense of other people as thinking and feeling beings, who have intentions and responses quite separate from them, but who, like them, inhabit an intensely personal world. Children demonstrate a sophisticated awareness of other people's multidimensional minds very early in life. They watch their parents and playmates and learn from them. But we now know that the most intensive learning goes on with siblings.

CHANGING THEORIES OF CHILDREN'S UNDERSTANDING

THE QUESTION OF how we know that a child is able to understand that another person has an active, independent mind, with her or his own distinct subjective focus, has long fascinated psychologists. The changing answers to this question over the past decades display the importance of bringing siblings into the picture.

It was once supposed that very young children could not grasp that other people had thoughts and feelings and needs distinct from their own. Instead young children were assumed to inhabit a world limited by "intersubjectivity." This arose as an infant became conscious of her own mental activity. A child learned that her own behavior affected the behavior of others. When she was hungry or cold or frightened, her body behaved in a certain way, and others might hold her, talk to her soothingly, or express stress themselves at her discomfort. Gradually an infant learned that she was displaying her feelings, and that her feelings could be understood by others. For some time, the established view was that children experienced their own minds and believed that other people shared their inner thoughts and experiences but could not grasp that other people had independent thoughts and experiences.

These views were not challenged until the final two decades of the twentieth century. Until then psychologists conducted their observations of young children in academic labs. These laboratory studies indicated that children were incapable of understanding other minds until they reached the age of six or seven years. Of course even very young children played alongside one another, but such play, it was argued, was devoid of mutuality. Other people in the child's world appeared to them as actors but not as thinkers distinct from themselves, not capable of taking a very different view of the world they shared. When a child appeared to "understand" what another was feeling, the academic argument went, then a child was merely projecting her or his own feelings onto someone else. Through self-projection they could socialize with others, but they lacked real understanding of other minds until middle childhood.

When children were observed with their siblings, however, these long-established theories were immediately overturned; with people they cared about, whose behavior and experience had profound effects on their own lives, young children's excellent mind-reading skills came to light. Judy Dunn and her colleagues observed children in their homes and interviewed mothers at length about their children.[4] She realized that if psychologists wanted to gauge what a child understands about the people who matter to her, then it is necessary to observe her in a setting that engages her, has emotional meaning to her, and in which she can best express her knowledge, without the constraints of a strange laboratory dominated by strange people. When we are dealing with very young children, the best setting for this is the home, among her parents and her siblings.

HOW CHILDREN DEMONSTRATE THEIR KNOWLEDGE THAT OTHER PEOPLE HAVE MINDS OF THEIR OWN

AS SOON AS children acquire the rudiments of language, they prove themselves to be active participants in a world of other people. Children as young as two are likely to comment on a sibling as a person with needs, wants, likes, and dislikes. Day-to-day speech and behavior show that very young children can understand the intentions, feelings, and actions of others who share that world.[5]

In Judy Dunn's observations of toddlers with baby siblings, the older child was adept at "explaining" the baby's thoughts and feelings: The baby needs feeding; the baby is tired; the baby wants her mother; the baby is interested, excited, happy. The toddler entertained the new sib by showing her toys, making noises imitating rattles or engines, tickling her, or making faces at her. The two-year-olds' "sensitivity to the emotional expressions of the baby, and the interpretations of his behavior, presented with clarity their beliefs and their understanding of the other child."[6] While they may not be able to judge the emotions of an unfamiliar person, or of a model representing a person in an artificial setting (as children had been asked to do in the laboratory studies), young children are skillful at reading, anticipating, and responding to the feelings and plans of their siblings.

Parents are well aware of a child's abilities. They encourage these abilities from a very early age, coaching a child to think about siblings as people like themselves. "How would you like it if she grabbed something you were holding?" "He just wants to be left alone for a while." "You'd be pleased, too, if you managed to do that." Many of these reminders are aimed at keeping the peace, but parents have also been observed talking to older children about a new baby in ways that encourage the older child to view the infant as an individual with a mind of her own. In families with a newborn second child, parents often talk to the older child about what the baby is looking at, what she might be seeing or thinking, why she is crying, and what will comfort her. In particular mothers draw attention to the baby's interest in an older sibling: "She's watching you," or "She thinks you're funny," or "She doesn't like that crying," or "She's wondering what you're doing."[7]

Children whose parents encourage them to take note of the newborn's mental activity do seem to pick up more quickly on the baby's individual responses, but siblings also grow close in the absence of parental input. In fact, psychologists who observe young siblings together have noted that when a mother is very tired, strained, or even depressed during the weeks after the birth, the siblings (especially sisters) are likely to sustain a particularly close relationship.

Children themselves take the initiative in eliciting responses from their siblings. They persist in coaxing a younger sibling to speak. They are proactive communicators, and when the younger child begins to talk, older siblings prove themselves excellent interpreters of what the infant is trying to say. They stimulate talk by gestures and gurgles. They infer the infant's feelings and desires, asking the younger child whether he or she has understood. "You want this—right? This one?" Older children simplify their speech when they speak to baby siblings. They shorten their sentences, repeat themselves, speak certain words clearly to accommodate younger siblings' developing language abilities, and paraphrase when they meet a puzzled or unengaged look. "Bring me the ball. The ball. The red thing. Red. Yes!" They display excitement and pleasure when it is clear that a younger sib understands them.[8]

Even children barely out of infancy themselves have the capacity to understand that other people have minds of their own, with a different perspective and different mental capacities. They are particularly articulate and expressive when they talk about a sister or brother.[9] When young children are asked to describe the personal qualities of their friends, their siblings, and their parents, they speak with far greater clarity and detail about their siblings than they do about either their friends or their parents. In describing a sister or brother, children use many more emotional terms, both positive and negative, than they do when talking about any of their other relationships.[10] Their sense of a sibling's individual character traits, her preferences and predilections, her winning ways and her irritating habits, are elaborately drawn by children who are only just learning to talk. So, once again, looking at siblings changes the entire picture of human development. A long-established theory about children's inability to understand the independent perspective and experience of other people is overturned as the remarkable ability to read the minds of siblings is observed. It is not that children *require* a sibling to develop or exhibit their knowledge of other minds;

but watching children with a sibling shows how quick children can be to understand that other people are independently thinking beings. Children have capacities for understanding far beyond what has previously been appreciated in standard theories of children's development.

This applies to all siblings, same-sex and mixed, but over time pronounced gender differences emerge in sibling behavior. Older sisters imitate a younger sibling more often and show more friendly interest in a sibling than does a brother. Same-sex pairs of siblings also relate in different ways from the very beginning of the relationship. Sisters and brothers exhibit a higher number of friendly interactions than do pairs of mixed siblings.[11] While same-sex siblings, over the years, often report more intensely focused jealousy, they also appear closer from an early age. Understanding and love connect with understanding and resentment to form one of the many configurations of the sister knot.

MOTIVES FOR UNDERSTANDING

THE INTIMACY OF siblings and the power of their mixed feelings emerge from the triangle of love, with the three points represented by the child, the parent, and the sibling. The first relationship, and the first awakening to other minds, comes in infancy.

The infant is wired to maintain and explore relationships, particularly with those who care for her. Children imitate grown-ups and learn how to be adults in their society by pretending they are. They imitate grown-ups when they boss their peers, sometimes to protect one member from what they perceive as an attack against her, or from a situation that arouses feelings they know another cannot tolerate. The language parents use is taken up in the subsystem of siblings. The moral mimicry—"You're a messy baby, aren't you?" and "You're naughty; you know you're not supposed to do that!"—allows a child to play at being dominant.

Parent and infant engage in a fascinating exchange of attention and response, whose moves are so closely coordinated, with such grace, that Dan Stern, who was the first to capture these unfolding interactions on film and video, called this interchange "a dance."[12] The mutual engagement can be seen as a sophisticated bid for survival in a world whose complexity requires long-term parental involvement. The parental attentiveness we need in order to survive plays a crucial role in our development of human understanding.

During the first year of life humans seem to need a warm, predictable attachment to another person for healthy development. And children need parents' engagement to continue, because they remain physically and socially vulnerable for a very long time. Humans are dextrous and ingenious, but they are slower than other animals to acquire skills to function independently. The complex society they have to adapt to requires an extensive learning period. So it is not surprising that siblings who interfere with this intense and adaptive relationship become a focus of hostility.

When a sibling is born, a child's world changes. The birth of the sibling and the accompanying changes in the older child's life have a dramatic effect on the behavior of the first-born child. It is not only a parent's attention and love that are at stake: The arrival of a sibling involves a constellation of changes. In the many families observed in Judy Dunn's studies of siblings, mothers reported that an older child was most obviously jealous when the father or grandparents showed pleasure or interest in the baby. They could be warm and affectionate to the baby, but in other respects clearly upset and disturbed by the events surrounding the arrival of the sibling. As Judy Dunn notes, "Almost all the children we followed showed signs of disturbance and unhappiness in addition to their interest in and affection for the baby."[13]

For a child born into a family with siblings waiting to greet her, the effect is different—but not completely different. Younger siblings, too, have a time in paradise, when their life seems to comprise only their overwhelming experiences of the wonderful and terrifying new world, and when the people who focus on them mark the border of their universe. The implications of the fact that there are other people with whom they must share and compete are episodic; but such awareness is nonetheless traumatic, as they gradually realize that others close to them, who interact with them, can threaten their unique status and their privileged position.

The tumultuous changes caused by a sibling are beyond a child's comprehension. After studying the effect of the birth of a sibling on young children for more than a decade, Judy Dunn reflected in conversation, "The child's misery is so unfocused. It is as if they don't know what they are so miserable about. In the middle of a nice game with mother, they burst into tears. Why they are so unhappy is that their life has been destroyed. Even more confusing is at the same time, many of them adore the baby. Children love babies. It's so unsettling, so painful . . . to feel and yet not have the faculties to understand your grief."[14]

This distress arises within a sense of self that is vulnerable to displacement. However careful the parents are to reassure and assuage, the trauma occurs on a deeply symbolic level. Children have a sense of urgency in getting to grips with who they are and how they can more or less stabilize a sense of themselves. A sense of self is, after all, crucial to a sense of being alive.

The emotional context in which siblings play, talk, and fight with each other, is a setting of real passion. The depth of conflict, jealousy, and affection goes a long way toward explaining why children grasp so early the feelings and intentions of their siblings. If you are competing for your place in your human world, it is important to anticipate the actions of someone who threatens you, and to do that, you need to read her moods or feelings. Empathy grows from the sympathy and compassion siblings have for each other, but empathy and understanding are also driven by the emotional power of their conflict with each other.

UNDERSTANDING: COMPASSION OR CONTROL?

KNOWING WHAT ANOTHER is feeling, and being able to follow her thoughts and predict what she'll do, involve the intimate process of empathy. We normally say we know someone well when we have a clear sense of what she'll do or say, and when we find it easy to explain why she acts as she does. Normally when we say we are close to someone, we imply both that we know her well and, on the whole, want to use this knowledge to keep her company, cheer her up, and protect her from the slings of fortune. When we look at empathy between siblings, we can see that having access to someone's thoughts, moods, and personal quirks and preferences does makes one feel close to that person; but such access does not always make one behave kindly toward them. "Thinking siblings," that is, registering the impact of siblings on psychological development, allows us to challenge stereotypes about empathy; and with this we can challenge stereotypes about girls' psychology and female bonding.

Girls' facility for empathy has been noted in a wide range of research. Girls emerge from infancy with a stronger basis for experiencing another's needs or feelings than boys do.[15] Their psychological development often resides in a deepening understanding of care.[16] Concern for, and sensitivity to, others often drives their words, their behaviour, and their judgment.

Such research findings both support and explain the observation that girls display more extensive awareness of a sister's moods and feelings than do either brothers or pairs of mixed siblings. For sisters, statistically, are more likely to share a capacity for empathy. But when we look at sisters, we see something that is all too often left out of readings of special female skills—the range of uses to which the facility for empathy can be put.

When we say a person is a good empathizer, we normally

expect that person to be good at observing other people. The phrase "women's intuition" does not mean that women come to know things in some magical way; it means that many women are good at catching sight of small changes in voice and behavior that some other people (both male and female) miss. From observations of children, and from the stories women tell of their sistering experiences, the skilled precision of sibling teasing is apparent. That precision arises from a deep understanding of the sibling. This understanding, or empathy, goes hand in hand with viciousness, sometimes occasional and sometimes systematic. Nowhere in girls' and boys' behavior is there evidence for empathy that is purely caring or sympathetic. Girls are quite capable of using their empathic skills to manipulate others.

Two decades ago two researchers noted, "Siblings know well the arsenal of weapons each possesses; they are usually able consciously to calculate, calibrate, plan and control their aggressive actions and hostile statements."[17] So it was that the quickness with which very young children learned how to *annoy* a sibling shattered the long-held belief that young children lack the capacity to get inside another person's head, to see what matters to another, to look at things from another's viewpoint. A two-year-old knows that her sister will be comforted by her favorite blanket, or distressed by seeing her favorite toy thrown across the room. She understands what meanings objects have to other people even when they do not have the same meanings to her.

Siblings, with their high access to one another, empathize with each other. This understanding stimulates sympathy and solidarity. It also leads to skilled playing on one another's "aggression keyboard." Siblings rile, infuriate, and distress each other; yet, as Ally says, "No one can comfort me like my sister."

SISTERS AND EMPATHY IN ACTION

WHEN WE LOOK at the intense empathy fostered in sistering, we can see that while empathy may perhaps be said to be hard-wired into the female brain,[18] it is complex; it may lead to care and sensitivity, but it may also lead to ruthlessness and cunning. If we are to understand the interpersonal world of women, so profoundly shaped by the capacity for empathy, then we must be clear about what empathy is and how it functions.

Siblings know more about each other than each voluntarily reveals to the other. This knowledge can be used to generate acute discomfort. When young children deprive a sibling of a favorite toy or blanket, they often have no wish to have it themselves; they are simply causing mischief; they take it away because doing so distresses their sibling.

This type of cruelty is far more likely to be reported by women when recalling either a sister or a brother than by men when they speak about their brothers and sisters.[19] It may be that women have better memories for this kind of treatment, or it may be that this kind of cruelty was experienced more deeply.

Beth, twenty-eight, reflects on what she calls her "horrible times" with her younger sister, Alexandra. She now adores and sometimes still fears her sister: "There was no playground bully who could hurt me like she did. Her put-downs were endless. One time I'd just persuaded our mother that I could wear my favorite coat to school. For some reason there was a battle about this. Maybe the weather wasn't right for it, but I couldn't wait until it got colder. Anyway I got to wear it. Just as Alexandra was leaving me in the schoolyard she said, 'That's just the kind of coat Judy would wear.' Judy was the girl I thought so revolting—you know how when you're a kid some people really make you want to throw up? Like I guess you learn to control that, but you don't when you're eight years old. We used 'Judy' as a word to describe things that made you ridiculous and disgusting. And when she said that I immediately saw what she meant, because it really had a frosted cake effect—sort of mohair and pinkish—and of course she knew that was something that would haunt me. I could be so pleased with something, and she always knew precisely what to say to shoot me down."

From Alexandra's point of view, her swipes at Beth were fair retaliation for her older sister's manipulation. She recalls how skilled Beth was at getting her to do things. "She used to say, 'Ok, you don't have to do it. And don't worry. I'll *never* ask you to do anything for me again.' It was scary, like a threat, like she'd let herself drown rather than ask for my help." Another tack Beth took, when Alexandra asked for her help, was to turn to her and say, "If you ask me one more time, I'll make you have it," and suddenly the toy or gadget or handbag she wanted was something sinister. Even the fact that she wanted it was sinister. "I felt trapped by someone who knew me so well. I could see what she was doing. I could see that she was tickled to death to be able to separate me from what I thought I wanted. But I couldn't do anything about it."

The ability to sustain a relationship with someone who may use intimate knowledge to hurt and humiliate is not easy. Alexandra sees this as a puzzle and as a necessity. "I love being with my sister. But even now it's not always easy. We can have such a lot of fun, but then she'll just say something and I want to kick her. There are times when I think I never want to see her again. But I guess getting mad is just part of the deal."

Often in sister stories, memories of cruelty inflicted are sharper than the memories of cruelties suffered. Knowing her range of fears, and having a shrewd sense of what a sister can and cannot tolerate, a girl is well placed to terrify and torment a sister; but even when she is the aggressor, she is likely to feel empathy.

Attacks on a sibling sometimes provide momentary pleasure, but they have a double edge. Sibling cruelty carries a moral message: When we hurt someone with whom we identify, we also hurt ourselves. So revenge on someone we love must be pursued with caution. Sarah recalls how she tried to get her sister, Ellie, to stop pestering her to play. "I told her there were lots of snakes under the house. We were in this lovely little cabin, on vacation, and she was running around and wanted to play outside with me, and I was tired so I told her about the snakes, and she just screamed, and wanted to go home, and I felt mean but satisfied. It's creepy, when you realize that you can take pleasure in being really mean. But then I got bored. The cabin wasn't fun anymore, because Ellie wasn't having fun."

When Fleur Adcock told her sister that her favorite doll had once been a real girl whose death they had heard about, her little sister thrust it aside, fearful of it, and never played with it again. The big sister's teasing was ingenious and effective, but it backfired: Fleur ruefully admits that the doll "was ruined for me, too."[20]

UNDERSTANDING AND REJECTION

THE CRUELTIES WE inflict and receive from our sisters seldom drive us apart. Sister empathy does not ensure compassion, but it does entail identification; and identification with someone who has characteristics and behavior we do not like is deeply disturbing. Wendy explains why she avoids talking to her older sister, Marcia: "I know exactly what she's feeling. I understand how she got there, sort of. I can see why someone who's grown up with my father could easily make a mess of her life. And that's what my sister has done. So when we're together, and I hear her go on about some other harebrained scheme, or hear her talk about the next dud guy she's hooked up with, I want to say, *I don't understand you.* But I do understand her, and that makes things worse."

The thought that terrifies Wendy is, This person is like me; this person is part of me; and I do not like her. So there is part of myself I dislike. But her attempt to create a permanent void is like disowning part of herself. As Stephen Bank and Michael Kahn say, "Every sibling, no matter how much he or she may dislike a brother or sister, recognizes that each person carries inside some part of the other." Disowning or cutting off a sibling is "really like severing part of oneself."[21] We may wish we could cast out a sibling who shames us, but rejection is difficult and painful. Among siblings we flick from rage to acceptance, and we learn to count the relational costs of holding a grudge.

These lessons and tensions persist beyond the cauldron of growing up. Wendy and Marcia each invest heavily in their own anger. Each is anxious to confront the other to explain what she feels, what has offended her, and why she is in the right. "I keep hoping things will improve," Wendy muses, "but then I talk to her and in two minutes I'm stuck in this cloud of blame." Even the most apparently straightforward conversations become "an excuse to list my faults and failings. When I have to tell my sister what I'm doing, or when I suggest she do something for the family, there's this awful pause. I can see her taking it in and absorbing the meaning, and then processing it according to her own lights. It makes me feel sick. She'll say, 'I know why you are after this.' Her voice can turn me to ice. I always want to kick myself for wanting to see her." Marcia says, "This isn't a small thing in my life. I try to make it small, you know, kind of accept it and box it up? But there's this sore spot that gets real raw when someone talks about her sister in a real positive way. I just don't have that, and it makes me sad."

We belong to our sisters, for better or for worse. Sistering gives rise to knowledge of the other, and this knowledge becomes part of the self. Identification through knowledge becomes a lifelong bond. Even siblings who on one level feel separate and disconnected retain the knowledge of each other's core identity. This remains as a legacy and a reminder of one's childhood past, submerged, unverbalized, and only partly forgotten.[22]

HOW SISTERS EXTEND MUTUAL
UNDERSTANDING
TO SHARED UNDERSTANDING
OF THEIR WORLDS

MUTUAL UNDERSTANDING is a process. As sisters look into each other's psyche, they pair up to look out, together, on the world around them. They confirm each other's perceptions and serve as a reality check. This begins in childhood, when they see the world differently than adults do. Together they have checking-up conversations: "Mommy's mad," and "Daddy said no?" and "He has big feet?" They often construct a private vocabulary, strange words and phrases that are meaningless to others but, to the sister group, have clear designations. "It's amazing," reflects Dan Stern, "to watch the whole communication system, the private language that brothers and sisters set up."[23]

In her book *Sisters*, Elizabeth Fishel reports that friends who happen to overhear one side of her weekly phone conversations with her sister believe that they must speak in a "private language, barely discernible even to those who know [her] best, a thick brew of intensity and high hilarity . . . and a patois of strange inflections and phraseology almost primitive in its litany."[24] Many sisters referred to a "private language" or styles of conversations and references that were closed to others, even to other family members. Some women said they were not aware of this privacy until they noted others' responses to it.

Ally, twenty-seven, explained: "It wasn't until my first husband said it drove him crazy that I saw my sister and I spoke what was just about a private language. There was a special rhythm to the topic of conversation. We're immediately back into the dramas of what my father is doing to us. We're talking about everyday things, but they're dramas. The little things Dad says, they can make you feel you're all alone in a corner. You're telling a story at dinner, and you're really into it and thinking everyone is following you, and he'll say, 'Sit yourself down, Ally, and stop showing off.' Or you'll try to join in the conversation and make a suggestion, and he'll look annoyed and say something like, 'Oh, sure,' and laugh. And that's your contribution sniped. Maybe you don't even catch it at first, because it's so little, and when you turn on him, he looks at you, like, *What are you fussing about?* He's cruel, and you're hurt, and then he turns to you to say, 'What's the big deal?' or 'What's your problem?' "

Ally's younger sister, Karen, says, "I don't know how I could have survived my family without my sister to help me make sense of it. My brother was pretty nearly destroyed by it. All these mixed messages that make you feel crazy. My father says to one of us that we're lazy and stupid, and then if we come back with something like, 'You're always putting me down,' he'll say he doesn't know what we mean, that he has the highest regard for us and would never say anything different. He told me that going to college in Chicago was fine, as long as I didn't care about giving my mother a heart attack with worry, and then when I told him I'd decided to go to Urbana, he said, 'Why are you giving up a chance to go to Chicago?' I was dumbstruck and said, 'But you said Mom would be unhappy if I went to Chicago,' and he said he'd never stand in my way, never even influence my decision, which now disappointed him. For my mom it's the same: 'We wanted you to make your own decision. We would never interfere.' Things like this—I have to go through them with my sister. I have to check I'm not imagining things. So I ask Ally, 'You heard him, didn't you,' and when she says, 'Yes, lots of times,' I feel so much better. The situation is the same, but at least I didn't feel mad. My brother has a terrible memory for things people say, so it's frustrating talking over what someone really said as opposed to what they *say* they said, and what they meant. And there's just no point talking to him about people's motives—well, those just don't matter to him the way they do to me and Ally."

Ally says, "Our brother just sits when we are talking. I mean, he sits and maybe sometimes listens. But my husband can't stand it. He can't see what we were talking about. He says it's impossible to follow, whether we we're talking about something that happened when we were kids, or about something my dad said the other day."

The sisters then go on to reflect on their shared histories, of life in their home after their mother died, when their father remarried. "Our stepmom thought we were excluding her on purpose. She'd get real huffy, and sulk, and our father would always see things her way. Sometimes he tried to explain to her why we shut her out. You heard him, didn't you, Kar? He said, 'They just forget about everyone else when they're together.' "

"Yeah," Karen agreed, "But then he scolded us: 'Don't be so selfish.' We didn't know what we were doing—"

"We were—you know, just trying to survive ourselves."

"Because we were left out—"

"When they married, we were left out."

"But we didn't mean to leave her out. We might have—"

"If we'd thought about it, we might have."

"But we wouldn't even say that—"

"We didn't see us doing that."

"No, we didn't see us as excluding her."

"So it was really unfair."

"Yeah, we thought Dad was being unfair."

"And she was being mean." They laugh.

"She was always mean."

This sister conversation stitches together shared words and paired views. Each woman identifies with ease the episode referred to. The sisters' ability to "read" one another's minds is demonstrated in this well-choreographed conversation. The sisters finish each other's sentences, and round off each other's thoughts.

Sister talk has a private register of historical references and deep contexts that are summoned up with a light touch. Ally and Karen are talking about the ordinary family cruelties that many of us suffer—and unwittingly inflict—from time to time. These are experiences that are difficult to catch, but in catching them we define and mold and manage them. Karen says, "It was so much better when we got brave enough to catch each other's eye across the table. With one look you're saying, *He's doing* that—and you feel you have some solidarity. You know, there's someone else who's saying, *This isn't right,* even though you know you would never be able to convince Dad of that. Like I said, I don't see how I could have survived it all without a sister. And now I can ring her and just tell her what he said, and she'll say, 'Typical.' She gets it right away. She gets why it's so maddening."

CHANGING KNOWLEDGE

THE INTENSE KNOWLEDGE sisters have of one another as children may be interrupted as siblings mature. Since the intimate knowledge of a sister is so closely bound up with her sense of self and of human understanding, such interruptions can be accompanied by anxiety and grief. Many of the women I interviewed spoke of a time when they feared they had been left behind and abandoned because a sister changed. Ally said that she watched Karen's absorption with her friends, and felt bereft because "I lost track of her. I lost any sense of what she'd do or say." As psychiatrists Stephen Bank and Michael Kahn observed, "one of two siblings can experience discontinuity in the relationship when the other changes sharply, wordlessly, and with a poignancy never totally assuaged by parental reassurance."[25]

Sasha, now twenty-three, says she is "very, very, very close to my sister," but that when she was fifteen, Vicki closed the door right in her face. "We'd been so close before, two of us, with Meg being the little sister who didn't understand anything because she was too young. We had our own language, a private version of pig latin and Spanish, which we learned from our friends at school, and we drove everyone in the family crazy by talking it. But then she turned fifteen, and she suddenly wasn't there for me. She still let me sit in her room and I'd talk to her, but she wasn't really there. It still—I can still feel how awful it was. Like a betrayal, you know? You think you have this relationship, and suddenly someone in it disappears, but not really, so when I asked her about it, I was just this nag. It still gives me the chills, when I complain about something she's done and she says, 'God, Sasha, leave it alone, will you?' She pretended she wasn't doing anything, and I was making a fuss about nothing. I think my mom saw how down I was, and said things like, 'She's a teenager, Sasha. She doesn't want us now.' She even once said, and this was really sweet, 'I still need you. And so does Meg,' but Meg just stuck her tongue out at me, but Mom was being sweet. I still worry sometimes that Vicki's going to leave me again."

When Sasha herself turned into a teen, her sister Meg said, "My big sisters were so much trouble that no one paid attention to me. I hated them both. And there's still that thing they have—they get together and they take up all the room in a house and breathe in all the air. Their bond is just so big you feel there's no room for you. What I learned from my sisters is how awful it is to be left out of everything and how easy it is to be sidelined." Meg saw her sisters getting new attention as they became difficult teenagers, demanding her mother's attention, stressing out her mother with demands to be allowed to stay out late or go to a party on a school night. "I hated my sisters then for what they were doing to my mother. I thought they were stupid and selfish. And when I wanted mom to say yes to something I wanted to do, I worried that I was just like them, and I couldn't really fight for myself the way they fought. I didn't want to be like them, so I felt really torn, and that made me even more angry.

"But when they left home, I felt abandoned. The real

world seemed to be someplace else. I wanted to know what they were doing. But we had this habit of bickering. You know, we couldn't talk without bickering. They call me, and I get excited about talking to them, and then the next minute they say, 'You're such a pigface.' So it's hard to deal with that, when I'm all up about hearing from them."

Some women said they felt so left out when a sister started doing grown-up things that they would copy her in order to keep up. Karen said that she started dating when Ally did: "I didn't know what I was doing. I didn't have any real interest in being with boys. But Ally was going on dates, and I wanted to be able to talk to her about that. I didn't want to be still the kid left at home who didn't have an interesting life." And Ally said, "I was mortified. I was furious. Here, it seemed I was finally free of that big-sister role of always having to be home to look after my little sister, and she was doing stuff that made me feel I had to look out for her still. Because it was obvious she didn't know what she was doing."

The closeness of sisters tends to take a hit in early adolescence—before increasing markedly in adulthood.[26] The different rates of growth, the upheavals in personality, the turmoil sometimes felt in the family, the different levels of adventurousness and rebelliousness, the critical edge of the adolescent girl, irritation, and intolerance—all contributed to this dip.

When someone close to us changes in some ways, our anxiety can be confused with jealousy. Karen said that she often needed to check in with her sister when something significant in her life changed. "It's not just to give the news, the way I always want to airlift news to my best friend. But there's this anxiety—I just want to make sure we're still the same. When

I ran for the phone after I got this promotion, my partner said, 'Oh, are you hoping she'll be jealous?' and that threw me. Was I? No, I just wanted to say, 'I'm still your little sister.' "

All this resonates with my own experience. If I could have given a name to what I experienced when I saw my sister's body change, and when I took note of her many private conversations with our mother, and heard our mother's whispered conversations with our father, I would have called it "betrayal." My sister appeared self-absorbed and self-important, and no one in my family was willing to reprimand her for it. Later my sister was to explain that she resented, suddenly, being an object of curiosity to me. She shut her bedroom door when she dressed, she wouldn't let me come into the dressing rooms with her when we went shopping, and she stopped inviting me to go swimming with her. "You made me self-conscious. You kept staring at me!" She herself felt betrayed because she was no longer the sister that her little sister knew.

Later what mattered was our new ability to speak our minds. The role my sister and I play and continue to play in each other's bid for sanity, in those lifelong attempts to free oneself from inherited but useless patterns of response, evolved during our verbal gymnastics in adolescence. We worked hard, together, to define the causes of our anger and frustration. We worked to place our sexual feelings in the context of attraction and repulsion, to read emotional meanings from our powerful and confusing responses. The greatest surprise and pleasure of midadolescence was the realization that we could use each other in this way.

The quarrels we each had, in very different ways, with our mother threatened to crush us; but together, taking these to each other, sharing our information, they became bearable. We could name our confusions. With friends there was an infuriating lack of understanding, in our view, of just how terrible these quarrels were. A friend would say, 'My mom's the same,' but I would know that no other mother would be the same, that no other mother's anger would bear down on her with such force.

To explain how and why my mother was so difficult, in my view at least, would require not only a family portrait of greater detail than I was capable of, but would involve the need to justify my feelings—because friendships set limits on what can and cannot be said. For all the family complaints swapped between girlfriends, there are things one often isn't allowed to say. With my sister we could talk and complain, without ever worrying that we were being outrageously dis-loyal. I understood exactly how angry she was, and how much she still loved our mother. I also had the same command of loyalty as my sister, so we could make our mother a monster when we talked to each other; but I knew I was safe from social exposure: My sister would never say to someone else, in mockery or disdain, "She has the most awful mother."

CONTINUING CONVERSATIONS

INTIMATE KNOWLEDGE LINKS one not only to the sibling but also to one's past. Siblings put one in touch with one's child-hood self, and with the old sibling issues. The role the sibling, and in particular the sister, plays in the growth of emotional understanding may explain why so many women say either, "My sisters are the glue that keeps me together," or "When I think of the bad relationship with my sister, I feel I am falling apart." The companion who helps give birth to our knowledge of human understanding is the companion we need to understand in order to keep our own sense of self intact. Yet the lines a sister speaks also hook onto old challenges and irritations.

In *Hanging Up*, her novel about three adult sisters, Delia Ephron traces the endless shifts in even the most ordinary of sister conversations. "I'll have the chef's salad," Eve tells a waiter as she lunches with her older sister, Georgia. Immediately Georgia challenges her selection: If it comes in a large wooden bowl, the older sister tells the younger one, "Then you don't want it. . . . It's too much. You'll get tired just looking at it." Whenever the sisters get together, they go back to old questions about who knows more, who looks better, and who's more successful.

Sister conversations become a delicate fencing match. In one phone conversation the middle sister and narrator, Eve, tells her older sister what happened in the hospital ward with their now elderly, demented father. As Eve relates the details of the day's incident, Georgia, the bossy, all-knowing elder, modifies everything Eve says: "You know how Dad has charm," Eve says, to explain how he got his way with the nurse; and Georgia explains, "Crazy-man charm, which is not to be confused with real charm." She is listening and understanding but also correcting her sister's statements.

Eve goes on to relate how their father boasted to the other hospital patients about Georgia's success as a magazine editor. At the time she was irritated and hurt. Her father's pride is focused solely on his oldest daughter. But she offsets her discomfort by entertaining her big sister with the story. Georgia is amazed at their father's rudeness to Eve, but she is also pleased by her father's special pleasure in her success. This distracts her, and she wonders aloud: 'Should I send a complimentary copy of the magazine to the ward?' Eve's rivalry then kicks in with cool mockery: "You mean so Doris, the nurse, can read about the perfect vacation on Majorca?" Georgia adeptly blocks this sisterly attempt to undermine her: "We don't run irrelevant articles like that, and you know it."

This sister conversation deals with issues that have life-threatening echoes. The father's favoritism of the older daughter is hurtful. At one time such a preference could have threatened Eve's physical life. Even now, when he is dependent on her, rather than she on him, his preference challenges her self-worth. The father was always difficult; now, in dementia, he is sadistic. He flaunts his preference by pretending to forget Eve's name, and then goes on to ask if Eve is jealous of her older sister. When Georgia is "gobsmacked" by this story, Eve is delighted and consoled: "I feel I am landing the biggest fish."[27]

Hanging Up, the title of the novel, refers to how telephone conversations end. The novelist also asks if, perhaps, to grow up and move on, we should put an end to these sister conversations which bring us back to old rivalries. The conclusion the novelist comes to, however, is that they never do end, that we never finish the exchange of views or the challenges to one another's position that we begin as children among our sisters.

In sister talk we see why life with the people we love is so complicated. In *Hanging Up* the younger sister hands her big sister this gift: Dad may be old and senile, but you are his favorite, the only one he really sees. In effect, Eve tells Georgia, *There is no need for you to give up your unique position.* This placates the older sister, but she still cannot accept her younger sister's taunt about her magazine. So, as a thirty-something woman with children of her own, the younger sister has to put up with the older sister telling her that she should not want the meal she just ordered. And as part of a sister threesome, the older two cannot back away from discussing, criticizing, and trying to straighten out the youngest sister. They glide from sisterly rivalry to sisterly alliance against a kid sister who may be an independent young woman but who is still positioned as "the baby," and who will never know as much as they do.

This is what sistering is: intimate and fun and infuriating. It is also potentially dangerous, in its precise knowledge of personality and personal history; but this intimacy also sharpens our vision of the myriad details of family history. Sister knowledge can change and grow with us, but it has a knack of roaming back to the old childhood frequencies in which we were focused on one another as companions, models, and rivals. You do not get easy or perfect love in the sister bond. If we could take this knowledge into other relationships, we would be well placed to redraw the map of love on more realistic ground.

5

"Just Like" and "Completely Different": How Sisters Find and Resist Family Roles

"WHEN I LOOK back on my childhood, the first thing I see is my mother, and then I see my father. They feature big, for sure. But when I go back into myself, the person whose presence I feel is my sister's. She was as much a part of that family as my mother was or as I was. In fact I often felt that she and I were the real family, and the others were somehow satellites. But I don't have a language to work it out. I know how to think about the ways my mother influenced me, and my father, too, but so much of my growing up was in tandem with my sister. The big things

I did were always shaped by some reference to what she was doing. And, you know, it wasn't only the big things. It was everything. From buying clothes to choosing courses at school and going out with a guy, my sister's choices were always part of the deal. But I don't think—even with the psychological sophistication I have a right to claim—that I can conceptualize this."

Felicity is a therapist who notes the absence of a psychological framework for identifying the role her sister played in her choices and preferences. Now in her forties, she senses the impact her sister has had and continues to have on her deliberations and decisions; but even as a professional psychologist, she lacks a conceptual framework to explain it. She understands the dynamics of parent power, which are associated with love and connection and fear of abandonment and urge to please, but the parallel force of the sister knot leaves her puzzled.

Sisters influence the formation of identity. We note similarities between ourselves and a sister who shares so many things with us. However intensely aware we are of a uniquely positioned self, a sister reminds us that we share an identity with her. Much of a self is constructed within a web of connections to others, and we share those connections with a sister. But a sister not only presents us with someone similar to us, she also reveals our differences. She challenges us to find our own niche within the family.[1] We search for a place that is not already staked out by another sibling. We mark a place that we can own. In so doing we engage in a relentless process of sibling differentiation. We work hard to define ourselves through "contrast effects." The genetic and environmental factors that make us alike also give rise to social and psychological factors that make us different.

INFLUENCE AND IDENTITY

WHEN WE THINK about how we become who we are, and what has shaped us, we are looking at many different things. There are the moods and events and eye-catching preferences that affect us when we make both life-shaping and mundane decisions. There are episodes and personalities that have a lasting emotional impact, that we reflect on with either pleasure or pain and seek either to repeat or avoid. Our humiliation in an arithmetic class at the age of seven can explain our reluctance, at twenty-seven, to take on an otherwise attractive job that involves presentation of accounts. There are also experiences that influence us at some level just below our normal radar. Whether we recall them clearly or have apparently forgotten them, they shape our patterns of decision and choice. We may, for example, barely remember our unease at a parent's hyperanxiety about traveling, but it may nonetheless shape our determination to be a confident explorer because we want to be different from the parental model or, perhaps, that anxiety has informed our own unease about being away from home. There are influences that can be measured and assessed by others, such as the statistically calculated effects of divorce on our educational aspirations, or of family income on our future careers. There are also the ideals and expectations we ourselves keep referring back to as we measure our successes and failures.

Alongside—and influencing—this personality system are the influences we name as we tell stories about the life we are living, stories about our places, both past and present, as actors in the world. Why did we go in one direction rather than another? Were we lucky in our life choices or were we plagued by misfortune? Were we unduly pressured, for example, by financial need or family expectations; were we held back by lack of imagination or confidence? What experiences were central to our personal history? How did these crucial episodes shape us? Who were the significant players in early assessments of our talents, our potential, and our human value? These stories help construct our sense of self, and we use them to make sense of our lives. And on these, siblings make an enormous impact.

The need to see oneself as unique runs very deep, particularly in the contemporary Western psyche. Being ourselves, and somehow taking ownership of ourselves, has vastly different meanings to different people; but self-recognition has become as necessary as air. In the sibling trauma we confront the terrifying possibility that we may be replaced, that our unique position can be lost. So, to overcome this fear, we shore up a secure sense of self. We know that we are in many ways like the people close to us. We know that we are embedded in the same family. We know that we have to compete with them for love and recognition. To secure our place we show others that we are special and distinctive—that we are, in effect, irreplaceable.

Identity is multiple and fluid. It is formed and modified by

experience and also by the words we find to describe ourselves. We define ourselves in part by constructing a map
alongside others. We see that others have abilities we do not,
and that we have capabilities others lack. We see that others
elicit different responses from people with whom we, too,
interact. We assess our strengths and talents as we compare
our own with those around us. Sometimes other people tell us
who and what we are, and their words, too, evoke comparisons. The most common points of reference within our families, when we are young children, are siblings. We may look
"just like Dad" or have "Mother's hair," but we are positioned
as sensible or impulsive, shy or outgoing, quick or slow, plain
or pretty in relation to siblings, and particularly in relation to
same-sex siblings.

When children grow up together in the same family, they
are as different in their personalities as are people from different families. For most siblings the differences are as great
as they would be if they were plucked randomly from the
general population. Even identical twins, who share identical
genes, are in many ways *more* alike if they were raised apart.
Growing up together, identifying with one another, is a good
way to ensure difference.[2]

SAMENESS AND DIFFERENCE

SISTERS ARE ALIKE in most of the ways sociologists care
about when they look at class and other social groups. They
have the same family background; they live in the same geo-

graphical area and are therefore exposed to the same social and financial spheres, the same healthy or polluted environment, the same peer culture. Families today tend to have fewer children, and they tend to have children over a limited number of years, so contemporary siblings are likely to be particularly close in age. As a result they are likely to share a very similar historical and cultural environment. The narrow age spacing increases the likelihood that they will spend a lot of time together, that they will develop social dependence on one another, that they will want the same things and compete for the same things, and that they will influence one another.[3] All these conditions may appear to promote similarities between them, but they actually result in differences.

When girls or women talk about their sisters, they initiate comparisons within the first fifteen minutes of their conversations. They talk particularly about being alike and being different. In part they may be imitating their elders, who search for and identify similarities between parents and children and between siblings. But whether they are twelve, twenty-two, or forty-two, they are careful to distinguish what other family members say about their similarities to a sibling and what they themselves believe. Sisters themselves are far more likely—indeed, twice as likely—to describe themselves as "totally different" from a sibling as they are to identify aspects in which they are "just alike." And those who focus most clearly on differences between themselves and their siblings are closest in age and of the same sex.[4] It is as though we were in a lineup, and our freedom, our sanity, and our identity depend on our ability to make differences stand out.

THE BEGINNING OF DIFFERENCE

AT THE EARLIEST stages of the sister bond, girls work to define their identity as distinct from a sister's. The older child uses her maturity as a marker for difference: "She's too young to play with my toys," and "She's too little to eat real food." What is probably too obvious to be a conversational point for others becomes something to be voiced, and underlined, by a sibling: There is the baby, and then there is me.

Children *become* adept at using categories of identity because they need to grasp that they are different from their siblings, that they are unique even though there are others who share that privileged relationship with parents.[5] They also need to keep track of what the new sibling requires from those around her, because they may have to compete to have their own needs met. They are fascinated by the responses she elicits in others. Why does a grandparent laugh when my sister speaks? a child wonders, and then decides, I'll try to please Grandma too, my own way, by showing her my toys, or jumping on her, or shouting loudly. On another occasion she reasons, If Mommy is comforting her because she hurt her chin, then I'll show Mommy I hurt somewhere, too, so she'll have to comfort me.

Another common sibling plot is: If these strategies do not work well enough, I'll use my knowledge of her to make her miserable, or I'll manipulate her so that she'll be naughty and get into trouble. Siblings constantly size each other up, and engage in borderwork—the activity of marking boundaries between one and the other.

WHY SIBLINGS CREATE SEPARATE IDENTITIES

AN EFFECTIVE WAY of establishing differences is to claim a special role in the family—the funny one, the helpful one, the troublesome one. These are often routes to forming different, distinct relationships with parents and other relatives. These differences offer the comforting proof that one is distinctive and therefore less easily replaced.

Of course, differences come about, too, because children *are* different, and inborn differences engender further differences. The differences sisters discover in themselves and each other, and the differences that others ascribe to them, impact on their highly individual relationships with other family members. Paula sees how difficult her sister Valerie is for her mother, and then decides to be "easy" to protect her mother and gain approval. "I never want to fight with my mom the way my sister does. She gets all anxious, and the whole house is just awful. But I get mad, too, and I want to do things Mom says no to, and then I want to argue, but I can't, because I don't want me to be like my sister, and have everything be like it is when Val is mad, so I just go away, and I feel awful, but at least I'm the only one who's feeling awful."

Paula resents her sister for setting such a poor example. "I don't want to be like that," she declares, but then does not know how to be other than opposite—the one who "never makes trouble and never argues." But to play that role is frustrating, and, in her view, makes her the container of all bad feeling. So she resents her sister for destroying her route to assertiveness.

"My little sister is so moody, and so difficult, I have to try to keep things together. Sometimes I hate my sister when she's bad-mouthing my mom. After they've had a real bust up, I want to stay with mom, talk to her nicely, kind of put things back together again. It's so awful the way Val tears things apart."

Children within a family have different temperaments. They have, for example, a different tolerance for stress and conflict—so one child is happy to argue her case, while another feels impelled to keep the peace. A temperamental difference such as this leads other family members to label them differently: "thoughtful" and "helpful," or "difficult" and "stubborn." Then the different sisters either adopt or resist these roles; and they establish different relationships with various family members. This is one of the many ways that natural differences lead to other differences.

SIMPLE DISTINCTIONS

IT DOES NOT take long, once I enter the house, to be aware that a sister group inhabits it. Everywhere is marked territory. One chair, set up against the table, has the name "Megan" carved along the back, and another, without a name, has stenciled ivy. Crayons and scissors are heaped together in the middle of the table, but the mats set in front of the chairs are distinct. A drawing pad is set on one, and a workbook on the other. These have been carefully name labeled. Upstairs on the door to their shared bedroom hand-drawn signs compete for vividness and size. It is clear that the embellishments on the signs have been made over time, in a phased competition, each name enlarged so as not to be smaller than the other. On one bed is a family of dolls, teddy bears, and a tiger, carefully arranged as a hugging unit. On the other is a higgledy-piggledy heap of soft animals, dolls, and cars.

In the middle of the floor is a line made with three-inch-wide green tape, straight and neat, dividing the room. "Megan's not allowed on my side of the room," Emma tells me, "but she comes in anyway." Megan then jumps on her own bed and starts arranging her stuffed toys in precisely the way the toys are arranged on the other bed. "See?" Emma tells me. "She always tries to spoil my things."

The seven-year-old feels that the five-year-old, in arranging her toys to imitate those of the older sister, is spoiling *her* things. And their mother says that Emma is often brought to tears by her little sister "always trying to do just what Emma does." Imitation was seen as an encroachment on what should be respected as her unique way of doing things.

While the older sibling is focusing on the differences between her and her younger sister, the younger sister is doing her best to learn from the very child who wants to say, *You are not like me!* All siblings imitate, but the rate of imitation is much higher in same sex pairs than in different-sex pairs.[6] As early as the second year of life, young children show more interest in siblings who are "like me" in terms of gender. Games involving imitation are much more common among same-sex sibling pairs. Older sibs will be pleased and amused by a baby who imitates them. When an older sib imitates a younger one, the younger often exhibits immense, body-absorbing delight. But once infancy is left behind, at any subsequent time in childhood and adolescence, "copying me" is threatening. It either mocks the other or infringes on her unique space.

BORDERWORK: CLASHES BETWEEN SISTERS MARK DISTINCTIVE IDENTITIES

"YOU CHILDREN CAN argue over snowballs in a blizzard," my aunt used to say to me and my cousins; and as a mother myself I witnessed my daughters, every autumn, engaging in routine arguments over the plentiful "conkers" that fell along an avenue of horse chestnut trees. Peeling away the spiny covers, they would assess the glossy brown chestnuts according to size and sheen. "This is a good one," and "This is a specially shiny one," and "This is a double one," and "There are three in this one," each would announce to declare that she had got the best one. Then they engaged in prolonged and heated arguments over who had seen which one first.

Each sister had her own collection bag that she hugged close, one satisfied, the other forlorn at the outcome of their negotiations. When we got home these bags would be put away, forgotten until they emerged weeks later during some ad hoc cleaning regimen. Dusted with mold, they were quickly discarded as smelly, useless things. Knowing the eventual outcome of their loot did nothing to subdue the emotion with which they fought over each one. Possessing each glossy conker was like claiming part of herself. Many competitions siblings set up are ways of marking distinctions from the other, and the differences are more important than superiority.

Dymphna, now eleven years old, recalls the endless and gratuitous contests her older sister, Siobhan, set up when she was a child. "Let's race to the car," Siobhan would proclaim, five steps ahead already as they left the house for the school run. "It never occurred to me just to refuse. For the life of me I don't know why I always tried to run. I always lost. Every time. But I kept being sucked into her stupid race. That made me mad, but I didn't have the sense to avoid it. If she set up a contest, I had to accept the challenge. I kept thinking I'd win this time, but I never did. And when I cried, she just laughed. Sometimes my mother laughed, too. I reminded her of that the other day. 'How could you take that seriously?' she wanted to know. I can sort of see why to her it doesn't mean much. But it does to me—well, it did at the time."

Being put in a losing position by her sister infuriated Dymphna. Winning and losing had no real significance, but the times when she "lost" and her sister "won," never felt insignificant because they carried symbolic weight.

In *Mixed Feelings*, Francine Klagsbrun describes her rage when her brother set up a contest to see whose ice cream would last longer. He managed, by devious means, to savor his longer.[7] The pleasure in triumphing over her, if only for a moment, was irresistible to her brother and infuriating to Francine. From a parent's point of view these are children fighting over nothing; from the siblings' point of view each is participating in a crucial battle.

In Tolstoy's *Anna Karenina*, Dolly sees her children squabbling at the dinner table. Their taunts, whines, and selfish demands fill her with despair. She feels that she has worthless, mean children. They are banished, dinnerless, from the table. She then finds them comforting one another and sharing the single dessert between them. Immediately she sees that these selfish children are also caring and loving.

The ridicule and sarcasm, the belittling and name-calling—the assertion of one's own importance that drive parents berserk and raise alarm about the basic goodness of their children—are forms of borderwork. "You're babyish," "Cry-baby," "Stupid," "Thick-O," "Tattle-tale," are means of saying, *You are not like me.* Pollution rituals—"You're not allowed to touch my things!" and "Get your cooties off me!" and "You can't sit next to me" or "You smell"—label one sibling as a lower caste. These are exercises at setting boundaries between her and me. The battles about whose toy it is and who sits where at the dinner table, are broad-based claims about who I am and who you are. The toy over which they are fighting is transformed into a meaningful symbol just so the fights can continue.

When grown-ups try to fix things so that they are "fair," or so that "each has the same," they inevitably fail. "The pieces are equal," and, "You'll have a turn, just like your sister" are placatory moves that fail to address the issue. Each sibling wants to be different, not the same; each wants to be special, not equal. Moreover children are sophisticated enough to understand that fair treatment does not really mean always being treated "the same." The endless and gratuitous contests siblings set up—"I have more than you," "My drawing's better," "I get to sit next to Daddy"—are rarely bids for real status. They are ways of constantly underlining, *I am different. I am not you. I have my own very comfortable place in this world.* A great many fights about who has more are really efforts to answer the questions, Where am I? and, Where are you? In other words, each is trying to determine, Is my own place safe and good? The challenge for parents is not to obliterate rivalry but to accept its inevitability.

BORDERWORK IN ADULTHOOD

IN CHILDHOOD THE threat to one's uniqueness is diffuse, so children fight over everything and anything. They work on "identity narratives," or stories of who they are and how they came to be where they are. They grasp at small things to stabilize a self that is as yet without the more or less established boundaries that adults generally have. How they dress, the arrangement of their toys, the length of their hair, and the roles they take in games become signs of either security or vulnerability. We may outgrow the enormous investment we put in such small things, but the concern that a sister is "copying" us, and therefore stealing our uniqueness, remains intact.

Julia reflects, "Felicity complained I imitated her, but that was the last thing I wanted. I just wanted to keep up with her, be worthy of her." Yet Felicity's response to the news that

Julia would be following her to medical school was clearly a throwback to an earlier vulnerability. "I got the news from Mom by phone. I pretended I was pleased. 'Oh, isn't that wonderful!' I could hear my voice go all squeaky. It was a weird experience. The walls seemed to move closer to me. I had trouble breathing, and there was ringing in my ears. I put down the phone and thought, Why did I answer that? I calculated that if I hadn't picked up the phone, if I'd missed the call that morning, I could have had a whole extra day without knowing this, and without feeling this deadness. I went to the hospital and went through the rotation schedule. I tried to appear normal. It was the feeling I'd get if someone died. But it wasn't exactly grief; it was dread. I wondered why I hadn't seen this coming. As soon as I could get away, I went for a long walk. You know, one of those walks where you're trying to walk away from everything?

"All this sounds like I was always jealous of my sister. I wasn't. I mean I never *felt* jealous of her. It sounds like I didn't love her. But I always loved her. It's just that I saw her one way. She was my little sister, little and cute, and always behind me. Then all of a sudden she was right beside me, and I had to look at her in a different way. I realized how comforting it was that she was little, how much I took it for granted. Then, there she was, saying brightly, 'I can do what my big sister is doing.'

"It took me a while to get my bearings. You know, when a feeling is so problematic, when you're sinking under it, you have to ask, What is this? I asked myself what was changed in my life, why did I feel this sense of doom? I tried to tell myself nothing had changed—because in one sense it hadn't.

I still had the same exams in front of me and behind me. I still had my projects, my friends, my apartment. Nothing was changed, but everything was being taken away from me. Suddenly I had nothing. And then when I saw what this was all about, I *was* jealous. So I felt worse, and I couldn't talk about it to anyone. How can you tell someone, "I'm jealous of my little sister," without looking like a twerp? But I decided, there and then, I was going to have to find a field in medicine where I was sure my sister would never follow.

"All this must sound awful. But I really love my sister and want to be close to her. I tried to focus on the ways this could bring us closer. But that first feeling about what this was going to do to me—well that's never left me. I'm still haunted by that feeling, that's so strong, that's like grief, but that has such a strange and shameful basis."

Many of the girls in my study spoke of the frustration they felt when a younger sister was able to jump over some hurdle—a driving test, making a complicated journey alone to another part of the country, getting a job, having a boyfriend—earlier than they had. Their anger was framed within the family setting: "It's not fair that my parents allowed her to do this before they let me do it." But the adult women, more aware of what it was they dreaded, spoke of "that ghastly fear that my sister can overtake me," or "a kick in the stomach, when you realize she can run way ahead of you."

These battles are not just for kids. Women said they remained interested, always, in what a sister was doing and where she was relative to them. Amid the love and pride there remains a tracking device set in motion by the sibling trauma: Is she in my space?

BORDERWORK WITH MOTHERS

IT HAS BECOME commonplace to say that women's identity is more intimately linked with attachments to people, while men's identity focuses on separation. The description of boundaries between self and other in women as "blurred" or "blended" has had enormous impact in highlighting the specific strengths women, generally, exhibit in empathy skills, and the different emphasis they generally place on responsiveness and care. But the model of girls' sense of self as continuous with others, and boy's sense of self as more separate and bounded, should not blind us to the importance that women, too, place on self-boundaries and self-differentiation. In many contexts girls and women are more comfortable emphasizing their separation from others than their connection to others. It is in the sister knot, in which girls sense, at some deep psychological level, that the threat of sameness is more prevalent, that the threat of difference and boundaries tend to be highlighted.

The battle that girls and women wage for their own identity can be ferocious. As teens they are quick to resist the deep identification they have with their mothers. They fight tooth and claw to say, *I'm not you,* and *I'm not like you,* and *You don't understand me.* In adolescence girls constantly and meticulously name their difference from their mothers. Their conversation is peppered with "identity reminders" as they tell a mother, "I know that already!" and "I'm perfectly capable of doing that myself!" and "I can figure it out for myself!"

During adolescence girls are likely to spend a lot of energy reflecting on the ways they are like their mothers and ways in which they differ. They struggle to define differences between a mother's history and personality on the one hand, and their own hopes for their future on the other. They also distinguish carefully between who they are and who their mothers think they are, between what their mothers expect of them and what they want for themselves. They pounce like an animal of prey on anything a mother says that indicates similarity or identity. "I used to feel the same way" or "What I would do . . . " is killed with exclamations: "I don't feel like you did!" and "I'm not you!" and "I want to do it my own way!"

As teens girls face the paradox of still caring deeply how a mother sees them, while being quick to accuse her of not knowing them at all. How people *see* us is as important as how they *feel* about us, so teens work hard to correct and update a mother's view of them. They challenge her habitual way of looking at them, and they remind a mother that her teenage daughter is different from the little girl the mother thinks she knows. A teen sometimes uses shock tactics to make a mother take a fresh look at her and assess her anew. Teens often voice their views more strongly and clearly than they themselves feel them; they then trace the effects of their borderwork on a mother as she gets to grips with her changing daughter. Fights between mother and daughter become a process by which a daughter forces a mother to recognize this new, not-quite-formed self. Fights sometimes spring from opposition to parental control and authority, but they also mark the identity border between mother and daughter.

Teens want to remain connected, but they also want to confirm a distinct self.[8]

CHANGING BORDERWORK:
THE CONTINUED QUEST TO FORM
SEPARATE IDENTITIES

WHEN ADOLESCENT BATTLES with a mother are at their peak, the childhood quarrels with sisters have subsided. The bickering borderwork with sisters becomes less fraught but no less significant. As girls are intent on trying out different personae—through hair styles and color, through body shape and exposure, through language and gesture—they often step far back from a sister. "There was this long cooling-off period when we were in our teens," Felicity said. "Julia was still important to me, but there was a coolness. We didn't fight so much, and we didn't talk so much. I'd find out what she was up to by watching her, not so much talking to her. Adolescence was not exactly a honeymoon, but it was a reprieve from those endless fights."

Often sister battles ease during late adolescence; yet whether one sister is "copying" the other remains an issue. Josie worries that her choices—what courses to take, what sports to play, what clothes to wear—are not original because they are similar to the choices her sister makes: "I often feel I'm copying Miriam, because a lot of stuff she does I do. And I don't want to be a copycat, but we are interested in the same things. She gets good ideas and I think, That's what I was thinking. When she says something, it's sometimes like that was on the tip of my tongue, but she's faster? She never believes me when I tell her, 'I was just going to say that,' and she says, 'Yeah. Right.' But it's true."

At fourteen, Josie is fighting to be original, and discounts a route on the grounds that her sister has taken it. When a sister decides to do something because it is "completely different" from what her sister does, she is as much influenced by the sister as she is when she copies her. Her teenage rebellion is focused more on defying the pattern set by her sister than on challenging her parents. Yet her sister remains the reference point in shaping her own life. Heading in the opposite direction is not really getting away from a sister's influence. Josie's decision is shaped by what feels safer, and that is to be different: "If we're both designers, then it's going to be obvious who's more successful. It's better doing something entirely different, so we can't be so easily compared."

In their teen years girls gain confidence in distinguishing their character from that of a sibling: "My younger sister and I both have terrible mood swings, but I've learned to handle mine more. My oldest sister just doesn't have this problem. She's able to sail through everything. She has a kind of serenity that's really wonderful, but it makes me feel she's set apart from us all. My little sister gets these awful moods when she cries and hits herself, and I remember just how I felt, like something's crawling inside you and you want to rip it out. I think I'm more stable now—you know, just hormones are better regulated. I can't stand to be with her when she's in one of her awful moods, because I know just how she feels. Helen, she's the oldest, is much better because she doesn't know—I think she has no idea, or doesn't think about how it feels, so she doesn't get distracted. She just sees that it's something to deal with, and she helps Josie deal with it."

At seventeen, Miriam carefully defines the difference in temperament among her sisters, also noting the similarities. When teens are unable to secure a sense of difference from a sister, they express frustration at being unable to mark, once and for all, their difference. I heard stories of girls who tried to *engineer* changes in a sister that would placate their fears that they were too much alike. Gina, now in her thirties, describes how she gave her sister her spare allowance when they were in their mid-teens. This apparent generosity was a strategy to get her sister to gain weight.

Sam, two years older than Gina, had a weakness for the sweet food that was forbidden in the house. Gina knew that Sam would "go as crazy over the stuff my mom was so careful to ration. I knew she'd spend the money on those little cakes she loved. Gooey little cakes in transparent paper holders, with violets on top and different colored sprinkles all around the sides. I made sure we walked past that bakery on the way home from school, and I gave her the money and told her to get herself something. I wanted her to stay fatter than me, and it worked. I also gave her packs of Oreos, and if our mom saw them she'd go, 'Who keeps eating all this junk food?' and I'd say, 'I bought some. Sorry, Mom. I won't do it again. I know it's bad.' That way Sam had no reason to hold back, because she wasn't in any trouble. At first I wasn't sure it was working, but then Grandma came to visit, and she took one look at Sam and said, 'You've been packing the calories away,' and I knew it was working."

Today she laughs darkly as she describes her motives. She is disturbed by the memory that comes alive as she speaks. At the time, however, she felt "beyond meanness, stuck in an obsession with putting my sister down." At a time when the questions Who am I? and Who will I become? present themselves so strongly from so many different directions, girls may grasp at anything to secure a superior difference.

Given the significance many girls put on body shape and weight, it is not surprising that differences in weight mark a sense of different selves. In their classic discussion of siblings the psychiatrists Stephen Bank and Michael Kahn present a case study of twin sisters, Vickie and Marilyn. Born with a broken hip and unable to engage in normal exercise, Vickie was much heavier than her twin sister for much of her childhood. When the hip mended, and Vickie became more active, she started losing weight. In response Marilyn started losing weight also. The sisters weighed themselves daily, usually in front of each other, comparing and commenting on any change. They cooked and ate together, and shared a fascination with food and an obsession with counting calories.[9] Marilyn became anorexic for a while, but as she improved, Vickie became severely thin. The twins used weight as a means of distinguishing themselves, one from the other.

For teenage girls weight is a subject of constant discussion, and sometimes it becomes an obsession. Gaining weight can make a teenager feel she is "no longer herself," and losing weight may allow her to feel she is becoming a person she likes, her true self. A parent's approval is often sought by losing weight. Gina said, "I know my dad was pleased when I was thin, and I knew he gave Sam a hard time when she put on weight. It wasn't just her private suffering I was after, it was also the flak she'd get from Dad."

With an adolescent's identity in flux, her new self seems deliciously within reach, all her own, buoyant and rich with promise; but the rapidly changing sense of self is also bewildering and threatening. When we do not know where we stand—because our place is constantly moving—we might put a great deal of energy into petty efforts to mark an intimate competitor as "inferior."

DISTORTED COMPETITIONS

IN THE TEENAGE years girls' sexual feelings and responses become a more salient part of their identity. Those who have had to scramble with a sister for love within the family also look to compete with a sister for new sources of love— usually in the guise of boyfriends. If the worst nightmare is having a sister replace you, then making a preemptive attempt to replace your sister as an object of love might offer some respite from fear.

Sisters naturally inhabit a world of comparison and competition. When someone pays attention to a sister, the other may act up or act out. In childhood a compliment to one sister raises the question in the other: Do I have the good qualities she has? or Do I have different good qualities? and Are the qualities I have better than hers, or less than hers? Within the sister frame an attribute of one sister can be experienced as a deficit in the other. Living together and being seen as part of a pair or a group highlights differences that sometimes hurt, differences that mean one is noticed and the other ignored. The sister knot introduces the threat of sameness, but it also introduces anxiety about the relative merit of differences.

Dorri is now in her late thirties, but her childhood memories of others' responses to her younger sister are both poignant and vivid: "Everyone wanted to touch my sister. Annette was so pretty, with a face I now realize was damn sexy—full lips that never quite kept still, but you also never knew what the movements meant. But when I was a kid, I only saw that people preferred her. They were drawn to her. And it was politeness that forced them to pay attention to me and ask me things."

Annette may have been admired for her beauty, but she felt that Dorri was their mother's favorite. "Dorri was the daughter who was loved, I thought, because she looked so much like my mother, and because they were so alike. So I decided, at the age of fourteen, to hate them both. I wanted to side with my father. He didn't get mad with me the way mom did, but I was always disappointed because he didn't side with me enough. I liked going on walks with him. I remember trying to get him to agree with me when I told him how maddening Dorri and my mom were. He said, 'You're so hard on your mother.' It made me fume, because I thought they were hard on me."

Annette used an easily recognized strategy. It is one Anne Frank describes in her *Diary*, as she witnesses an alliance between her mother and her older sister Margot. Her father offers sympathy but avoids the role of ally in her wish to denigrate the mother. Of course this does not deny the enduring love in the sisters' bond. However much Anne complains about Margot, she also describes the good times they have when she climbs into her sister's bed: "It was a frightful squash but that was just the fun of it." They read selections of each other's diary; they talk about sex; they are "thick as thieves."[10]

Rivalry rarely pushes out love, but it does complicate the relationship. Annette says, "I would take her boyfriends. Every one I could. I never thought about whether I liked them. I liked them simply because they liked her. At that time my entire sense of what I was worth was related to what my sister was worth. Eventually I was able to move on. I changed so much. . . . But even today Dorri can't believe I won't steal men from her. Yes—even though she knows I'm gay! When her marriage broke up she was sure I'd played a role in it. She accused me of having an affair with her husband. This was absurd. There was no basis for this, just her twisted mind."

Choosing lovers, and watching whom a sister chooses, is partly social learning and partly rivalry. The primitive panic at seeing anyone focus exclusively on her sister left the teenage Annette with a desperate reasoning: If my sister chooses someone, he must be someone I want. If she has him, then I should try to take him. This distortion derives from the diffuse focus that really belongs to early childhood, when anything the other has is desired. The flashpoints of sibling rivalry normally diminish as one exercises one's own identity. But when the fear of annihilation by a sister remains in the foreground, a syndrome I would call "relationship theft" recurs. This was demonstrated by the cellist Jacqueline du

Pré in the breakdown that preceded the diagnosis of multiple sclerosis: She explained to her sister, Hilary, that she needed to have sex with her brother-in-law; and Hilary, terrified by the betrayal but even more terrified by her sister's illness, gave her reluctant "blessing."[11] In her extremity Jackie sought some proof of a triumph in the sister knot. As Stephen Bank and Michael Kahn sympathetically reflect, "When children are compared physically from birth on, their identities and sexual unfolding often develop inextricably, in ways that reassurance and praise cannot undo."[12]

The most threatening betrayal a lover can commit is to fall in love with your sister. The cliché of a best friend stealing your man is a variation on this theme, since best friendships among women borrow heavily from the experiences of sistering.[13] Sexual intimacy is a way of being privileged: One reason this intimacy can be so satisfying is that the partner becomes, if only momentarily, the most important person in the other's life. Dorri fears a grotesque parallel to sharing the family's love, resources, and care as she accuses Annette of trying to share her husband. This accusation leads Annette to reflect, "On one level there was absolute devotion to my sister; and on one level there was absolute hate." When these two extreme feelings abide, without being integrated and modified, these exceptional distortions occur.

LABELING THE DIFFERENCES

THE URGE TO highlight differences between oneself and one's sister is shared by the grown-ups of the family, who often join in sibling borderwork. "Annette is the pretty one; Dorri is the smart one," is only one of many examples in which parents affix labels to each child as they note each child's need for her very own perch. While their aim is to reassure each child, in adulthood sisters complain bitterly about a parent who has doled out such labels. "How could either of us benefit from these categories?" Annette wondered. "What I heard was that I wasn't smart and that Dorri wasn't pretty. When she said I didn't have to worry about going to college because I was pretty, what could she mean, other than that I was stupid, and that Dorri was smart but ugly, or unwantable?"

Labels are not simply things that we stick on and peel off at will. When we hear them often enough from people whose views shape ours, we incorporate them into our sense of who and what we are, and what we can become. We may resist others' descriptions of us, but these return to mock or question our own self-definitions. Even when we establish how inappropriate they are (as Annette does when she realizes the irony of her adult position vis-à-vis that of her childhood labels), we resent their long-term sticking power. "My sister is living the conventional life—the dutiful mother, the put-upon wife, the one who keeps house and cares for people. I'm the one earning my living with my intellect, teaching at a first-class college; and I'm gay, with a partner who is far more domestic than I am. But I was always the one who was good at housework and caring, so I was always called upon to tend my mother when she was ill. I was even sent to take care of my sister when she was all stressed out with her college finals. And I was pleased as punch to do this stuff because I thought that was all I could do." Even in her twenties Annette had accepted a caring role; so, when her sister was struck by depression, she was summoned to look after her and the children. "I was glad to serve," Annette said, amazed, now, as she reflects on her story. "I dropped everything to take care of her. I thought that's who I was. I thought that was my role, and that gave me my value."

The sisters, now in midlife, remain wary of the emotional violence that has raged between them. Yet, as is so often the case, each sister has a different story about the family and her own position in it. Dorri, who was given the label "the smart girl," said, "I've always had this sense of there being a definite end point to my abilities. I do well one day, and people will take it as an indication of potential, but I know that it won't go further. That's my one trick that I've shown them. My mother knew this, and she tried to boost my confidence. She was always telling me I was clever.

"But I knew Annette was smarter than me. I knew in the end she was more capable. There was something in her that could go far. My father saw this, and that's why my mother didn't look out so much for her. Well, partly because my mother was so needy anyway, but also because Annette had my father to root for her. Now Annette says we tried to sideline her into a caring role. But being able to cope with our mother and younger sister and brother was really something. To be able to do that when you're fourteen, fifteen, and sixteen—that's really something. So why she felt diminished I don't know. We always looked up to her, always. And when I asked her to come to stay with me when I was in a tizzy over my exams—well, that was because I thought only she could manage things. I was in real bad shape. I needed her. Why is she pretending that that was putting her in a corner?"

The flickering questions What do my family labels mean? and What are her labels worth? tease us long after we have left home. This uneasy dance does not always end; but when we understand our use of labels and the purpose they serve, we are better equipped to manage them.

SURVIVING OTHERS' LABELS

"DO NOT LABEL your children" is the first piece of advice Annette said she would give to parents seeking ways to minimize sibling troubles; yet labels continue to be handed out. To some extent this is an outcome of the way we look at people. All families scan their children for similarities and differences. Their tendency to compare and contrast siblings is echoed in fiction and in fairy tales: Elinor has sense, and Marianne has sensibility; Rose Red is sexy, and Snow White is chaste; Cinderella is good, and her stepsisters are bad; Cordelia is loyal, while her sisters are natural-born betrayers. Whether there are two or three or four sisters, there is a tendency to distinguish pairs of sisters in matching and opposing sets. In stories and in myths, in films, in history and in our lives, we often feel we can see a person more clearly when we compare and contrast her to another.

Negotiating similarities and differences may be so confusing that we abandon all subtlety and go for "just alike" or "completely the opposite" for the sake of clarity. After all, if I am the opposite of a sister, then there is less risk of her replacing me. Family myths may evolve in response to this need. We put a stamp on one as the extrovert, one as the introvert, one as the sportswoman, the other as the scholar. The good/bad, the nice/nasty, sometimes follow from these misplaced comforts. Polarizing labels, however well intentioned, bring rigidity, and differences lose their subtlety and mutability. Instead of providing reassurance, they constrain us.

Well into adulthood women brood angrily over inappropriate labels. As adults we can often argue our way out of the constraining views, even while we continue to feel their pinch. But young children, too, are adept at providing a counterlife to those dominant family stories which label one child as "sweet," the other "pretty," and another "smart." While siblings listen to the family history—about their births, their first steps, their early behavior, and their likely futures—they also make fine distinctions between what a parent sees and what they themselves see. Among the most important people in their world is a sister, and the psychological sophistication they show in very early childhood—a sophistication driven by their need to make sense of the other people who matter to them—is developed further as they define their views and contrast them to those of a parent. Children's probing minds are not at the mercy of others' simple stories.

Ceri, now twenty-five, carefully distinguishes her view of her sister from that of her parents. "They always thought my little sister wasn't as smart as me. I think they still think that. I mean, they think it in the face of all evidence to the contrary. And it's not that they don't love her. They do. Maybe that's part of it. They love her and she lets them, and loves them back, so there's something still babyish about her. Even at twenty-one, she has that baby sweetness in her. I so liked being older and being seen to be smarter. I relished it!

"But I also loved playing with Andrea because I thought she was so smart. I watched her understanding things, and ordinary things would become interesting by watching her look at them. I learned to love animals through her. I used to be very frightened of dogs, and I was in the park with her once and this dog lurched toward us.

"It was barking really loud, and I think it was big, nearly as big as her. I was terrified, and I shouted at her to get away from it. I was too frightened to go to her and pull her away, and I think I must have been crying too hard to shout as loudly as I wanted to. She just stood in front of that dog, and you could see her whole body rippling with pleasure because the dog was jumping up on her. And when he jumped up, she patted his head and giggled. When his owner finally came to restrain him, I marched up to her and said, 'Why didn't you go to the other side of the gate? Why did you stand there like some do-do bird?' See, dogs weren't allowed in the sandbox area, and she could have just walked through the gate. And she said, 'I wanted to see him jump. I saw his whiskers. *Up close.*' Then we started fighting. I think I pushed her, because the next thing I knew my mother was holding my arm and jerking it and shouting at me not to always hit my sister.

"My mother always worries about my sister. I mean she *worries*. This is worry big-time. This is any-minute-something-awful-is-going-to happen worry. She worries about me, too, but maybe I don't see it so much, because the worry kicks in when we're not around. And it's all because she thinks we can't take care of ourselves. She just doesn't see who Andrea really is. And because I do see—well, I've always known what she's really made of."

Andrea's take on the parents' view is somewhat different: She feels the parents are responding to her self-doubt. She is anxious that her sister does things she cannot do, and did things at her age she cannot do now. But she also says, "Without Ceri's belief that I could do more, I'd be much less confident. It's funny how she gets mad at Mom when she worries about me, because she says I can do that stuff. The other day, though, she said to Mom, 'Don't ask her to do that all by herself,' and I thought, 'Well, I can do that.' And thinking I can do even more than my sister thinks I can do makes me realize how much confidence I've gained."

SEPARATE LIVES

WE BEGAN THIS chapter by looking at how sharing a family environment makes siblings *different* from one another.[14] Children seek out "contrast effects" to secure their distinctive sense of self. But we must also note that, within the same family, children actually experience a different environment. For all the concern about being alike and being replaceable, children are genetically different, and they have very different experiences within one family. One sibling grows up with a bossy sister, and one does not. Parents may be strict with a child who is by temperament impulsive, and lenient with a child who is timid, who does not step over the boundaries even when she has the chance. Parents behave differently with one child, who clings to them, than they do with one who constantly bolts ahead. Children spot and exploit and complain about these differences: But they are inevitable; and these differences in parental behavior become incorporated into a wider network of influences.

When parents talk about themselves and their children, they often marvel at how different they themselves are with different children. Rachael explains the different rhythms and moods she has in the presence of her two very different daughters, Megan and Emma: "With Megan, you have to talk all the time, I can't get a moment to sort out my own thoughts; but Emma plays happily by herself, and just turns around from time to time to see if I'm watching, and so I can be more relaxed with her." Judy Dunn found that mothers talk about different things they like about their different children—the playfulness of one, the easy pleasure of talking with another, and the worry over a third; and these differences in children lead to different behavior in a parent. Dunn heard a mother describe herself as a "different kind of person" with the child she fusses over, who is so easily alarmed and upset that she herself acts highly strung, compared with the easygoing self that comes to the fore when she is with another child. Dorri, now herself a mother of two girls and a boy, says, "We were so hard on the way our mother treated us differently. When we were teenagers Annette accused her of having a multiple personality. I mean, she was that different. She was real playful with our brother. She talked nonstop with me, constantly telling me what to do, but she'd ask Annette a string of questions. With Annette she seemed a lot younger and less sure of herself." The way a parent behaves to one child in her family is intimately related to how the other children behave toward her and toward each other.[15] Different parental behavior creates a different environment for the different children.

All of us share a major proportion of our genes with one another: More than half our genes are identical to those of other primates. When we think about heredity we think about the other genes, the genes we don't share with everyone else. Siblings share roughly half of these nonuniversal genes with one another. The influences we usually think of as environmental—the effects of parents, siblings, and peers— are also affected by the genetic similarity of the siblings.[16] Since parents treat different children in different ways, they are more likely to treat similar children in similar ways,[17] so children who are genetically similar to one another are more likely to have similar family experiences. But genetic similarity does not guarantee actual similarity; genes are expressed differently in different environments, and part of our environment consists of individual experiences with other people. Heredity—the way some character traits are passed on and some are not—is as much about difference as it is about similarity.

Families themselves change during the course of a childhood. Deborah Tannen says that "sisters and brothers are born into the same family, but it's a different family when each is born."[18] For families themselves change. A first child is born to inexperienced parents, probably to younger parents, at a special time in a family's emotional, financial, and geographic history. One child grows up with a happy mother, supported by a partner, but her younger sister sees a mother tense and alone. One sister lives in a roomy house, and another has to share her room with a stepsister who seems like a stranger and intruder. One child grows up in a family who has to watch every dollar spent, while another, in the same family, experiences a large suburban home and a family relaxed about its spending habits. One child has to adapt to other family members, so may be forced to "grow up" when a new baby demands time and attention.

Divorce and death make an impact on all family members, but affect different siblings according to their age at the time of the event: A three-year-old's world is destroyed by her parents' split; a teenager's domestic and social life is disrupted; but a twenty-year-old, however sad about the breakup, experiences very little disruption to her day-to-day life. The timing of a parent's illness also impacts different children in different ways: The older college girl feels guilty but distant, while the younger one has to perform day-to-day care tasks. In every family there is a complex network of influences—between siblings, between sibling interaction and parents, between parent and child and child and parent.

A single family is not a single homogeneous environment but a bunch of little microenvironments, each inhabited by one child. And these differences leave legacies: Mary Beth and Marge, now in their fifties, look back to see a different mother. Marge sees her as full of fun, active, resilient, and confident; Mary Beth sees her mother as dull, depressed, cautious in her outlook, filling the future with distasteful dangers. For when Mary Beth was a child, their mother was undergo-

ing treatment for breast cancer, while Marge, in early childhood, had a mother who boasted about "never being sick"
and "having no time for illness." Mary Beth saw her father as
concerned, full of empathy, but somehow helpless. Marge
saw her father as "selfish"—something Mary Beth can make
no sense of, since his protectiveness was aroused by his wife's
illness. Marge feels she is doing her mother's bidding by moving away from home, being adventurous and casual in the
daughterly tasks of checking in. Mary Beth feels she is doing
her mother's bidding by staying near the family home, carefully drawing her parents into the life of their grandchildren.
The sisters have had the same family but not the same family
experiences, and their interactions with family members have
been shaped by different aspects of the same parents. They
discover this gradually, and only in adulthood, as, like so
many sisters, they cross-check memories and meanings.

Even when the significant features of the family remain
unchanged, the imaginative and emotional meanings of
shared events are construed differently by each member. We
are different from our siblings both because we have inborn
differences, so that we look upon the same world in different
ways, and because our worlds themselves are different. Yet,
fearing that we are really the same, we highlight and develop
further personal differences.

When we look at human psychology from a sibling perspective, the shifting spaces between ourselves and others
take on new significance. We negotiate the comfort of sameness and the threat of difference on the one hand, and the

pleasure in difference and the threat of sameness on the other. We are flexible and creative in laying out similarities and differences between all family members. A sibling perspective allows us to accept that difference is constructed for particular uses, and that we have to question its use. Sometimes the differences we construct are creative and expansive; but when we stick to rigid definitions, either of ourselves or of another, we may be trying to preserve a defensive separation that is not actually there. If our aim is to say, *I am nothing like you; we are completely different*, then we are seeking a false and unnecessary comfort. Rigid contrasts "assure" us that we are special when we lack the confidence that we are unique. An analysis of the sister knot shows us both that we are different and special; it also explains why we so often come to doubt that we are.

BUILDING A WIDER PICTURE FROM DIFFERENCES

THE NUANCES OF the sister knot ultimately allow us to appreciate our difference and distinctiveness in the context of a close connection. For so many of us the awareness that other people are thinking, feeling beings, with their distinct subjective experience, unfolds in a sibling relationship. A great pleasure in being among sisters stems from the endless comparisons and contrasts of who we are and what we experience, and how we maintain intimacy and empathy in the context of difference.

In her play *The Sisters Rosensweig*, Wendy Wasserstein

shows three sisters comparing experiences and asserting individual variations, even in the ordinary activity of drinking wine.

> GORGEOUS: Drinking goes directly to my feet. Does it go to your feet, Pfeni?
> PFENI: No, my head. Directly to my head. What about you, Sarah?
> SARAH: In my hair. I feel it in my hair.[19]

The first sister begins by describing the effect wine has on her, but she then turns to another sister to ask whether the experience is the same for her. Pfeni explains that wine affects her in a different way, and immediately asks the third sister, Sarah, about her experience. The sisters pass themes from one to another, building up a picture of their present experiences, their past, and their vision of a future. Together they compile a whole experience. The differences are variations on a theme, and the sisters bond by noting their differences while sharing their experiences.

When we realize that we inhabit a world in which we share our life-giving relationships with others, we can no longer take for granted that primitive grandiosity in which those we love focus solely on us. We consequently see each personal intimacy in a broader context, in which everyone has relationships to other people. Throughout our lives we both maintain and modify the comfort zones for others' labeling of us, for the stability and rigidity of the features by which we identify ourselves and recognize others. We see that others who are very much like us are also important to the people we love, and we often shuffle our talents and personalities to secure a favorable position in the shifting arrangements of our interpersonal maps. Accepting the intricate challenges to one's egoistic claims is necessary to our survival in a world of other people whom we can love and respect even as we know they take up places we ourselves might want.[20]

6

Protection and Resentment

n *Little Women*, that classic novel with sistering as its central theme, the peacemaker Beth March scolds her sisters for arguing. She says, "Birds in their nests agree," and so sets up a cosy model of sibling harmony. Chicks, bundled and warmed together, each with its beak raised and open, each awaiting a turn for the family share of food, present a soothing image. Yet no analogy could be less appropriate as a model for sibling harmony and safety. The reality of chicks in their nests reveals how vicious sibling rivalry can be; but in raw nature, too, we witness the powerful urge of siblings to protect one another.

NATURAL BEHAVIOR

WHEN WE OBSERVE birds in their nests what we see is far more disturbing than the roughhousing, teasing, and bickering commonly observed among human siblings. Several species of bird routinely kill their siblings as they jostle for food and warmth. The female black eagle, for example, lays two eggs, the second a few days after the first. When both eggs hatch, the slightly older chick is likely to be bigger than its sibling, and will constantly peck its smaller nest mate. There are chilling observations of a black eagle chick attacking a younger sibling within a few hours of its birth. When the younger tries to receive a scrap of meat offered by the parent, the attacks escalate. The younger chick typically dies within a few days, and during its short life is subjected to repeated assaults. In one series of observations, the younger chick was attacked on thirty-eight separate occasions, and had over fifteen hundred distinct pecks by the nestmate. But the younger chick did not die of wounds alone. The larger chick lays first claim to the food available to the entire brood, so the weaker chick is likely to starve.[1] In one study an older chick had gained fifty grams of body mass, while the younger died at eighteen grams below birth weight.[2]

Around two dozen other avian species display equally ruthless behavior. The pattern is similar: Two eggs are laid, and if two chicks hatch, one routinely slaughters the other. Another example of ferocious rivalry is found in the sand tiger shark.[3] The battles begin in utero, when one embryo devours its embryonic siblings. Brutal, and beyond parental control, but within the womb's protection, the embryo that develops more quickly is the one that survives.

In other species attacks may be less direct. One common strategy is for the strongest chick to bag the cosiest place by the parent's body. Since, at high altitudes, chicks require proximity to a parent's body to keep warm, this is not just a counterpart to the bullying human sibling who claims symbolic victory by pouncing on his mother's lap and proclaiming, "This is my place!" or "I got here first!" The chick with the greatest strength (usually the one hatched first) pushes and bullies the other chicks in order to get the warmest, most protected spot. Needing less energy to keep warm, and best placed to get the next lot of food the parent offers, the stronger chick has the best chance for survival; the weaker chicks that fail to secure their own warm spot by the mother usually die.

It seems that chicks are programed to work on the assumption that food may be scarce, and that it therefore makes good sense, in survival terms, to ensure that they get enough. Getting in first is the best way to get enough even when there is not enough to go around. A preemptive attack on a possible food rival, who is right there with you, and doesn't present a direct danger to you because he's smaller or less aggressive, seems to make good survival sense. There might not be a food shortage at present, but since it is the sort of thing that can happen sometimes, it is good to play safe.[4] This may explain why perfectly equal shares do little to quell sibling rivalry: Human siblings, too, may be looking beyond actual family provision to possible survival conditions, when competition will be a life-or-death matter.

Human parents are not alone in making efforts to control sibling fights. After all, a parent invests in each offspring and hopes that as many of her children as possible survive. Pelican parents have been observed plumping down firmly on their chicks to keep them both warm *and* out of each other's way. As in human families, the fighting starts again as soon as the parent stands up.[5]

Some people would argue that this unflinching look at avian sibling aggression mirrors behavior they are all too familiar with in their own family. According to Frank Sulloway, each child wants more than its fair share of family resources, while the parent wants to distribute resources where they'll do the most good; so siblings, he concludes, are natural rivals.[6]

Keeping the peace between siblings, to many parents, seems like stemming the tide of nature. Children have on average nearly five fights with siblings every day;[7] in very early childhood, between the ages of eighteen months and twenty-four months, a younger sibling has a "conflict incident" at the rate of about eight an hour.[8] In their popular book *Siblings Without Rivalry*, Adele Faber and Elaine Mazlish quote a parent as saying, "I don't know what will happen first. Either they'll kill each other or I'll kill them."[9]

Sibling rivalry is as pressing a topic for parents as it is for the children themselves. Parents have a great deal invested in each child, and put enormous effort into waylaying sibling arguments. Parents feel intensely involved in the quarrels their children have with one another. There is something infuriating and unignorable about your children fighting one another.

This just might be the aim of some sibling quarrels: As they broadcast their hostility, siblings may in fact be cooperating to get parental attention. A recent and intriguing study by Rebecca Kilner shows that some nestlings work together to demand food; when they display competition with other chicks, their parents work harder to bring them food; and when they fight with one another, the parents bring them more food than they would if only one chick demanded feeding. The chicks *appear* to compete against one another, but they are actually cooperating to get a more satisfactory response from the parents.[10] This creative reading of nestling behavior can make new sense of the apparently choreographed bickering of human siblings, too: In fighting and squabbling, sisters and brothers work together to make sure they all have a parent's full attention. Cooperation is sometimes mistaken for rivalry.

NATURAL PROTECTION

CHICKS IN THEIR nests do not tell us what is going on between any individual human sisters, but a close look at animal siblings sheds new light on familiar family behavior. Human parents are more persistent than black eagle parents in defending each child. Generally they are careful about allocating resources so that all their children can survive, but human history is full of stories about siblings coming to blows over the division of family resources. The Book of Genesis contains eleven descriptions of sibling rivalry, including one brother's challenges to the other for a father's (or father figure's) love and favor: Cain and Abel, Joseph and his brothers, Esau and Jacob.

Laws of primogeniture, which kept the size of the family wealth intact by stipulating that the family property be passed to the oldest son, continued to shape themes of sibling rivalry and resentment. Family behavior is not the same as animal behavior, but there are uncomfortable similarities. Because wealth and rank passed from father to son, it was brothers who competed for the family goods; and sister relationships have not been given such prominence.[11] Yet the zoological tales of sibling rivalry are not gendered: Females and well as males compete for survival.

There is another equally significant evolutionary side to rivalry; and that is an inbuilt genetic push to protect one another. The guiding principle of evolutionary psychology is that genes are selfish,[12] which means they work out ways to reproduce themselves. Until about forty years ago natural selection was widely believed to function for the good of the entire species. Survival of the fittest was seen as the survival of an entire species or community, operating under a concept called "group selection."[13] Steven Pinker notes that the tooth and claw of nature were then seen to operate *between* species; the fatal unpleasantness *within* species was ignored. Now it is the genes that are seen as "selfish," and it is survival of the genes that operate adaptive behavior.[14]

This does not mean that people are selfish; indeed, people are primed to love one another and care for one another and protect and cooperate with one another and these responses and behaviors foster the selfish drive of the *genes*. As Pinker also says, "Sometimes the most selfish thing a gene can do is build a selfless brain."[15] However, this shift in perspective is not easygoing or benign. On the one hand the implication seems to be that it is my genes I care about, not those of my species or group or friends. But it does mean that I care about my sibling, because siblings share approximately 50 percent of my own genes.[16] If evolutionary arguments have any relevance to the behavior of individual humans, then it makes very good sense to suppose that siblings have an investment in protecting one another.

This explains the bridge between sibling rivalry and sibling protection. Two siblings are pretty much equivalent, in genetic terms, to oneself. So a mechanism that predisposes us to accept a serious risk to ourself, while saving two siblings, can, on average be to our advantage: It may save the genetic material in the other two siblings, and we may after all get away with the risk to ourself. Long-term studies of helping behavior in various birds and mammals have shown lots of minimother effects, or what is called "nonbreeding helpers." Many species are good at distinguishing degrees of relatedness, for example, between half and full siblings. Looking at survival from a genetic point of view, a gene often achieves survival not only through its offspring but also through its siblings. The protective urge toward a sibling, the "maternal" roles sisters, in particular, so often take toward one another, are not altruistic in evolutionary terms; they secure the survival of one's *own* genes.

The tension between sibling rivalry and protection is so marked and so regular across species that zoologists use a formula to describe the likely "calculation" made when a sister or brother is in trouble: How close a creature is to another (in the sense of how many genes they share), how likely its protection is to be effective, and how much its action "costs" (in the form of food or risk) are all weighed up according to some inherent gene-preserving mechanism.[17] This does not mean that siblings of any species crunch genetic data and perform a risk analysis every time they act protectively toward one another. According to the principles of evolutionary psychology, the argument would be that "the mental programs for familial love were calibrated in the course of evolution so that love *correlated with* the probability in the ancestral environment that a loving act would benefit copies of genes for loving acts."[18]

We do not make a calculation when we act protectively or when we look out for ourselves; but the impulses to protect and to attack are adaptations to the environment we are likely to live in. Familiar characteristics of sibling behavior, both in terms of rivalry and love, are, in this argument, likely to be shaped by evolutionary adaptation. We are geared to be sociable and, to some extent trustworthy, because living in a society gives us individually a greater chance of survival. We are geared to be rivals to siblings to compete for family resources, and we are geared to protect our siblings because they share our genes, and in protecting a sibling, we are ensuring the survival of our own genes.

SISTERLY PROTECTION

THIS BRIEF FORAY into research by zoologists and evolutionary psychologists provides an intriguing framework for sibling bonds. The patterns in the animal world cannot be mapped directly onto relationships between human siblings; but these studies suggest how forcefully the sibling bond shapes behavior in many species. They also highlight the abrasive dynamic between sibling rivalry and protection.

Sisters' protective responses to one another, however fierce and effective, are balanced against shrewd self-interest. Catching this balance in action challenges simplistic assumptions about women's orientation to care for and protect others. The bedrock of protectiveness has an evolutionary base: It is an adaptation that protects one's genes. In addition the urge to protect grows from sibling experiences, a common family history, the mutuality of understanding, and a strong identification among siblings. The urge to protect is so strong that many sisters in my study said they were confused and resentful of its force. The urge to protect a sister sometimes came into direct conflict with their own self-interest, and they resented the force of that protective urge.

Siblings have an intimate sense of what each is feeling. Family griefs and constraints and cruelties experienced by one sister can be swiftly transmitted to another by means of a single gesture, word, or look. The empathy one sister feels for another is described as "immediate," "overwhelming," and "like it's happening to me but worse." Distress over a sister's distress comes, in the words of one woman, "like a wave of panic."

Children as young as fourteen months of age show awareness of a sibling's distress and take steps to provide comfort. A two-year-old can see that her sister wants a toy, is crying because it has been taken away, and will wrest it from the grasp of another child to restore her sister's contentment. But the same two-year-old is also capable of wrestling with that sibling for a toy, for a place on a parent's lap, for the larger piece of cake. The fierce impulse to comfort and protect resides alongside a child's willingness to cause distress and deprivation. From a very early age children are alert to the often minor but deeply felt cruelties a parent may inflict on children as she instructs them, warns them, and keeps them from driving her nuts. A child is sometimes pleased to see that a sibling is in the line of parental anger, but she is often anxious to console her when she is the target of someone else's scolding.

Carol is now twenty-seven, and says she is just beginning to emerge from the tension between protection and resentment that shadowed her childhood. "Liba was nearly two years older, but I was constantly anxious about her. Whenever I heard she'd done something bad, my stomach took a dive, and I tried to monitor her more closely. But she was so stubborn and so impulsive! Liba had this really bad temper. Until she was . . . oh, I think it wasn't until she eighteen, she was a terror. Ordinary things just set her alight. Now: What I'd say considering it now is that she is defensive. Maybe even with a paranoid streak. The kind of schoolyard teasing that would just be like a prick to most people puts her in a rage. Someone might call out, 'Hi, curly!' and she'd stew about it and mutter and ask me if her hair was really that much curlier than so-and-so's. She'd go quiet, and I'd be scared, not so much of what she'd do, but of what would happen to her when she lost it.

"I was always worried she'd be really rude, and get into

real trouble. I also worried that she'd get hurt. I got this image of her somehow drowning in that silence. Maybe because I couldn't breathe, I thought she couldn't. I felt so responsible! She was two years older than me, but I felt responsible because she just didn't get the hang of things. And that made me feel so trapped, so I felt sorry for myself, too. I really resented her, because of what she made me feel when I was trying to protect her."

Carol sees this protection as something that is "ripped from her": "It was so different from anything I felt for anyone else. I wouldn't say that Liba and I got along. I felt very competitive with her, especially with our dad. He thought Liba was so smart. I'm sure he followed all the rules in the book, and didn't directly compare us, either favorably or unfavorably. But I knew what he felt. It's the small things you pick up on. I could see that leap of delight when she did well, and the more polite pleasure when I achieved something. It's the range of interest he had, how long he'd focus on her when she spoke. And so I really resented her. But there was this other thing, too, and I know it won't go away. It's sort of needing to protect her because I love her; but I don't feel that I love her."

For the once-difficult Liba, her younger sister was an anchor. "I was often aware of her—this little blur in my peripheral vision. A sort of center of something. You could feel her concentration. She protected me? Is that what she's saying now? Well—now, I'm really trying to see that. She was there, and I knew she was sometimes anxious. You know, I hated how she worried about me, and was embarrassed by me. Well—I'm really taken aback by this. Because, yes, I did like her being there, especially at school, which I found really hard. Sometimes I had a real hard time. I knew I was always the weird one, and I never got it. Never got why. So it was always comforting to have Carol beside me. But I didn't realize she was there for me, you know, because she thought she could do something for me."

The protection Carol provided has shaped her life; she says, "It's probably the reason I never had children. I'd been there, and it was too great a burden, and I did all I could, but it clearly wasn't enough." The pressure to care for a sister when one does not have the adult's power, either in the world or in the family, is not easily forgotten or forgiven.

Carol and Liba are stunned by what one gave and the other took. Protection may be effective, but it also puts the protector in a stronger, or one-up, position. Between siblings who want to prove their superiority to each other, protection offered to one is often minimized by the sibling who benefits from it. Mismatched sister stories about who protected whom were common.

PROTECTION AND EMBARRASSMENT

OUTSIDE THE FAMILY sisters' social worlds overlap. Yet children are keen to be their own person, free to construct new identities among their peers. Such infringements lead to clashes between two worlds, competing personae, and competing loyalties.

Miri had many responses to her younger sister's needs. She recalls the annoyance she felt when her sister, Elizabeth, three years younger, ran up to her during recess, crying and complaining because her plastic raincoat got torn. "I was playing with my friends, and I was so annoyed when she came near me. I couldn't be both her comforting sister and my friends' friend. The two just didn't go together."

Miri recalls the hot shame and pity she felt for her sister when she peed in the classroom. Hearing some girls talk about it during the lunch hour, she wanted to weep with resentment, and also was plagued by images of her sister's pouting face. "You could tell when she was sad. I always wanted to hug her when she went into that moody slump. But I hated being seen as someone who loved a kid who would pee in school. I had to wait with her for the school bus, and I knew what she'd been through that day, but I kept my head turned away from her, and didn't look at her or allow her any opening to talk to me about this. I told her not to sit next to me on the bus, and she let out this little whimper but did as I said. It was only when we got off the bus and were nearly home that I took her hand, and she burst into tears, and even then I wanted to kick her before I comforted her in the usual way."

Sisters often express ambivalence about their feelings of protectiveness. The tension between wanting to respond to others' needs and wanting to be left to get on with one's own life becomes a familiar theme in women's psychology. While this has been highlighted in discussions of mothers' powerful but ambivalent responsiveness to children, it has not been explored in the context of siblings.

Miri, twelve years after she had shared a school playground with her sister, still confronts the wish to accommodate her sister on the one hand, and her reluctance on the other. "Elizabeth rang me last week and asked whether I could stay with her and give her moral support when her fiancé's son comes to visit. She's terrified he won't like her, and that she won't know what to do with him. My boyfriend saw me scuttling around and switching my schedule, and said, 'She's your sister, not your kid.' But she's my kid sister. For her I'm her family, and it's important for me to be there for her—even though it's sometimes a pain."

Being a good sister can be as tricky a challenge as the more familiar one of being a "good mother" or a "good wife." What others can ask of you and what you can ask of others are crucial questions, and impact on a woman's sense of being "good" or "bad." These questions are salient when a sister has special needs.

Janet's young sister has Down syndrome. "I was always told I should be grateful for being normal. . . . Well, my gran used to say this, and I think my mom sometimes thought it, but maybe she never really said it. But Ashley seemed to be the most important person in the house, and sometimes I felt that no one cared about me and my problems never mattered because I was supposed to be okay. I was more jealous of her than I would have been of a sister who was much smarter and prettier than me." Now nineteen, Janet looks back on the years, from when she was eleven to the time she was sixteen, when it was her job to pick her sister up from school on her way home.

"Then we'd go to catch the bus. Sometimes I had friends with me. And sometimes it was okay. But she was so friendly, and she wouldn't leave them alone. She kept on patting them and grinning, and she talked to me the whole time we were on the bus. Every day she'd say things like, 'I like that store,' and 'There's the cat. Janet! Janet. I see that cat.' She could get hysterical and giggly, and I was so embarrassed I wanted to punch her. I hated her, and I hated my mom for making me do this. I'd tell her to shut up, and then she'd close her mouth and look down at her lap, and I'd get mad because she was making me feel bad. But then she'd forget all about it and start mouthing about everything again. It wouldn't be so bad if she just spoke quietly. But everything excited her, and when she was excited she'd scream. 'There's a CAT!' I made fun of her. I was really mean. But she never got it.

"But when other people teased her, I lost my temper before I even knew I was angry. You know what I mean? I could always see the teasing about to start, and I got good at staring guys down, or just ignoring them and distracting her. It got around that you couldn't mess with 'that funny kid' without having your face scratched by her sister. That reputation sort of surprised me. Because most of the time I wanted to scratch Ashley's face. But I didn't. I just hit the guys who teased her."

The primitive identification between sisters makes each vulnerable to embarrassment and shame at the other's behavior. Each is not wholly oneself, but part of a family unit with which one identifies closely. Each is implicated in the other's identity, and the social standing of a sibling is never a matter of indifference to oneself. However different the sisters Janet and Ashley are, Janet says, "I feel part of me is her. And when someone teases her, it's every bit as bad as me being teased— even worse, maybe, because it's not just what I feel it's also what she feels."

*   *   *

Protectiveness has a hard edge. There is an inevitable ambivalence embedded in our concern for others. The impulse to prioritize concern for others is a central issue in the psychology of women. For example, How much do we want to give to others? and, How far are we pressured by social norms and the burden of others' opinion to take a caring role, often at the expense of self-care? The embedded tension between protection and resentment, which women and men share, hooks up with the social norms of women as carers; this increases the tension between meeting their own needs while also responding to the needs of others. A sister's worry is that she will not be able to limit her protection, however much it costs her. The range of ambivalence within the sister knot opens our eyes to the fact that caring for others and looking out for oneself is a hard-wired dilemma of social evolution, and finding the best balance presents humans and other species with the need to perform tricky calculations.

TAKING A MOTHER'S ROLE

SISTERS' CARE FOR one another is widespread.[19] The maternal roles sisters take toward their siblings has been noted in cultures with extended families, such as India, Kenya, and the Philippines,[20] yet it often goes unnoticed in our everyday life. In a recent study of primary-school-age children in Scotland, sibling caretaking was found to be a common experience, and was viewed positively both by the siblings who were carers and those who were cared for.[21]

This common pattern also raises common problems, particularly among girls and women who often experience uncomfortable maneuvers into a caring role. Karen believes that she was manipulated into a caring role by her father, who said, "My supper always tastes better when you make it," and "I only enjoy this program if you watch it with me." Ally's mother insisted, "I need you to take care of your little brother," and her grandparents reinforced this with, "You should help your mother," as did the neighbors who said, "You're so *good*, the way you help your mother." Often family roles are shaped by gender: *You're the man of the family now*, or *It's up to you be a mother to your younger brother/sister*. While many children gain competence and confidence from taking on caring roles, the burden can force a premature facade of maturity that forcloses their ability to explore, experiment, and test their talents.

I first interviewed Sarah Ann for a study on development and growth in midlife women. When Sarah Ann spoke about her goals for the fifth decade of life, she kept returning to her development as a teen, when she had had to look after her younger brothers and sisters. When a family is marked by the death or illness of a parent, everyone suffers; but it is usually the best-functioning female, regardless of age, who does the most work toward sustaining the emotional, psychological, and practical well-being of the other members.

By the time she was fifteen Sarah Ann had taken over the care of her younger sister and half sisters and brothers, while her mother remained in a drug-controlled depression. "I loved my sisters and brothers," she said, "and I was glad to look after them, but always there was a secret selfish self quietly watching the door." She described "a reckless nature that breathed along with every careful step I took."[22]

There was only a three-year difference between Sarah Ann and her sister, Shena, but the mother's illness affected each sister differently. While Sarah Ann stayed at home and took on domestic chores, Shena sought social distractions from the uneasy life at home. The sisters remained close, but Sarah Ann said, "I really resented her. I gave up an awful lot to be reliable so she didn't have to be." But Shena insists, "Sarah Ann didn't have to be the good daughter. She could have gone off when she wanted. Sometimes she sounds like the family martyr, but in our mom and dad's eyes she was the golden girl, always reliable. I felt like nothing next to her."

Now Sarah Ann looks to midlife as presenting an opportunity to reach back to the spontaneity and adventure and recklessness she had to forgo in order to be the responsible one, whereas Shena wants to prove that she is reliable, as reliable as her sister. "I hated being cast as the flighty one. I still resent it. You know, she'll look at me, and suddenly there's this thing in her look, like it's not worth her while asking anything of me." But Sarah Ann recognizes the shift in roles. "My little sister is now looking after me. She is doing all the organizing stuff I need to do for this 'gap year' I'm planning. She'll look after my dog. She's taking me to the airport and will take care of the car. I feel my kids have a mom on site. It's good to know your kids have that, even when they're supposed to be grown. I thank her, and she says, 'Yeah, sis, you've done a good job on me.' Twenty years later what I did for her is still important for both of us. At least that's how we feel on a good day. But sometimes she denies I did anything for her, and goes on about what she does for me. We can turn nasty. We can turn on a pin."

Sisters may feel guilty that the urge to protect has limits; they feel guilty, too, that they resent a sister; and this guilt often is expressed by bagging the role of rescuer and denying they have ever been protected by a sister. In *Motherless Daughters*, Hope Edelman describes the sister tension that was shaped by the caring role into which she was maneuvered when her mother died. At the age of seventeen Hope became the housekeeper, the family chauffeur, the one in charge of that domestic schedule. School time and dentist appointments and shoe replacements became her problems. Edelman uses the term "mini-mother" to describe the role that was foisted on her.[23] She seemed to split in two; part of her had to grow up, suddenly, to become the domestic manager, while the teenager who was grieving for her mother got left behind.

The need to be "the strong one" continued to rankle as she grew into womanhood. In her twenties, when her younger sister announced that she was leaving New York for Los Angeles, Hope was terror stricken. How could her sister abandon her? When Hope then protested, her younger sister pleaded with her not to make a fuss. The younger sister herself was anxious about the move. She explained to Hope, "I need you to be strong for me," but Hope countered with, "I can't always be the strong one. . . . I don't want you to leave." The younger sister's response was, "What about when *you* left for college when I was fifteen?"[24] This accusation stunned

Hope: She had seen, clear as day, all the care she had given others; but she had been oblivious to their continued need when she escaped to college.

Mutually supportive, the sisters are also mutually dependent. As a result the younger sister remembers being "abandoned," while the older sister remembers being forced to care for her. Each sister is defensive about how much she can give and how much her gift is appreciated. Sisters who take on minimothering are driven by doubt about their capacity to protect and fear lest too much is required of them. Yet research shows that whatever care an older sister is able to provide is effective: An older sister can prevent the behavioral and emotional problems that otherwise occur in children who suffer parental loss.[25]

In one study of isolated children, younger siblings (about one-third) said they confided in an older sister even before they turned to a father, when a mother is not present;[26] and about half mentioned an older sibling as their only source of help. It has been found that sisters provide mutual support when they face problems with other children at school, when they face the distress caused by maternal illness, or when they themselves suffer childhood falls and scrapes and the routine colds and flu. Social workers have noted similar sibling bonds among those who are threatened with separate fostering arrangements. Offering protection to a sister can anchor one after the loss of a parent. Bobbie says, "I don't know what I would have done when my mother died, if I didn't have my little sister to look after." But being looked after by Bobbie had a different meaning to her sister. Now in her fifties, the younger sister says, "Bobbie is always so bossy. When my friends complain to me about an interfering mother, I say, 'You should meet my sister.'"

The discrepancies in sister stories about protection are the basis of lifelong arguments about who gave what to whom, and who owes gratitude to whom. But the effectiveness of sibling support is beyond question. Anna Freud and Sophie Dann studied six children who lost their parents in World War II, and who were brought up together in concentration camps. They saw themselves as a family group, and formed a connection that is described as "social siblings." The children, bereft of families, constructed their own family unit. After their release from the camps, Anna Freud and Dann observed the children's "unusual emotional dependence on each other," and the "almost complete absence of jealousy, rivalry and competition."

These social siblings were emotionally indifferent to the grown-ups who came into their lives. For the most part the adults around them were merely providers of material goods. The siblings used their interactions with adults to get things for themselves and one another: "When one of them received a present from a shopkeeper, they demanded the same for each of the other children, even in their absence." These children had remarkable emotional and mental stability, which they derived from one another, and their greatest anxiety was about being separated.[27]

When the environment is frightening, when parents are threatening, rejecting, or invisible, siblings, write Stephen Bank and Michael Kahn, "are not minor players in the family drama: they are the stars: the villains and the heroes who play a significant role in the child's life-and-death struggles for attachment, separateness and identity."[28] An age-old model of siblings starring in their own survival story appears in the familiar tale of Hansel and Gretel. The brother comforts the sister from the fears of the lonely night, the children warm each other, and the sister finesses her brother's freedom from the witch's cage. With a father who is too weak to save his children from the stepmother who wants to hoard the family resources herself for her and her genes,[29] the siblings look to themselves for mutual comfort and protection.

GIVING AND INGRATITUDE

interesting

[THE QUESTION, DO you understand and appreciate how much I have done for you? raises powerful feelings. It is linked to questions about who is capable of generosity, whose love is worth more, and who has the emotional intelligence to act effectively. These questions impinge on our self-esteem. The capacity to love, to connect with others, and to see that one's love is effective are crucial to our humanity. Between partners, between parent and child, these issues are perhaps the most pronounced, but they also are heated issues between sisters, partly because the impulse to protect is so strong, and partly, too, because these questions link up to cultural norms of women's worth.]

The most striking case in my study involving questions of love and gratitude, protection and resentment, is that of Gina and her sister, Sam. When she was in her twenties, Gina developed an inflammation of the filtering part of her kidneys, which, because it was painless, progressed until she suffered severe kidney damage. Sam, who was two years older, knew little about the severity of her sister's condition until her mother phoned to say that her sister was suffering kidney failure.

"We were sisters," she says flatly, when I ask her whether they are close. "We sometimes fight, and we sometimes hate each other, but she was always part of my life, and I think I knew I always loved her. There was a time in our teens when I was intensely jealous of her, and wanted her to get fat, so I wouldn't look so bad next to her. Then there was a kind of cooling-off period, when we just weren't that interested in each other. I had my friends, and she had hers, and at that time friends seemed more important; though I sure see now that they weren't. When our mom phoned me and told me how ill Gina was, it was like being hit by a tornado. I had a house full of kids, mine and some of their friends; and I kept walking around the room in circles thinking, This can't be happening. I never worried about her the way my mom worried about all of us. But all I could think of was how I was going to get there, and whether I'd take the kids or leave them with someone."

In the end Gina's only hope for a normal life was a kidney transplant. Sam was tested and found to be a match. "When I heard this, I felt two things, right at the same time. I thought, 'Well, good, that's solved,' and I also felt as though chains were being clamped onto me. I wanted to run as fast as my legs would carry me. There was only one choice. I mean, there was no choice. But it was still difficult. I mean, *boy*, was it difficult! I listened to the doctors' spiel, but that didn't mean I understood anything. I knew I didn't understand, and I knew there were things they weren't saying. Not that they were covering up; but they just went from one step to the next step, and I knew it just wouldn't be like that. That was their story, but this was my body. I really didn't want to do it! There! I've said it. I don't think I've said it before. But they said, 'You're a great match!' I heard this scream inside me, this No-no-no!

"But I couldn't say no. I didn't want to say no. I wanted to do what I could for my sister. I wanted her to live. I sure didn't want to go through life being the sister who refused to give her sister a kidney. But I also thought of my two children, and my husband thought of them, too, and he thought about himself, and his parents thought about him and the kids. But I didn't really understand how deep their feelings were until afterward. It took me so long to recover. I mean, I got better, and she got better, but I was so low for so long, and I feel there's a real difference in me since I have only one kidney, but the doctors tell me there's no physical basis for that, which means that it's all in my mind. But it's there. And we— I mean me and my husband, and not just us, his family too— resent the way I was pushed into it. Not that I really could have done anything different. My mother-in-law says some really shocking things. Well, they're shocking, but I still kind of agree with them. She says it wasn't right because I have children and Gina doesn't, and that was never taken into account. But, even thinking about it now, I don't really see any other way."

Sam pauses for a few moments, then takes a deep breath. "What bugs me every day is that my sister and my parents just take it for granted, and I don't think any of them see what it cost me. I don't think my sister is grateful. She's thankful she's well now, but she's not grateful to me."

Gina, on the other hand, is bewildered by Sam's belief that she is insufficiently grateful. "Of course I'm grateful to her. I owe her my life. Of *course* I'm grateful." She is clearly hurt by this accusation. Though she has heard it before, she pauses to reflect on it. "What choice did I have? Other than to ask this of her? And what does she think? Does she think I wouldn't have done it for her? Does she think that she's the only person who'd do such a thing for a sister? And does she think I should always be thanking her? Like we should never argue, never just be us, because she's done this big thing? It *is* a big thing. I know that. But we're still two sisters who sometimes disagree and sometimes criticize one another. Am I supposed to love her like some saint, or in some super-duper way? I love her like a sister, like I always did. But now that's not enough."

The act of protection is not always appreciated for the same reasons that maternal care is not always appreciated. It is taken for granted; and it is taken for granted because there are times when it is so necessary that one cannot imagine being without it. The tension between gift and debt within a family is always difficult to negotiate. Sam and Gina are, of course, a special case. The gift of a body organ, the demand one makes on the other in order to survive, is seldom so crystal clear, and the aftermath so clouded by resentment and love.

RESCUING A SISTER

MANY SISTERS, HOWEVER, imagine that they would like the opportunity to offer a life gift to a sister. Pride in protecting a sister was a common reference, and some women recalled elaborate childhood games in which they vied for the role of rescuer. Jessica remembers that she often got into trouble with her parents for trying to enact her protection fantasies. "When we were kids, I set up games where they'd be in trouble; I had to be a firefighter or surgeon or policeman. I made a harness for lowering my baby sister from her bedroom window to the yard. When my mother saw what I was doing she started screaming, 'What are you doing? Are you trying to kill her?! You're trying to kill her!' She was in such a fury that she threw the hairbrush at me and cut my cheek.

"I kept the harness. I found it when I was clearing out my room during college, and I thought, 'This isn't bad.' It followed all the rules about knots and stresses, and the rope was really strong. I was so relieved, because my mother's reactions slammed those games into the ground. She acted like I was really trying to kill my sister. But when I got out that harness and gave it a good look over, I thought, 'No, I wasn't trying to kill Adi. I just really liked the idea of saving her.'"

When the dramatic games were brought to a halt, Jessica turned to storytelling. She wove together tales of adventure and danger, with the three sisters as the main actors, but she, invariably, gave herself the role of rescuer. The stories were sometimes written down, and sometimes simply spoken. The plots became more and more elaborate. "It was something I looked forward to, the chance to engage in my private movie theater. I had fantasies of saving my sisters from an earthquake or flood. I worked on the stories at night, before I went to sleep. I went through them in my mind on the long ride to school. Oh, it's all coming back to me now! The scenarios were cheesy, but they were so lovely! My favorite was dragging my sister just in time from a collapsing gateway.

"I was twelve when that quake hit Pasadena and a woman was killed near UCLA by falling cement. I wanted to be in that situation with my sisters so that I would be able to show how I could save them. The best scene that I made up and then kept playing over in my mind, was when I got this amazed look from my mother, who realized that she'd never properly appreciated me before, but that was really an afterthought. Her admiration was just a perk, though; the main thing was imagining how I'd feel when my strong arm tugged my sisters to safety. Doing something like that would be wonderful. Like having a success so clear I'd never again have to wonder whether I was really worth anything. Today I still want to see that my sisters are safe. I'm a mother now, and I'd tend to my son first, but that feeling about my sisters is still there."

While their brother was playing games of danger and rescue on an imaginary battlefield, Jessica's landscape was home and neighborhood, and the possible dangers and rescues there. These games and fantasies bring together the wish to be the stronger one, and the goal to obtain the most parental approval; the entertainment in seeing a sister in peril, and the deep satisfaction of being able to protect her effectively without harming oneself. In this cross section of sister play we can see the abiding mix of protectiveness and selfishness within human bonds.

ANXIETY AND PROTECTION

STEPHEN BANK AND Michael Kahn describe a girl who "lived with the daily apprehension that her brother would act 'bad' if not supervised closely by her." Whenever she heard that he had once again behaved badly, her anxious monitoring of him increased. The psychiatrists observed also a nine-year-old girl whose "sleeping and waking life was so preoccupied with worry about [her brother] that she often withdrew from contact with other people. . . . She seemed to feel that his obnoxiousness and immaturity were a . . . burden that she would willingly but resentfully carry for a lifetime."[30]

In fantasy the urgent call to rescue a sister is enjoyable, but in a child's everyday life, it evokes acute anxiety. Am I able to be as brave/strong/clever as I need to be to save her? is a question that comes upon a child like a nightmare. A two-year-old, seeing a large dog approach her baby sibling, flaps at the dog and, unable to shoo it away, displays extreme distress that subsides only when an adult takes charge. When Emma's five-year-old sister, Megan, gets into a temper, declares she is running away, and leaves the house, her mother calmly asks the seven-year-old to bring her sister back. Emma races down the street and screams when she sees Megan step up to the curb.

When her younger sister refuses to come with her, Emma grabs Megan's collar and pulls her toward her house. A passerby scolds Emma, "You shouldn't be so mean to your little sister," unaware of the protective terror that spurs the older sister on.

Children show great distress when a sibling, too young to look after herself, is separated from them. Liba's early memory of a family holiday is being in a trailer park, where her sister, then three, liked to jump out of the trailer and pick the wild daisies. "Carol was always running away. She'd spring on her chubby legs and race through the grass. I told her to stay close to me but she wouldn't listen to me. I was so cross because my mother wasn't looking out for her properly. She was blabbing on to her friend, and Carol thought running away from me was funny. No one cared how dangerous it was. I had to look after her all morning because no one else would."

This resentment is similar to the anger a parent feels when a child puts herself in danger and refuses to obey the commands shouted to her at the top of a panicked parent's voice. It is anger aroused by fear and by anger at the person who arouses that fear. When the protector is herself a child, a panicky collision occurs between the sibling's danger and one's own uncertain capacity to protect.

In the sister interviews there were twice as many references to feelings of care, concern, meeting needs, and offering help and protection than there were to rivalry. Seeing a sister in trouble, and being terrified by danger posed to a sister, were commonly mentioned as among "the strongest concerns I have about a sister." This protectiveness is as complex, makes as deep an impact, and elicits as much ambivalence as does rivalry.

When one sibling is badly treated, sister empathy can be so intense that a girl will risk punishment herself rather than leave her sister undefended. Stephen Bank and Michael Kahn describe the sisters Julia and Melanie, who find different ways of dealing with their difficult father. The older sister, Julia, left home after a series of battles with her father. Melanie then became distressed by the false and humiliating accusations her father brought against the absent sister. Defending her sister (who was not there and would not actually suffer) seemed necessary to her—even though it led to her being beaten by her father.[31]

Empathy combined with impotence results in intolerable levels of stress. At one stage of her life Ally resented her mother's bizarre behavior more on her sister's behalf than on her own. Her inability to protect her youngest sister inflamed her anger toward her mother. "Our mother was giving Karen these toothpaste sandwiches. My little sister had to take slices of bread stuck together with toothpaste to school. Mom said that she was fed up with her for forgetting to brush her teeth, so she would make sure she got that toothpaste in her mouth if she wanted to put anything in it. She once mixed cat food in her soup. She said Karen had to learn what really bad food was like if she was going to complain about the food served at the table. She said Karen stuck up her nose at her dinner once too often. And she made her sit at the table until she ate it. Her voice was like an iron rod ramming through you. I hated my mother when she did things like that to me, but Karen just felt sad." Still struggling with her impulse to protect her youngest sister, Ally encapsulates protection and resentment, as she remembers, "Then I hated Karen, too, because I couldn't protect her."

PROTECTING A SISTER, PROTECTING THE PARENTS

A FAMILY CAN be mapped with crisscrossing lines of loyalties among its members. Sometimes sisters quarrel because one judges the other to be insufficiently loyal to a parent (as Ellie resents her sister for being hard on their mother) or too compliant (Shena says Sarah Ann did not have to stay at home to be "the good daughter"). Sometimes sisters are loyal to one another to form a protective alliance against difficult or abusive parents. But Hannah explained that the underlying reason for protecting her little sister was to protect her parents from being bad parents.

"Our parents were always working. They'd say things like, 'As soon as we get this account sorted, things will settle down.' One day my mom was rushing around the house and swearing and slamming drawers because she couldn't find some document or some invoice. Elina and I just cowered somewhere, talking real low, because our mother always shouted at us when she was in that mood, no matter what we said. Just when she was at the door she turned and put on this smile and said, 'Daddy and I are opening the West Side store today. As soon as it's up and running we'll all take a trip.'

"I think I nodded because I knew she was still in a mood and would shout if I didn't do the right thing, but something clicked, and I thought, That's a lie. It was scary thinking that so clearly while she was right there. But I nodded and took my sister's hand, and our mom sort of sighed and smiled some more, and when she went out, Elina plopped down on the floor and started one of her tantrums. There was a maid home, I guess, but no one who would help Elina. Connie was upstairs with her friends, and it was just Elina and me. I always looked out for her. I wanted to know whether she had any mishaps on her way home from school. The things she told me sometimes made my heart turn. She said, 'Tommy told me I was stupid,' or 'The teacher said I couldn't do music anymore because I forgot my recorder again.' I see now that these are just everyday hiccups in a kid's school day, but then they seemed awful, and made me feel so sorry for her I felt sick. I had no perspective. All her dramas were my dramas. I couldn't tell the difference between the little and the big things. Once she dropped some money in a shop, and she knew she'd lost some money, but she wasn't sure the money on the floor was hers because she didn't see it drop, and so she came crying to me because she'd lost her money, and I wanted to strangle her because she needed someone all the time. But I decided, there and then, Okay. She can have me. I'll be her person. I'll take care of her."

Hannah is the middle of three sisters. From that vantage point, she said, "I made a decision to look out for my neglected little sister. I could see she was struggling. She was lonely and no one was really paying attention to her. There are these images I have of her: picking a scab on her skinny knee, and suddenly I realized our parents didn't notice her and didn't explain she shouldn't do that. And I told her, I must have shouted, because she burst into tears and said, 'Everyone's always telling me off!' Taking care of her wasn't going to be easy. I kept getting things wrong, so very wrong, and I really wanted to help her. So I thought, Well, I'll just keep at this. I'll keep at it and I'll learn. To this day I'm not sure she knew what I was doing. I was the bossiest sister, the one who was always finding fault with her. But to me she was someone I wanted to look out for. That's become something in my life. And it's something I've been proud of, and comforted me when *I* felt neglected by our parents, too. I get very impatient with her now if I feel she's not raising her kids right, or if she's with the wrong guy."

Hannah's sister Elina does think she is bossy, but says that arises from her competence. "Hannah is so smart, and she always has an answer. You know how you sometimes wonder, Should I buy these shoes or the other ones?, Is it better to get a six p.m. flight or one at noon?, Does it make sense to take the kids swimming first or get the groceries first? When I ask Hannah, she comes out with the answer, as though there really is a good answer, a right one. She has this habit of sitting back when she makes a decision. Her chin goes into her neck and she gives me this look, and then after she gives her pronouncement: 'What I think you should do is . . .' Then she makes this slow big nod, like she's listening to herself, hearing how right she sounds."

For Elina this is comforting, but also it is annoying. "I don't want to feel like the inept little sister forever." Many of the decisions she makes are influenced by her determination not to be inept. She describes how, at age twenty, she moved to a different city. "Going to a new place was exciting, but mostly I was scared. I really wanted help, but I was more worried about being pathetic and getting help, so I went alone. I did everything myself. When I finally found somewhere to live, and I was so relieved: I can really do this! You know, that feeling of amazement because you've been able to do something. I'm thirty-three years old now, and I still get that feeling. And it's always followed by this rush of love I'll always have for Hannah. Because she is the best sister ever. Connie is the oldest, but Hannah is somehow the biggest sister. She's the one I think of when you say sister. Hannah is all that's good and infuriating in what I see when I hear the word sister." Hannah remains watchful of her sister. She is uneasy about what she calls Elina's "religious fanaticism." "She's inflicting it on her kids—on my nieces. And she shows disrespect to our parents, because they are more lax in their ways." Once the position of protector is taken, it is difficult to relinquish.

"Here I am, a thirty-seven-year-old professional woman with my own life, worrying about my little sister who is herself over thirty and has her own life. But when I see what position she's taking, when I see what she's doing to my nieces to make them conform to her views, I feel ashamed. There's a nagging sense of guilt. I carry it around because I feel responsible for her. I feel bad about what she's doing. I worry about her, but I'm also furious about how it's making me feel. This is such a strong thing, and no one talks about it. Do other people feel this? It's such a strong thing. It feels like it should be common, but I don't know anyone else who deals with this."

The close identification between sisters, particularly between sisters who have a history of care and love, carries the burden of "sororal alert." Sisters who look out for each other throughout their lives face the moral hazard of feeling ashamed if a sister's behavior does not come up to her own standards. "She makes me feel guilty, even though, strictly speaking, it has nothing to do with me. This is poisoning our relationship," Hannah reports. "There are times when I feel bad about myself, because I feel bad about her."

Stories of sisterly protection uncover an ancient ambivalence about self and other. We are not fully distinct from those we love. This connection is compounded by cultural pressures on women to take on caring roles. When we connect to a sister, we feel that she is part of us and we of her. This gives the bond strength, but it also reveals the limits of our control over who we are. The bond between sisters is another reminder that our identities are changed by those we love.

PROTECTION, FEAR, AND STRESS

WITHIN THE FORCE of the sister knot, protection is activated in response to danger, and the perception of danger initiates a stress response. When we explore the dynamics of sisters, however, we have to challenge assumptions about how stress functions; for established assumptions about human responses to stress have been formed by observing stress in males. What we learn by looking at males cannot always be easily extrapolated and applied to women.

Stress has traditionally been modeled as a flight or fight response, because it is the model that males are likely to follow. In men stress primes the body to fight or flee. In this way stress prepares them, physiologically, either to attack the danger head-on or to avoid it. The pattern of females' response is different. Faced with danger, a female will naturally experience a lot of what males experience. Girls and women, too, undergo physiological changes that increase heart rate and blood pressure. In females, too, stress responses mobilize energy and divert it to the activation of muscle power. But their stress behavior is not so clearly shaped by the urge to flee or to fight.

The anthropologist Shelley Taylor analyzed female responses to stress and discovered that female stress is more accurately characterized as "tend and befriend."[32] Faced with a predator, a female tends to her young and bands together into groups for protection. The first thought of a woman confronted by a predator would be how to save the child; that is the "tend" part. Being vulnerable, she bands with other women and their offspring and seeks strength in numbers; that is the "befriend" part. Competition has survival value, but so do care and cooperation. This response would have had survival value to hunter-gatherer ancestors, and would thus have been passed on to subsequent generations of females through genetic and social reinforcement.

A sibling of either gender can feel empathy and an urge to protect; but it seems to be a particularly prominent pattern among sisters. The genetic and social pressures to protect cannot be distinguished from one another. Sisters battle with both social expectations and primitive impulses. And even while sisters protect each other, they mark out the meaning of their behavior in the context of sibling rivalries.

Sam wonders whether the fact that her parents (implicitly, perhaps) expected her to be a willing kidney donor to her sister means that her parents love her sister more and value her own health less. Gina knows that they are sisters and will always be sisters. They are willing to die for each other; they care for each other, and they are easily irritated by each other. With a touch of poignant comedy, the sister who is strong enough to be protector then seeks acknowledgment of her life gift from the sister she has protected. The sisters protect each other, and then go on to bicker about the usual things. As in all relationships grounded both by ancient responses and everyday interactions, the large acts of generosity and protection do not obliterate the smaller irritations.

The sister knot presents a stunning challenge to an idealized love that is all giving; it poses a challenge to the question of whether any relationship can be totally devoid of selfish interests or resentment. The love in the sister knot shows that connection and protectiveness inevitably conflict with our own interests and needs. The challenge of close relationships is not to find a perfect one but to negotiate their mix of demands and blessings.

PROTECTION AND EMPOWERMENT

A SISTER'S URGE to be a capable protector is a powerful theme, nowhere more powerfully portrayed than in Alice Walker's novel *The Color Purple*. When Celie is abused by her stepfather, she determines to put herself between the abuser and her younger sister, Nettie. The cruelest act her careless and negligent husband commits against her is to deprive her of contact with her sister: "You took my sister away from me; I say. And she was the only person love me in the world."[33] When Celie discovers that her sister is alive and thriving, she begins, for the first time in her troubled life, to "strut." Her pride in having protected her sister goes deeper than anything else. It goes deeper even than her romantic love for Shug.

Though separated for most of their lives, the sisters keep their connection alive. Each sister can tell her deeply personal story to one of two figures only: either to God or to her sister. Telling a life story to a sister is far more than sharing family news: It enables Celie to make sense of what threatens to be an ugly life. She survives through the strength and pride provided by the sister bond. As with Bobbie, the ability to care for a sister is a supportive, not draining, activity.

Celie is dominated by men who themselves have been brutalized by segregation and poverty. When she helps Nettie escape this social structure, Nettie takes Celie's two children with her. The aunt then loves them, rears them, educates them. The sister who is protected by her older sister acts as mother to the protector's children. Some of Alice Walker's mythic force as a storyteller comes from this revelation of the link between sistering and mothering. Celie "mothers" Nettie by protecting her, as her own mother fails to do, from the abusive stepfather and the abusive society that shapes the stepfather's behavior. Nettie "mothers" Celie's children by raising them in an educated and capable family. Walker then marks the link between protecting a sister and acting selfishly, in the evolutionary sense of ensuring that one's own genes have a good future. The illuminating and imaginative narrative of *The Color Purple* supports the biologist's calculation based on the selfish gene: When Celie protects her sister, she also protects the person who will care for her children. Because she protects her sister, Celie's own children thrive.

When we take a sistering perspective, the tension between protection and resentment reveals itself as an inevitable offshoot of human connection. The urge to care for others is set within shifting balances between the various interest groups that reside within a single person. Points of tension and resistance are inevitable in a fully realized psyche. It is impossible to resolve all the dilemmas of caring. Instead we see that the natural and social environment constantly presents us with tough decisions, and these are a consequence of our multiple interests and attachments. As sisters care for one another, they tune in to the personal costs of caring. They confront questions about what others need, about the cost to themselves of meeting those needs, and about how they themselves benefit from protecting those they love. The dynamics of the sister knot once again provide us with a grounded and contextual view of human emotion, human responsiveness, and the nuances in attachment.

7

Sisters and Friends:
The Interweaving of Female Bonds

ONE OF THE most common themes in sister talk is that of friendship.[1] Two sisters in early adolescence, Siobhan, fourteen, and Dymphna, twelve, describe a closeness "like friendship, but closer." Siobhan talks of the "telepathy" she has with her sister. "We share a whole bunch of private stuff, so it's easy to get a big idea across," and Dymphna says, "We speak the same language, so you don't have to spell everything out in order to understand what the other's saying." Siobhan notices that she and her sister take short cuts to understanding, whereas with other people, even other girlfriends, explaining how you feel can be cumbersome, slow, and frustrating.

Among sisters this rapport survives distance and endures prolonged absence. When Amy, at eighteen, goes off to college, her younger sister Carrie says, "When we talk, we get right back to where we were before. Even though she starts putting on this I'm-so-grown-up pose when she comes home, like she's left me far behind, when we're alone it's back to where we were." And Amy says, "I've made wonderful friends in college, people I'll think of all my life. But Carrie and I—well, we trust each other. We can tell each other anything. There's this safety net thing I just don't question." This trust is echoed by mature women who have tested that safety net. Marge, at fifty-five, and her sister, Mary Beth, fifty-one, have been through illness, divorce, financial reversals, and geographical upheaval; they have also been fiercely at odds over their mother's poorly worded will and a shared boyfriend, yet Mary Beth says, "Whenever there's a crisis I know I can call on her, and I known she'd be there for me. I trust her like a friend, and more than I trust the woman I call my best friend." And Marge says, "I've known my sister all my life. Our parents died, and she's still here. I've seen lovers and husbands go, but she's always in my life, and always will be. She'll be with me longer than anyone else."

The prominent role of siblings as friends has been overlooked simply because most studies of friendships look at friends who are not also relatives. "We're not related, we're just friends" was a message Lillian Rubin contemplated in her book on the importance of female friends.[2] But in her London study of married women's friendships, Pat O'Connor[3] found that for half of her sample of sixty women, their most intimate relationship was with a sister, rather than a friend or a mother.[4] A sister offers mutual understanding and support and a long-term knowledge of one's disappointments and hopes. When the bustle of childhood competition subsides, women find a reassurance, a permanence, in a sister who is also a friend. Even among teenagers, when friendship groups take on a life-or-death significance, a "real best friend" is often a sister.

It is *sisters*, not siblings in general, who speak about their relationship in this way. Whether looking at affection, a sense of shared history, identification with each other, ability to talk easily, or to confide in the other, women tend to describe themselves as "close" to a sister. In Francine Klagsbrun's study of siblings, it emerged that sisters had the closest relationship of any sibling combination on all measures of closeness. Among her sample of 272 siblings, ranging from the age of nineteen to seventy-one, 61 percent of women reported feeling "close" or "very close" to their sisters, compared with 48 percent of men in regard to their brothers and 46 percent of men and women in relation to their opposite-sex siblings.

Whatever intimacy women experience with men—either as brothers, lovers, or friends—most say there is a different quality to their bonds with sisters and with girlfriends.[5] As Susie Orbach and Louise Eichenbaum write in *Bittersweet*, their classic book on women's friendship, "For many women, intimate relationships with women friends, sisters, aunts and co-workers are a bedrock of stability in their lives."[6]

The cross-referencing of sister to girlfriend opens up our understanding of how each relationship impacts on the other, as girls make sisters into friends and friends into sisters. The process of searching for an idealized sister in a friend and discovering the ideal friend in a sister highlights yet again the significant role the sister knot plays across a range of close relationships.

PRACTICING FRIENDSHIP

THE SIBLING SUBSYSTEM of the family has been described as the first laboratory in which children can experiment with peer relations. Within this context children support one another through the daily round of frustration, excitement, shame, and delight. They learn to claim attention for themselves, and they learn to accept their own time on the sidelines. They learn how to include one another in their games, and how to isolate and scapegoat one another: *She can't play with us*, and *She started the fight*, and *It's her fault*, are moves familiar to siblings. In their sibling world children learn how to negotiate: They bargain, they plead, and they offer trades to get their own way or to avoid getting into trouble. And, of course, they also learn how to compete.[7] Jostling for position near the parent, vying with one another for attention, and grabbing what they want are skills first practiced among siblings.

In early childhood, however, friends and sisters are distinct categories. A friend is someone who is outside one's family, someone very different from a sibling. These friendships are based on companionship, often on simply having someone to play with, but they are also rich with physical comparisons and interactions. Girls groom each other, with hair brushing and cosmetic facials; they compare skin tone and body shape; they try on each other's clothes, and dress each other up in endless fantasy games. Their meticulous comparisons suggest the importance of twinning and contrasting, which are activities central to sistering. But peers are not regarded in the way a newborn sibling is, as a potential threat to a child's interests.[8] Their interactions with friends have many rough edges; young children's social skills and tolerance of interpersonal frustration are still rudimentary, but however fraught, their relationships with friends are, at this stage, less intense than their relationships with sisters.

It is when talking, understanding, and empathizing become important features of friendship that the theme of "sister" steps in as a significant feature of friendship, and when sisters are referred to as "friends." While the dramas of girlfriends are enacted in the school cafeteria, in telephone conversations, in email chat sessions, and in peer-group hangouts, sister friendships are maintained through shared knowledge of personal feelings and family experiences. In both relationships girls begin practicing the private talk that is to characterize their relationships with women, either sisters or friends, throughout their lives.[9] Women discuss personal topics for far longer than men do. They share detailed information about their daily lives; and, above all, they talk about how they see the world and what they think and feel about it. They need a friend to understand them and to respect their views; they need to feel they are not alone in their world, that they are one of a pair.

FRIENDS AS TWINS

THE PAIRING OR "twinning" that girls experience with a sister is then taken up again in friendships. By the time they reach middle childhood, girls begin to replicate a sister bond in friendship. In friendships, when the threat of being exactly alike lacks the primary force it has in the sister knot, *difference* is actually more threatening than comforting. Hence, among girlfriends, the similarities are emphasized, the differences are muted.

An abiding hope in girls' and women's friendships is to experience someone as fundamentally like oneself. In our study of girls' and women's friendships, Ruthellen Josselson and I found that girls' descriptions of their friendships, and their explanations of what made the friendship, were filled with references to discoveries of shared experience, shared thoughts, and a sense of being "just the same."

A girl's urgent declaration that she is "just like" her friend arises from her attempt to make her friend into a sister. When girls talk about a friend, they often start by asserting the fact that they are the same, and then go on to list the specific ways in which they are the same.[10] This pairing gives one a sister figure; the friend, while representing a sister, allows one to maintain, quite safely, a sense of oneself as unique and uniquely valued. Alice, age ten, sets up a framework in which she and her friend are "twins." They share similarities, at both a minor and a major level. In friendship, unlike sistering, the twinning process is governed by her and chosen by her. Alice cites similarities as a justification and proof of friendship. She says that her best friend understands even "the silliest things about me; I told her I like the bath so hot I had to inch down in it real slow, and she said she did too, and her legs went red as lobsters, and I said mine did too. And we eat apples exactly the same way."

In friendship twinning is safe. Alice takes the "good" part of the identification (the companionship, the comfort in finding someone like oneself), and discards the part that could threaten her (the sister aspect that challenges her place in her personal world). She hopes to find in friendship someone she can love as a sister but who cannot replace her in her family.

A friend, after all, does not threaten one's sense of self the way a sister does. She thereby begins a process of constructing a sister, in effect a twin sister, from a close friend.

As adults, in the special pleasures of talk, women continue to enjoy the excitement and humor of being with someone fundamentally like them. They seek a friend who reflects back to them their own image. "That's exactly how I feel" and "I know just what you mean," are cries of pleasure at recognizing a twin.[11] It is thrilling and consoling to discover another sister, a sister one chooses, a sister who does not present the threat of displacement in the family. Friends represent a sister without presenting, initially at least, the threats of displacement that arise in the sister knot.

WHY THE SISTER KNOT
SHAPES GIRLS' FRIENDSHIPS

GIRLS' FRIENDSHIPS HAVE many connections to sistering, many that boys' friendships do not have with brothering. First, girls tend to form smaller, family-size friendship groups. They tend to avoid the larger gregarious herds that boys hang out in.[12] Most commonly they play in pairs; they also play in groups of three and four, comfortable conversational groups, where each member can focus on the other. Rarely are girls' close friendship groups larger than this. Their playing styles, too, have a family feel, whereby girls check up on each other's mood and contentment. As young as five, they refer to the other's acceptance of or satisfaction with the game ("She likes playing this skipping-rope game," and "She always lets me be the teacher") and complain about someone who has an uncooperative attitude ("She thinks she's too good to be the messenger," and "She never takes turns").

The way girls control each other in play is closer in style to parental control than the authoritarian persuasion demonstrated in typical boy play. Girls are more likely to say, "Why don't we do this?" or "Let's try it this way?" than to issue direct orders. When they run into disputes about the game, they tend to put an end to that particular game. "Whose turn is it now?" and "Who's not playing fairly?" and "Who made the wrong move?" are all questions that can lead to conflict. While boys throw themselves into arguments about the rules to preserve the integrity of the game, girls have been observed to end the game in order to bring the dispute to an end. They "play something else" rather than continue with something that breeds disharmony. Like a parent, their priority is keeping the peace.

It has often been said that girls do not fight openly with their girlfriends because they do not know how to fight face-to-face. It is said that the social environment girls experience does not provide them the opportunity to declare openly that they want something or to stand up for their rights. Yet, among their sisters, girls are as adept at fighting as boys are. Twice as many boys are involved in fights outside the family, but within the family girls are just as likely to come to blows.[13] The fighting they engage in with their sibs is both open and direct, sly and subversive.

Girls get good practice fighting with their peers in the family, but raging against someone you know you love, and someone with whom you closely identify, is painful. In a context in which sisters are more likely to feel linked to one another, and in which there is additional social admonition against conflict, there is a natural naive desire to obliterate it. Horseplay among siblings may be fun, but real conflict is terrifying. Since girls' friendships aim to create a perfect sister, they try to avoid arguments.

So different are friendship groups from the close relationships within the family that some researchers argue that different parts of the brain develop in tandem with different contexts of play. The social module of our brain is composed of at least two subsystems. One specializes in dyadic relationships and one specializes in group influences. The first subsystem, the one that specializes in dyadic relationships, is ready at birth, ready to lock into the parent-child passion. The other subsystem that deals with groups takes longer to assemble and functions quite differently. While dyadic relationships are based on things like dependency, love, and hatred, "groupness" is based on recognition of peer-group similarities.[14] Group participation is essential to grooming children as a cohort, but this does not in itself involve intimate personal bonds. The latter mode of socialization seems to inform boys' friendships far more than girls' friendships: these remain steeped in the dyadic mode. Girls' friendships are played out as profound personal relationships.

WHAT HAPPENS WHEN
TWO DIFFERENT BONDS ARE MIXED

THESE PROFOUND, INTIMATE bonds are not easy. Negative passions between sisters are higher than between other sibling pairs, and negative passions between girlfriends are more common and more heated than among male friends or mixed friends. Women hold on to their anger vis-à-vis a sister or a friend for longer than men do with either a brother or a friend.[15] While some women say, "My sister is my best friend," or "My two sisters are closer and dearer to me than my best friend," others conclude, "I've given up hoping that my sister can be my friend." From both a positive or negative perspective, sister bonds are viewed in the framework of friendship.

Just as female friends are likely to be "closer" than male friends, in terms of intimate knowledge of one another and detailed updates of personal information, and just as female friends are more prone to sudden and brutal divisions, so too are sisters, more than brothers, likely to be either very close or violently opposed to one another. In the realm of sisters, and in the realm of girlfriends, feelings are passionate, mixed, and sometimes polarized. To find some reprieve from these complications, girls test out places of safety, sometimes among their girlfriends and sometimes among their sisters. In each case they are exploring what is good and what is terrifying in a close relationship to someone with whom they also have to compete for a place in their social world.

When the sisters Siobhan and Dymphna say that they are "best friends," they mean that, much of the time, they are like girlfriends enjoying the goodness of friendship. References to their friendship cover a range of common features—affection, understanding, mutual interest, and delight. However, girls' and women's friendships, like their relationships with sisters, have dark, terrible aspects, too.

Sistering becomes an important theme in girls' friendships just when the sibling trauma is reawakened by the new threats of the social displacement girls experience as they leave early childhood behind. An uneasy counterlife of girls' friendships emerges at around the age of eight or nine. It is when children become capable of sustained and complex social maneuvers that girls' friendships take on the distinctive passion and occasional cruelty that give "mean girls" such prominence. In earlier years there may have been tears, tantrums, and fallings-out, but none of that systematic meanness that arises at the cusp of puberty.

This is when girls become aware that some funnel of development is ahead of them. At this time they are, in some social sense, taking a big step away from their families. Their friends take on renewed emotional significance. They glimpse that wider world and realize that the problems of the sister knot extend beyond the family. The emphasis on loyalty and perfect harmony that girls and women, in different ways and at different stages in their lives, place on their friendships with other women, are attempts to deny the instability of such attachments. By pledging loyalty ("We'll always be friends"), by carefully naming the relationship ("You are my best friend"), girlfriends assure themselves that no one will replace the other.

But they also engage in a dark exploration of their fears about inclusion and exclusion in this wider social world. The friendship group, or clique, is their family outside the family. They "practice" confronting the fears awakened in the sibling trauma. They set up endless, invidious competitions among their friends: Who is nicer, who is prettier, who is liked more. These questions are unanswerable, yet among themselves, girls constantly try out answers and lay siege to other girls who presume to be secure in their position: "She's always showing off," and "Who does she think she is?" girls demand of one another. As friends begin to stand in for sisters, girls look at a friend and wonder, Does she have what I need to be absolutely secure in my relational place? Their efforts rest on a fantasy about what one needs to be included in the group and accepted by the others. They wonder if, outside the family, there will be that "the perfect girl" who everyone likes to be with, and who has all the qualities that ensure that others will love her.

Few women, and fewer girls, are not sometimes shadowed by the ideal girl. For me there was JoAnne Baldwin, an academic high-flier, a cheerleader with a flawless complexion, whose pleated skirts hung perfectly on her slender hips, who would choose just the right college, just the right job, just the right husband. I admired her qualities but was also crushed by them. I would never have to worry about being loved if I were her, I thought. I would not feel cowed by my older sister. I would not feel overwhelmed by my clutch of beautiful and smart cousins. I would be the perfect girl and no one would eclipse me; no one would take away from me the love that I really thought could be easily lost. I would not have to envy anyone if I were JoAnne, and my place in the world would be secure.

I now realize that what I craved was to be someone who was protected from the sibling trauma, someone who would never face the threat of having her status among those she cared for challenged.

For fourteen-tear-old Tess it is her "friend" Gemma, whom she "really hates being with, because she makes me feel awful, but I want to keep an eye on her. I want to know how worried I should be. Whether something's happened that puts her far ahead of me. Sometimes I'm happy, and then Gemma will tell me something, like she's having her room redecorated, or she's just had this really nice time with her boyfriend, who's being really nice to her, and I'll realize I'm not happy at all. You know, she says something or just looks a certain way, and it makes me realize that I have nothing, really, that I'm nothing." As Tess struggles to identify what it is she envies about Gemma, and why she focuses on Gemma's qualities, she says, "There's just something that makes her wonderful. I just know that everyone she wants to love her will love her. It isn't just one thing. It's everything; but sometimes, when I match up to her, like I play real well in basketball or something, or when I see her mess up, I feel relieved. It's like—well, today I don't have to worry. She's not going to make me nothing today."

The envy of "the perfect girl," or the woman who is "the perfect mother" or who has "the perfect home" or "perfect marriage," is an ideal that we construct as a false resolution to the sibling trauma. We shall never be perfectly safe within relationships. These are based on human dynamics, and people and circumstances change, casting up unexpected glitches and hurdles. In a social context in which we may be unsure of who we need to be in order to be loved, we suppose that we would after all be safe and secure in love if only we embodied an ideal.

THE RATIONALE OF EXPOSING ONESELF TO CRUELTY AMONG GIRLFRIENDS

GIRLS OFTEN RESIST their idealization of another girl by turning on her and denigrating her. They are not the terrorized dependents they were when they first experienced the threat of displacement with its associated fear of annihilation. They now want to take some control over the fears aroused by envy and displacement. They reach beyond the confused whining and deliberate naughtiness they engaged in at an earlier stage. They now exercise their power to choose whom to include in their group, and they practice excluding other girls from their group. The selection process is based on little more than whim: Girls know that they, too, might be thrown out of the clique on another occasion. They play on a knife edge with inclusion and exclusion.

Clique dynamics are exercises in fear management. They enact fears about relationships and their implications. Time and again girls reveal themselves to a "best friend" whose heart—they should know from experience—will soon change. Over and over girls trust an alliance that now protects them but—they should know from experience—will soon wound them. Again and again girls return to a friend who teases, taunts, or betrays.

The point and purpose of these exercises are missed by parents and teachers who despair of the friendship wars, and by the researchers who believe these wars can be overcome with their wise words.[16] They accept that sibling squabbles are essential but do not realize that friend squabbles are, likewise, necessary—that girls continue their learning about connection and affection and competition and resentment. As a mother watches a daughter suffer friendship wounds, she asks, *Can't she take in that this girl is poison? Why does she keep going back for more? Does she really think this girl will change? Why doesn't she just stay away?* It is time to ask this question in a different way. Instead of asking it to vent frustration, it should be the first step in the search for a genuine answer.

This repetitive behavior, witnessed in many aspects of childhood play, is an attempt to overcome fear. It is a version of what Freud called "the repetition compulsion." Freud observed children enacting and reenacting scenes that they found disturbing. In the game of a two-year-old child the concepts of "here" and "gone" were engaged, and Freud saw that the child was reenacting a version of a parent's arrival and departure. The child found the parent's departure distressing but had no control over it. A parent's movements, "here" and "gone," were part of the child's daily routine but beyond his comprehension or control.

At first Freud puzzled over why a child would deliberately replay events that bothered him. He concluded that by reenacting a troubling event, a child could gain a sense of mastery over it. Repeating patterns one fears is a kind of psychological practice, whereby one prepares for the events that will inevitably recur. Repetition is an attempt to reduce the anxiety level accompanying these events. It allows us to anticipate and meet challenges or surprises without being overcome by anxiety.

This then provides the answer to the mother, who, when she sees her daughter being battered by the friendship wars, demands, "Why do you remain her friend? Why don't you just stay away from her?" Her daughter is not fooled into thinking that her mean friend will change. Her daughter wants to return to the fray so that she can ponder and placate and then paralyze the dragon of envy. The purpose of friendships in childhood and early adolescence is not to avoid mean girls but to manage them. If girls can repeat the heartache of loss and displacement in this context, then they are better equipped to survive in a world of sharing and changing relationships. Mean girls are a necessary rite of passage.

CAN WE SUCCEED IN FINDING
AN IDEAL SISTER IN A FRIEND?

MANY OF THE most profound and puzzling aspects of girls' friendships can be seen as attempts to move away from the ambivalence of the sister knot. Instead of loving and hating the same girl, the attempt in friendships is to love one girl totally or hate one girl totally. The notorious instability of girls' friendships results from bound-to-lose efforts to perfect a relationship. In response to these hopes and their inevitable disappointment, the idealization/denigration effect comes into play. For girls' friendships appear either as enduring, harmonious bonds or as deeply uneasy social alliances in which true conflict is veiled.

We see friendship in one frame as enduring, cooperative, and supportive or in another frame as backstabbing, drenched with envy, and aggression distorted by various sweet disguises. We need to step back to see an integrated whole. The delights of sistering are shadowed by fear of our sister as a replacement. This is compounded by fear of our own anger toward someone we love and with whom we closely identify. How much better it can seem to seek female bonding in same-sex friendships, when the perks appear similar to those of sisterhood, and the dangers are reduced. By looking at girlfriends and sisters side by side, we can make sense of each and integrate the positive and negative aspects, just as they are in day-to-day life.

The shift from sister to girlfriend, and back and forth

again, is captured by Jane Austen in her wonderful novel *Emma*. In the opening pages the author poses the question: How is a young woman who is "handsome, clever, and rich" going to fulfil her need for a sister?

Emma is motherless and has a father who is a timid invalid; but her most pressing relational need is for a sister. Her much older sister, Isabella, is married and lives so far away that Emma will not be able to see her until Christmas, which, Austen notes, is three *long* months off. Since Isabella's marriage Emma's need for a sister has been fulfilled by her governess, who is described as "less a governess than a friend." The quality of that friendship is immediately explained, for "between *them* it was more the intimacy of sisters."

The governess herself marries, however, and Emma is bereft once again. Emma's need for a sister is now too urgent to be wise. She scoops up Harriet as the most promising sister material available. Younger and less attractive, and much less clever than Emma, she is also malleable and grateful for Emma's attentiveness. Moreover, she lacks Emma's wealth and social position. Hence Harriet seems like an ideal sister. She is a daily companion with whom Emma can share everything without putting anything at risk.

Jane Austen writes frequently about sister love. She shows how sisters can provide the imaginative space within which a confining life can be tolerated. Romantic disappointment, social humiliation, and relative poverty can all be borne happily enough, as long as one enjoys the daily conversations and comforts of a sister. But it is in the novel *Emma* alone that Austen explores the *ambivalence* that dwells within our fundamental need for a sister. For if Emma finds in Harriet a friend who really stands in for a sister, then she has a sister-friend who will also awaken the primitive fear of being displaced. If Emma has in Harriet a friend who cannot stand in for a sister, then she does not feel threatened, but she has an unsatisfactory friend. The ideal friend, who represents a sister without awakening the sister knot, cannot be found. Emma's adoption of Harriet as sister is successful, and hence Harriet threatens to displace her. In constructing a sister out of a friend, Emma comes face to face with the sibling trauma: Harriet wants to become Mr. Knightley's true love, thereby ousting Emma from the relationship she sees as rightly hers.

Emma's pride in her ability to understand the emotional world is misguided. She makes grave mistakes in her assessments of who should love whom. She also fails to realize whom she herself loves. But the driving error of her ways is to think that she can have a sister without confronting the sister knot. When Emma discovers that her place in Knightley's heart is safe, her relief mirrors a fantasy triumph over a sibling: Emma, Jane Austen writes, begins to "catch and comprehend" that "Harriet was nothing; that she was everything herself."

On one level this is a happy ending, because it provides Emma with her desire; but it is also a sober ending, because it is a reminder that while we seek a sister in a friend, we awaken our primitive fears when we succeed. It is sobering, too, because the discovery that a friend cannot be a sister is disappointing.

This often-read novel has been made into several films, and transposed to modern-day suburbia in *Clueless*. The tenacity of the novel's appeal rests on its remarkable exposure of the tensions between the longing for a sister and the complexities of the sister knot, and their reappearance in the world of friendship.

SISTER TROUBLES CAN LEAD TO FRIEND TROUBLES

WHETHER WE SEE our sisters as "good" or "bad," or whether we have experience of both, sister relationships make their mark on our relationships with other women. However broad and mutable human relationships are, the women I interviewed caught sight of sister problems in any unease they had with female peers. Some women report that having sisters is more demanding than having female friends,[17] and some report that abiding tensions with a sister make them wary of female friendships. Donna, twenty-five, whose childhood unease with her sister remains an unpleasant feature of her life, struggles with a form of envy that bears the stamp of the mean-girls mode. However carefully she reflects on it and resists it, she suffers its power. "When Susan came for the interview, she immediately set my nerves on edge. The way she dressed, the way she answered me—it had that 'superior persona' that I recognize from high school. I couldn't even tell you whether I liked her—I mean, professionally liked her, because that's what I was there to assess. I hate how she makes me feel. The men were so cool about assessing her, but I just felt blinded by something—I don't know—a kind of irritation? Maybe even rage. She's the kind of woman my mother would love me to be, I remember thinking. That's how my dad would love me to dress. I also could see her being the star of the boardroom. She'd make me invisible. I'm telling you all this, but I'm also deeply ashamed of it.

"On one level I could justify it. Really, she wasn't the right person for the job. You know, she liked talking, but I never noticed her listening. She didn't show signs of being a team player, and she could lead, maybe, because she had that self-assurance—but I knew I'd feel awful being led by her. I don't often get rattled. But she frightened me."

Hearing stories from women about the bitterness among women who share high-level careers,[18] it seems that the new professional woman may, at times, be much closer than she would like to the thirteen-year-old "mean girl" gossiping about another girl in the hall at school. The social displacement girls often feel threatened by during this transition reactivates the sibling trauma. It can awaken, too, throughout our lives, when displacement threatens us. The trigger is not any particular woman's superiority but a superiority that she links to a particular kind of woman—the woman a parent would like, a woman who would take one's own place as the daughter to be proud of or the colleague others admire and appreciate.

The meanness of envy is experienced by women who are not themselves mean. What girls and women describe, when they speak about envy, is an awful and primitive feeling, a fear both of being envious and of being envied, a sense that envy—whether they are the one who envies or the one who is envied—can destroy them.

Envy is a throwback to an earlier threat of displacement, which we experience as a threat of annihilation. We respond with an urge to destroy the person who threatens us, and we are terrified by this urge because it is also a wish to destroy someone we love. Girlfriend problems arise in relation to this concern—to love those we are attached to, to define ourselves in the context of similarities and differences to those with whom we feel we belong, to confront the fear that someone will replace us or outdo us. In the sphere of girlfriends, too, we have to learn to accept that we are one among many, and learn how to stabilize ourselves in the whirlwind of others' claims and attributes. We need, in short, to survive in a world with other people.[19]

REDISCOVERING THE SAFETY OF SISTERING

THE TRICKY BASELINE of girls' friendship can now be redrawn. Girls' friendships continue the learning curve that goes on within a family. They provide a testing ground for relationships in general, the joys and the limits of human love, and what we can expect from others.[20] Connections between girlfriends are described in either very good or very bad terms by girls, who themselves struggle to integrate the good with the bad.

The kinship category "sister" carries an emotional punch for most women, whether or not they have a sister. However, girls who are sisters and girls who are not sisters will seek sisters in friends for different reasons. Sisterless girls seek to exercise their potential for sistering. They may also be operating with an idealized concept of what having and being a sister consist of. Girls with sisters often seek in a friend someone to duplicate the pleasures of sistering while avoiding the complex relationship that comes with a real sister.

The themes of solidarity (supporting one another) and of twinning (being alike) emerge in both sistering and girlfriend stories. So, too, do stories of loyalty and betrayal, belonging and envy, and, envy's companion, exclusion. In each context girls and women ponder ambivalence against the background of simplified feelings and characteristics—"nice," "mean," "good," "bad."

Mixed feelings are difficult to name and difficult to acknowledge, so girls learn to patch up the problems and make good use of what is available. Donna has been through the friendship wars, and, like every young woman, knows the deep discomfort of envy and being envied. But still she hopes that with her girlfriends she can avoid the echoes of uneasy rivalry that emerge as she speaks about her sisters. She has two "best friends," one of whom she sees regularly. Talking through the dramas of her daily life, either at work or in the serious play of her social life, provides comfort and entertainment and the opportunity to see things from another perspective. She cannot imagine living well and keeping sane without her girlfriends; but her sister offers her something different, sometimes more difficult, but only because, as she says, "There's a directness with her. I'm more assertive. I guess you could say that I risk more. I'm insistently myself, and in her face to boot!" While she loves her friends' enthusiasm for her success, she knows how to be careful in conveying her own excitement: "I want to tell them, but I also know

I have to hold back, especially if things aren't going well for them. I love it when they're excited, but I know I have to be ... Well, I have to be kind of measured when I tell them about my new position. The only person I really crow to is my sister. It's her I'll tell—straight out—that I've landed another high-profile client. I can feel the knife go in, and I think, This is just something you have to deal with. I get terribly *unsettled* if I think a friend is envious. But I figure, with my sister, we're pretty well matched."

From friendship to sistering, Donna explores the effect she has on others and her need to assert herself with others. Between sisters envy is inevitable but ultimately bearable. However, in her experience it has spoiled the relationships with her sister; so, among friends, Donna thinks that anything that might possibly trigger envy should be avoided. To keep friendship safe she has to limit her honesty.

The compulsion Donna has to show herself as she is, with her sister, has a parallel in fifteen-year-old Carrie's growing awareness of how safe the sister knot can be, in comparison to friendship. She had done something which made her feel bad, and she wanted, urgently, to speak to a friend in order to find relief from feeling she is "the awfullest person in the world." But to get this relief she had to expose herself, revealing unattractive motives and unseemly behavior. She can tell her friend, "I did the stupidest thing, and if you tell anyone else, I'll die." She can talk to her friend, and know her friend won't appear to judge her.[21] She can offer this as a secret, which she hopes will protect her: She will both reveal herself and find comfort in another's understanding, but protect herself from being fully known in her social space. But she also knows that secrets are not kept. Falling out with her friend would now be extremely dangerous, because what she has revealed may become fodder for gossip. "But I can talk to my sister. She'll get it. She'll be sorry for me. She'll understand. It's not like she's going to spread it around school and judge me."

Girls in their teens still vacillate between friend and sister. In adulthood, however, women describe firmer distinctions of sister roles and girlfriend roles. It is far easier, Lucy explains, to tell her sister, Meng, that she failed to get the job she applied for, than for her to tell a friend. In her thirties, Lucy feels that the competitive element with her sister has been largely laid to rest. With her friends, envy issues remain less digested, less easily placated. She has friends who will root for her, but she feels her sister is the safest option. Telling her sister about the job is telling her news, and telling her about her current mood ("down" and "discouraged"). She says, "You can put up a false front to a friend, but not your sister."

With sisters there is an informality that comes with the pleasure of regressing to a younger self, but there is also the danger of earlier rivalries rising up. While we continue to work out the sister knot with our friends, we continue to need our sisters. Carson McCullers's sister, when asked about the quality of her relationship with the writer, replied with barbed common sense: "We were sisters—sometimes intimate friends, sometimes enemies and at times strangers."[22] Managing the different affective tensions provides the lifelong lessons we keep relearning as we accept the dimensions of all human attachment.

As in sister bonds, girls, in their friendships with other girls, explore the borders of connection and identity, mutual understanding, twinning, and anxiety about displacement. As in sister bonds, girls' friendships combine love and resentment. Cross-references from one to the other are common: A sister is a "best friend"; the solidarity among female friends is a "sisterhood." Yet friendships and sibling relationships have different deep emotional structures. Highlighting how these attachments overlap, intersect, and diverge allows us to see why they take the forms they do, and clears age-old puzzles about the nature of female attachment.

Girls may seek a perfect sister in their girlfriends, but the tensions and connections found in the sister knot also shape friendships. Declarations of sisterhood between girlfriends, however genuine, deny the ambivalence of sistering. They set up the fiction that one friend's status among one's family of friends, or in one's wider social environment, will never challenge the other. The "perfect understanding" that girls proclaim as they embrace a girlfriend aims to remove the sting of ambivalence among sisters. The threat of displacement is denied by the norms of female friendship, which declare that everything can be shared, always. But the politics of their friendships that emerge as girls take their places among the multiple regimes of social status and social approval show that the terrors of the sibling trauma are salient here, too.

By understanding how the sister knot influences the emotional maps we follow in our relationships with others, we can see that status play among girls is a means of working through the terrors of displacement within the home. Hierarchies of popularity are attempts to name a place of "safety" from which one cannot be ousted. The wicked pleasure of the dominant girl, who has control over which other girls are "in" or "out" of groups, is something others fear, loathe, and long for.

When we bring to girls' friendships the perspective gained from thinking about siblings, the contradictory aspects become integrated: The compulsion to see a friend as one's twin, and the discomfort with difference; the conversational styles that mark mutuality and the distortions brought about by envy; the sense of an enduring bond and the volatility of cliques—all take their shape from the dynamics of the sister knot. The hope is that in friendship the sister knot will be controlled or avoided; in fact, friendships work by reproducing both aspects of sistering. That is their difficulty and their strength.

8

Group Dynamics Among Sisters

FROM A VERY early age children learn to fit in with and make an impact on the highly complex relationships between different members of the family. Human survival depends on functioning within a group, and kids learn fast. While the grown-ups in the family try to set down the rules by which the family functions, children acquire skills in systematically influencing the behavior of people who matter to them. Sisters often join forces to work this family system for their own needs, or in response to the needs of the people they care about. In this chapter I look at the subtle and sophisticated cooperation among sisters as they suss out and regulate their family systems.

In early and middle adolescence the sister pair, Tess,

fourteen, and Beth, eleven, already show explicit awareness of how they operate in their home, both to accommodate and to influence the family unit. Tess talks about her sister in terms of how she is defined by their parents. "Beth is the dream girl, the one who always knows what to say. Everyone praises her because she's 'helpful' and 'nice.'" Tess then goes on to explain many of her own characteristics as a response to her sister's place in the family. "I don't see any point in competing," explains Tess. "So I don't. I don't bother trying to be pleasant or nice or helpful."

She notes her sister's compliance and the praise it earns; this provides her with an excuse to exaggerate what she calls her "narkiness." Tess says her mother is "always telling me off and always praising Beth," but that her grandmother is "quicker to understand, and says she was really moody as a kid, too. When I make Mom mad I feel like I'm some sort of bad person, but Grandma always makes me feel okay. We have this special closeness. Beth's sweetness—I mean, she is a real sweet kid, she has this—I don't know, something yummy and lovable—is cute most of the time, and I *like* having her as my sister. But it's nice with Grandma because sweet doesn't go as far as it does with Mom."

Tess grasps the opportunity to establish a contrast effect, thereby ensuring that she is clearly different from her sister; but this is not her only aim. Tess and Beth bicker with each other, each wishing to disturb the other's position in the family system: Tess sneers at Beth for being "such a dumb sweetie-pie" and for being complacent about her parents' approval; Beth scolds Tess for "always upsetting everyone." Beth, with her lower tolerance for others' stress, works to keep people calm. Resenting the praise this attracts, Tess sometimes opts for negative attention; she decides to be difficult because her sister is nice. On the other hand Tess is sensitive to Beth's anxiety when voices are raised and anger expressed: "Tess always rushes to comfort me when I get shouted at," Beth says. "She makes funny faces to cheer me up." So Tess regulates her sister's anxiety: When it rises beyond a certain point, she becomes the peacemaker and protector; but when Beth's anxiety is low (that is, when Beth is "complacent") Tess steps in to raise it again.

These sisters appear to be at odds, but they are actually engaging in careful choreography that impacts the wider family group. Tess manages, with her special brand of "narkiness," to bring her grandmother into the family as a useful member. She says, "I'm so glad Gran is here now. It was awful when Granddad died and Mom thought Gran should come to stay, and Dad thought it was a really bad idea. There were awful fights. Mom even cried and called Dad "mean." It was awful. And when Gran first came, Dad was in a bad mood the whole time. Now everyone's okay with it, even Dad, who says I would send him to an early grave if it wasn't for Gran."

By demonstrating that the grandmother is useful, Tess makes sure that her mother and father do not quarrel over having the grandmother in their home. While her sister minimizes family stress by being "good," Tess minimizes it by being "bad" and manageable only by the grandmother. The sisters have devised a way of reconfiguring the family system. Instead of being a closed unit that is disturbed by the grandmother's presence, Tess and Beth manage to construct a broader group, wherein the mother is supported by one daughter's compliance, and the father is placated by another daughter's compliance exclusively at the hands of his mother-in-law. Each dyad: mother to daughter, sister to sister, child to grandmother, father to grandmother, can only be understood by looking at how the family functions as an entire group.

Sister dynamics often evolve according to various members' strengths and weaknesses. One family member develops skills that disguise the weaknesses of another. Harriet Goldhor Lerner describes how, when her mother was diagnosed with endometrial cancer, her older sister became the strong one in the family. She commuted to college, and also organized the home. She cooked, cleaned, and ironed, competently and without complaining. Harriet, the younger sister, however, demanded clothes that the family could not afford, made a mess of the living room and kitchen as soon as her sister cleaned them, and acted up in school.[1] One sister responded to the change in how the family functioned by taking on the practical tasks that their mother now could not do. Another sister responded with diversion tactics: people were so anxious about her that they had reprieve from their anxiety about the mother's illness. Each sister took a complementary part in tweaking the family system so that it would function as close to normal as possible.

COOPERATIVE ALLIANCES
WITHIN THE GROUP

THE TENDENCY GIRLS have in their friendships to form special pairs has been widely observed.[2] I have found that sisters, too, however large their sibling group, organize themselves into emotionally significant pairs. These bonds are sometimes negative and sometimes positive; the importance of the relationships is sometimes informed by love and sometimes by hatred.[3]

Dora and Maria have, for decades, on and off, formed a close sister pair within a larger sibling group. The oldest two of five children, these sisters became dominant and often dark forces in each other's lives. Dora says of her feelings toward her sister Maria, "We were astoundingly close—not so much like lovers, but like an elderly couple. There was this shared sombreness and responsibility. We'd come home from school together, and know that together we'd have to face whatever our mother presented when we opened the door. It might be outraged silence or some kind of explosiveness. We knew how to work together. We never said anything, but we had the moves down pat. It made me think that Maria was forcing me to help her, so I hated her, too."

Their mother suffered from bipolar disorder, and the sisters' roles (particularly those of the oldest two) were to protect the mother when she was low, and to keep the family safe when she was high. Together Dora and Maria managed their mother, and tried to reassure the younger sisters and brother. "Maria and I looked to each other. I would watch Maria watching my mother. I had this routine of asking her, 'You think things are okay?' which meant, were they okay with our mother? Would we get through another day? I think I saw the signs before she did, but I still asked her and when she said, 'Yeah, things are okay,' I would just love her to bits. It was like a great big hand was coming down from the sky and stroking me. My sister. I still feel that overwhelming love and trust, because no one else can know what it felt like to be there. No one else shares that part of me. Whatever I feel about her or think about her, I know we're forged together."

When their mother swung into a high mood, they tried to protect each other. "She didn't need us then; or if she did, we couldn't do anything. We were powerless, and useless. She'd start clearing out the house. That usually meant she'd start throwing everything away. I tried to hide things I really cared about, sentimental stuff, notes from friends, party favors, or presents from my aunts that I really liked, things that I liked to have because having them made me feel I was lucky. But I could never hide them well enough. Your own distress didn't matter when she was high. She just looked at you and laughed, and I never knew whether she was laughing at you or just thought you'd made a great joke. Maria would fish things out of the trash. We'd try to distract her. I'd keep her out of the room where Liz and Rita, our two younger sisters, were studying, and we'd all make sure the younger kids got ready for school and had what they needed. I now realize how furious we were. When she was 'up,' she was real aggressive. She'd say the most awful things.

Her mother, when gripped by a manic phase, found her own criticisms of Dora hilarious. Dora was utterly wounded by them: "'Cutting me to pieces' isn't a metaphor; well, it didn't seem like a metaphor. The things she said cut me to pieces, and I thought I would never be able to move again, never be able to go outside and face people because they might think about me in the same way. Then either Maria or Liz would say, 'That's a madwoman talking,' and I felt a weight fall from me. But we could never totally reassure each other that what she said was nonsense. The fact that our mother thought like that about us, even for a moment, even when she was certifiable, was hard to let go of. But we would talk about it, and no one of us ever got bored, talking over the things she said, and explaining to each other why what she said wasn't true, that we weren't to blame for everything that was bad in the world."

And, like a comfortable elderly couple, they protected their three younger siblings—two sisters and a brother— from their mother's highs and lows. Even today, in her forties, Dora views the younger sibling as people to accommodate and care for: They drop by her home, unannounced, and she offers bed and board. "Maria would do the same for them. They're like our kids. The real, thick sister bond is between Maria and me."

In her experience of the sister knot Dora notes an aspect of cooperation that is generally ignored: "I've learned that there is a subtle line between cooperation and coercion. Maria and I crisscrossed it when we worked together. There's something creepy about the whole thing, how close we were, and how wary that made us of each other."

SISTERS AS THEIR OWN SUBFAMILY

DIANA, ROSALIND, KATE, and Sue form a very different group of sisters; but they too form emotionally significant pairs. They are really, in Diana's view, "three different sister pairs. The relationship I have with Rosalind, who's only fourteen months younger than me, is deeper than anything. It's not all good, but it's deep. Kate and Sue are so much younger, and what I feel for them is much less intense."

The sisters reflect on the past minisystems that have driven their frantic jealousies and power plays throughout childhood and adolescence. Now at twenty-nine, twenty-eight, twenty-three, and twenty, they look back, good-naturedly, to the sistering that played such a large part in their lives. Sue, twenty, still sees herself competing with Kate and Rosalind for her oldest sister's favor. "Diana has a vividness that I just don't see in anyone else. I once thought no one could match her. Sometimes I'd look at her, and my guts would just ache with envy because I thought she had this magic center, that where she was was the center of the world. But sometimes I thought I didn't have to envy her because she was my sister, and I had her as my sister, and all I needed was to be real close to her. I always wanted her to focus on me. I wanted to be special to her. You don't have any idea how hard I tried. I tried to be funny, and I tried to be sulky, and I tried to be awful. She was always calm with me, and affectionate, and hardly ever told me to get out of her hair even though I was always hanging around. But I never make the impact on her that Roz does. Even now, I can catch myself thinking, That will make Diana take notice. But Diana just carries on with the same old tolerance, you know, kind of amused, not at all phased. She sees me as *one* of her sisters. But she always introduces Rosalind: 'This is my sister.'"

Sue feels like a rival with one sister and tries to get another sister's love and attention; while Kate, twenty-three, feels that she was "the one who was always left out. I spent a big chunk of my childhood in a sulk, thinking, No one cares about me.

No one asks me things first or comes to me first to play. They are always ignoring me." She felt excluded from her sisters' magic circle of jealousies and preferences. "Roz stood by Sue and tried to comfort her when she couldn't get enough of Diana, but no one cared what I was feeling."

Here sisters work within a subsystem that has its own triangularity. It is *almost* self-contained and seems more salient than the young women's relationships to their parents. Rarely did these sisters speak of their parents, so vivid was their own dynamic sistering system. The triangularity of rivalry took place within the sister subsystem. And their mother confirms, "When these girls are together, they don't see anyone else. They come home at Thanksgiving, and I'm shouting at them to do this or that, but they never pay any attention. It isn't because they're lazy. They're glad to pitch in and help. They'll take over the kitchen themselves. But when they're together, they don't hear me. They don't have to fight with me, either. They just vie for attention among themselves. It's as if I don't really exist."

During her second year in college, Kate, the third sister, was raped. The sister dynamic then changed to form a protective unit. Rosalind said, "The bickering we'd been doing for years and years seemed utterly stupid. I couldn't remember what any of us had complained about. We all feel it's something that's happened to *us*." While the sisters themselves are reluctant to say more, their mother says, "They're such a tight-knit group, and the fighting has virtually stopped. Kate's survived because they've helped her. And because they all seem to share her experience, she doesn't feel ashamed."

Many sister alliances function as a protective mechanism within the family. Karen and Ally say they are close because "Mom is so difficult. Without each other I don't know where we'd be." And Ally says, "we don't want to compete for attention, because we don't want her attention. She's so difficult." The two sisters look at each other and nod.

But in another sister group of three, the middle sister, Amber, thirty-one, and the youngest sister Cathy, twenty-nine, team up against their older sister, whom they describe as "nasty." Cathy says that their mother tries to be fair to all three of her daughters but fails, because "she is afraid of Kelly, who's the oldest and really, really mean." Amber says that she and Cathy "put up a united front. We have to, to get anything out of our parents. Kelly can't stand it when Mom gives us anything. She complains about being left out, and she complains about her kids being left out. You should see Mom's face when Kelly says things like that. Mom is a sucker, and right away she buys whatever Kelly says. See, Kelly's the only one of us with kids, and I think she frightens Mom into thinking she won't be allowed to see her grandchildren if she gets on the wrong side of her." Cathy looks quizzically at Amber. "Right?" and Amber concurs.

"All this makes me feel so awful," Cathy explains. "If Amber didn't back me up, I'd feel like I deserved all this. I might feel Kelly was really better than me."

"She sure isn't," Amber insists.

"That's what I need to hear. See? That's why we need each other."

Amber and Cathy go on to explain that they did not always feel this way. "Kelly is always picking arguments with Mom," Amber says. "They always fight. When our dad left, Kelly lived with him for a while, because things were so awful with Mom."

"That was horrible," Cathy adds. "Remember the day he left? He told us we had to choose between him and Mom. And Kelly just reached for her stuff and said, 'I'm coming with you.' I couldn't believe it."

"The two of them leaving—"

"Yeah, that was the worst thing, that Kelly left too. That she left *us*."

"Good thing we had each other. Mom was a wreck."

"She was really a wreck. When Kelly came home again she wanted all the attention. The house was so loud when she came back."

"But we kept out of it."

"Yeah, we were all right. We had each other."

Cathy describes Amber as "generous with time and money. She helps me out when Mom is afraid to, because Kelly will complain if she does." Amber describes Cathy as "the best anchor I have in this family. She'll never betray me, the way the others have." For these sisters cooperation confirms mutual support and recognition of each other's goodness, as they contrast it to a third sister's "meanness."

In each sister group "sister" takes on multiple meanings. There are "good" and "nasty" sisters; there are "strong" and "weak" sisters; and these emerge in the context of family dynamics and family circumstances. What it means to bond with a sister has to be seen, always, against a shifting background of family systems.

THE RADICAL FORCE OF SISTER DYNAMICS

FOR HARRIET GOLDHOR LERNER and her sister, cooperation was a means of preserving the family's status quo; Tess and Beth cooperate to facilitate a change on the family as the grandmother comes to live with them; Maria and Dora cooperate to allow a family on the brink of destruction to function at all; Cathy and Amber together bandage the wound of their older sister's rejection and subsequent disruption. These sister pairs aim to preserve some status quo in a family; but some sister pairs cooperate to set a radical agenda. They *appear* to aid the smooth-running family system, but they are either resisting family norms or protecting other siblings from being harmed by an abusive status quo.

Amy protects her sister, Carrie, by confronting the mother: She tells her mother not to worry, not to be overprotective, assuring her that she knows precisely what Carrie is doing, and that there is nothing wrong with it. The older sister uses her ability to reassure the mother in order to manipulate her mother into giving permission for the younger sister to do what she wants. When Dymphna gets in trouble with her father and is sent to her room, Siobhan brings up her dinner and says, "You should admit what you did. Don't lie. You're not a good liar. Admit it and say, 'Dad, I'm so sorry. I didn't realize. I won't do it again.' That's what you have to do to stay out of trouble." Siobhan teaches Dymphna the "real" rules of the family.

In another sister pair the older sister distracted the mother when the younger sister was making her "getaway" on a date, and the sisters would lie for each other, presenting the other as an alibi, so that each could do what she wanted as long as they met up before reentering the home.[4]

These two pairs of sisters develop strategies for doing what they want to do in spite of family rules and restrictions. Other examples of sisterly cooperation show more courageous and longsighted defense of one sister against the dominant family system.

Protectiveness, an issue in virtually every sibling theme, often drives sisterly alliances. Compromises and pacts, barely acknowledged at the time, are made in psychological extremis: *We can't let her be hurt as I have*, or *We can't let her be constrained as I have*, or *If the family can do that to her, it can do that to me*. These are sometimes impulsive, and addressed to a specific occasion; but they can also develop into long-term strategies.

The dynamics of long-term cooperation in a defensive sister pair are mapped in Jane Smiley's Pulitzer Prize–winning novel, *A Thousand Acres*. It is about the economic roller coaster that Midwestern farming families rode in the 1980s; it is about the isolation and grief of childlessness, and about the myriad unspoken cruelties committed by a patriarch, and about what daughters owe even a cruel father; but, to me, Jane Smiley's novel is primarily about three sisters and the remarkable alliance two of them form to protect the third from the blight of paternal control and abuse.

Two of the three sisters in the Cook family follow their prescribed parts. They live on the family farmland and, with carefully chosen husbands, engage in the work of the farm.

They have well-established rituals for dealing with their father's displeasure; they are quick to placate his easily roused anger with "a proper appearance of remorse." While an argument with their father is, in the two older sisters' view, a matter of father management, the youngest sister, Caroline, insists on looking at the actual rights and wrongs of each argument, and cannot be persuaded by her oldest sister to toe the line. Whether he is drunk or whether he is in a rage, she speaks her mind, confident that fairness and reason will prevail.

Ironically the youngest sister is the least compliant because the older sisters have been the truly defiant daughters. When Caroline was a teen, her older sisters provided cover stories so that she could lead the normal social life their father's strictness disallowed them. They barely acknowledged their purposes to one another, yet they firmly guarded her against the sexual interest they knew their father would have in her once she moved beyond puberty. So successful were they in protecting her that Caroline, as a woman, can love and honor her father. Having grown up under her sisters' protection, she thinks they are "bad women" and "ungrateful daughters" when she realizes they hate and fear their father.

Ginny and Rose, the two older sisters in Jane Smiley's novel, have the strongest bond, based as much on identity as affection. The close identification the older two sisters have with each other makes teamwork natural. The close identification they have with their younger sister makes protection essential. They use their knowledge and hard-won wisdom to protect the younger girl from the abuse and control they experienced.

But Ginny and Rose can barely name their own suffering without checking up on the other's memory and experience. Ginny depends on Rose's capacity "of remembering, knowing, judging, as if continually viewing our father through the crosshairs of a bombsight." Having "shared" their father as a lover in adolescence, they replay this in adulthood by taking the same lover. Even their sexual jealousy is shaped by the sister bond: When Ginny imagines her sister next to her lover, Jess, she imagines the bone, flesh, and odor of her sister rather than of the man she loves. Her jealousy consists in the realization that she is not Rose: All her life Ginny had identified with Rose, followed her reactions to something, and assumed "that differences between Rose and me were just on the surface" and that beneath, "We were more than twinlike, that somehow we were each other's real selves."[5] Once again the image of "twin" is used as a prototype of sistering: The experience of being and having a twin may be exceptional, yet the sense of twinning is common among sisters.

Jane Smiley's rendition of this close sister bond grasps the ambivalence within the identification. Beneath the surface we are one, Ginny thinks; therefore I want what you have; you are taking something from me because it is mine; but my jealousy of you dissolves as I realize that we are really one. On the other hand, what also emerges in Jane Smiley's description of sistering is the realization through rivalry that sisters are not "each other's real selves," and that each has to engage in borderwork to construct that separate self. But the shared identity allows them to work together seamlessly, tacitly, to save the third sister. Caroline's life, in consequence, is so different from theirs that she does not recognize herself in them. The sister knot, consisting of identification, love, and envy— becomes a basis for a sister contract between Ginny and Rose.

When sisters cooperate with one another under immense family pressure, the bond that arises from cooperation is often mixed. Dora says she is wary of her closeness to Maria. Their shared work on the levees built between their mother's mood swings and their younger siblings had been too painful to be a source of shared pride. The sister pact sprang from mutual understanding of their mother and of the harm she could do to the family; it has resulted in mutual resentment at the high costs of their valuable enterprise.

Recognizing oneself in another is a mixed experience. We find reassurance in the identification of a soul mate, but when what we have shared is drenched in shame and suffering, we may not always be comforted by what we see. Yet, since most of these sister alliances have a positive, protective aim, and are formed as survival networks, the resolution would seem to be in recognizing their fundamental usefulness. Rosalind points a route forward: "We all feel that what's happened to Kate has happened to us. And I sometimes catch myself thinking, You stupid girl, why did you let this happen? You know, why did you let this happen to *us*? Because it's so hard sometimes, keeping her spirits up and nudging her: You know, you always want to make sure she just keeps going. But being together like this, and all doing what we can—well, it's a way of discovering how we all work together for each other. And that matters more to me, to all of us, than having an easy time."

9

The Power of Sister Stories

S ISTERS PLAY A special role in our lives as witnesses to
our pasts and partakers in our efforts to piece together
family portraits and family histories. What happened
when, and who really said what are just a few of the very
basic elements we may want to check up on as we make sense
of the experiences that have made us who we are.

"Did Mom really say that?" Sasha asks Vicki, to check up
on what she is telling me about their mother's common ways
of scolding them.

"You bet!" Sasha replies, "Don't you remember? She'd
say, 'I'm not shouting. I never shout!' And she'd be screaming it at the top of her voice."

"I used to think that screaming must be different from shouting."

"I know! Remember when Aunt Gabs was staying? And she said, 'What's all this shouting about?' And you said, 'She's not shouting. She's just screaming.' You were so serious. The rest of us were convulsed. Remember?"

"Yes! But I just remember you laughing at me. I was horribly embarrassed and confused. I wish someone had just said the obvious thing—"

"Like, 'Mom shouts a lot'!"

"Yes! That would've been good to hear."

"Well, that's how it was."

"At least what I remember now makes sense."

Sisters also work to puzzle over deeper stories, about motives that explain others' behavior. "I only realized, after talking to Amber, that our mother is afraid of Kelly, just like us," Cathy says. "It explains why Mom doesn't defend us, when Kelly's mean, and why we have to tiptoe around her, because you never know how she's going to take what you say. It makes me see Mom in a different way. I feel let down, but at least it makes sense."

The heightened role that personal talk plays in women's relationships, along with the deep identification among sisters, opens into sister-talk that ranges from casual family gossip to historical and psychological analysis. Women tend to talk about their parents and typical family behavior far more and far more directly than do brothers or even brother-sister pairs. Ordinary topics are mined for nuggets of meaning. As grown women, sisters whooped with delight when their memories came alive, and when they were able to make new sense of past experience. Looking back together at their family is a significant sister activity.

"Whenever we're together Annette and I launch into discussions about what was really going on. We keep peeling things back, maybe layers we've peeled away before. But there's always something to uncover. Always something we want to check up on," Dorri explained. "We were just talking, and Annette said something about how hard it was to talk to Dad. You tell him something, and he goes all stiff. Then there's a long pause, and finally he'll say something, but it's all stilted and formal. I hadn't thought about this in years, but as soon as Annette started describing that it—she called it 'daddy's stiff pause'—it all came back to me, the number of times I got so angry when he did that."

While Annette and Dorri "keep peeling things back" as, together, they look more closely at their pasts, the four sisters Kate, Rosalind, Diana, and Sue, rejig their sympathies and alliances as they exchange views. "In our family it was always Mom's feelings that seemed to matter more than anyone else's. She was tired or she was unhappy, whatever. And Dad always warned us girls not to bother her too much. We were always told stories about the hard time she'd had as a kid, with no money, with her difficult father. Remember?" Sue asks her other sisters.

"Yes. Always. We heard those stories constantly. But when Dad's company folded, remember how patient he was? It must have been awful for him, but all he did was comfort her and reassure us," Kate said.

"It must have been awful for him. But he was so good at dealing with it. 'That's business for you. You have to roll with the punches.' That's all he said. I know more about it from reading the newspapers than from him," Diana said.

"Did Dad really have a hard time?" Rosalind asked the others. "Did we ever comfort him? We usually ignored him."

Sue and Diana laugh as they recognize the aptness of this description. "Yeah, we did. But he didn't seem to mind. Did he?"

And Kate admits, "I sometimes felt sorry for him, but mostly thought he wouldn't notice us even if we did pay attention to him."

In conversations such as these, sisters work together to achieve deeper understanding and more balanced views.

Many sisters made repeated efforts to resolve confusion. They revise family stories with an interest and passion that few people outside the sister group can understand. They add to and challenge one another's accounts; they root out the pockets of silence or deception to give coherence to family myths or stories parents may have told them, repeatedly, about others' needs and character and history. They constantly reassess the family versions of who had power, and to what effect, of who was to blame and who tried to mitigate the harm done.

Ally and Karen say they provide a lifeline to sanity in sorting out what was really going on in the family. Ally and Karen discovered together how their father manipulated them. "Not big time, not anything you can write up in some textbook," Karen explains. "Just little things that make you feel guilty, unless someone else can say, 'Yeah, he shouldn't keep asking you to do things for him. He shouldn't make you feel bad if you say no.' And my sister can do that. And we talk about how long it's gone on, and how it took us a long time to catch on. Mom always says, 'You always have to criticize everyone.' And she says he's just being him, and we're too critical. If I didn't have Ally to refer to, I'd think it was all in my mind. And I'd think I was crazy."

The stories we tell about our family are also stories about ourselves, how we came to be who we are, and what roles we take within our family. This narrative identity helps us make sense of ourselves, our experience, and our personal environment. As Karen notes, confirmation that our personal stories make sense to a sister, can offer deep assurance of our sanity. But sisters feel bound to the same family, and the story each tells of the family matters greatly to the other. Jean, seventy-one, says, "I love talking things over with my sister. We go over and over things that happened in the past. That way they become mine again. It's sad to forget what made your life. And it's easy to forget. When I talk to my sister I remember so many things. Or she'll mention something, and it will suddenly be there for me. And that's wonderful."

WHAT HAPPENS WHEN SISTERS' STORIES DIFFER?

SISTERS WHO CONTINUED to enjoy one another throughout their lives often enjoyed constructing and reconstructing family narratives. Questions such as What is our family like? and What made it like that? are enthralling. The experience of one sister becomes a point of reference. In matching views and memories, sisters sometimes discovered how their family stories differed. They were often amused and amazed, and experienced something like revelation, when they discovered that one was holding on to a very different story from the other. They would then try to make sense of the other's different memories, as they do in Nergis Dalal's memoir about her life with her sister.[1] Nina asks her sister whether she remembers the school they attended as children. "It was the only part of our childhood that I would change. That awful grim building and those bloody nuns." Nergis stares back, astonished to hear this negative description of what she remembers as a lovely building filled with kind nuns. Each is amazed by the other's memory, yet each recognizes the other's story as true.

Now the sisters' memories lie between them "like a bridge"; the different memories of a shared past link them and also comfortably mark each as the individual she is. Such sister moments allow us to discover the reality of our individuality. This discovery may reassure us that, after all, we simply are different; but because we are also connected, the differences add another layer to our own experience.

But different stories are sometimes seen as betrayals: *How can you say that about our mother?* or *How dare you think that about our father?* and, of course, *How can you say that about me? About us?* Siblings can challenge our memories, not simply as accurate but as "fair" or "cruel"; and they may then condemn us for the stories we tell. They, like us, are passionately committed to the interpretations that inform our ever-present memories of life-shaping people and events.

The most vehement long-standing fights between sisters were informed by opposition to views about their childhood, their parents, and their experiences within the family. These often occurred when one sister felt, as Marjorie Williams did, that she "was raised in a family full of lies—a rich, entertaining, well-elaborated fivesome that flashed with competition and triangles and changing alliances."[2] Marjorie and her sisters then allied themselves according to whose story they believed: Was one sister really anorexic or just normally thin? Was the father's assistant accompanying him on vacations as part of her work or something more personal? Resisting the ubiquitous lies in the family, Marjorie Williams drills deeply for truthful accounts of the family. When one sister resists the other's efforts, each distances herself from the other.

There were sisters who were close whose stories often differed; but some differences on important points, and on points one cared about, sparked conflict. Gill says, "I can't stand the prissy way Frances talks about our family. Like they never did anything for her. Some of things she says happened are outrageous. She thinks Mom was selfish. To hear her talk you'd think our mother never did anything for us. She says Mom was a bully, and that she spoiled our chances of seeing our father. Her memories are so twisted. Even little things, about who said what when. It's outrageous how unfair she can be."

Different stories about our shared pasts can threaten the stories that build up our personal narratives. While some differences add new perspectives to one's own history, other differences threaten to dislodge the identity they help construct. Was a mother kind, loving, and playful? Or was she con-

straining, cold, and vindictive? Sisters seldom agree to disagree on such matters.

One of the most surprising findings in this study of sistering
among adult women is the passionate investment each woman
has in her version of the family system. Not only did most
women want to preserve and protect their particular version,
but they also wanted their version accepted by a sister.

The passionate attachment each has to her own story of
how the family works gives rise to passionate clashes when
another sister lays claim to an inconsistent story. Whether, for
example, it was a father who was verbally abusive or a mother
who was withholding is an opinion about which sisters were
rarely inclined to disagree amicably. Which parent, for example, is deserving, which is victim, and which is villain are
questions that divide sisters. The shared identity developed in
childhood, from mutual understanding and empathy, makes
intolerable clashing views of the people intimately involved
in our lives.

THE CONSEQUENCES OF CLASHING VIEWS

GOOD SISTER TALK is filled with reflections and retellings of
what was really going on in the family. But some sisters tear
each other's stories to shreds. The distance between the sisters
Ceri and Andrea is marked by their very different accounts of
their mother's character and motives. Ceri explains, "Andrea
sees Mom as controlling and critical. Whenever I mention

Ma, she'll make this face. It's like she knows the real story I'm telling, and I don't. So I say I'm going to see Ma, and she asks why I'm at Ma's beck and call. She has the knack of remembering things when we were kids and twisting them, so I don't recognize anyone in them. She says Ma clucks around us, that her ways are self-serving, because she's always telling us how much she's doing for us. The awful thing is that for a while I see her that way. Ma walks into a room, and says, 'I'll just clear this away,' and 'That carpet looks good since I cleaned it.' But basically my sister changes her into a different person. The whole family seems awful, the way she tells it. She says our brother was always spoiled, that all he had to do was walk through the door for my parents to treat him like royalty. She even says our house is crummy, that no one in our family cares if the roof is mended or the sills are painted. You get this litany of complaints about everyone. And these aren't conversations you can avoid. They come up whatever I do. We just have totally different views of our family, and I think she's warped and mean."

So painful are these clashing views that the creative gossip natural among sisters dries up. Rather than deal with genuine joint attempts to construct coherent stories, some sisters freeze their memories and views, both of their families and a sister whose perspective counters theirs. "Freezing" one's view is a way of insisting that one's own version of the family system need not be changed. As a result we refuse to test our story. We "don't want to talk about it," or we dismiss what another family witness says: "Baloney!" or "Whatever," or "Think what you want."

In some cases sisters refuse to see one another because

they know that they will discuss their family, and then the story they want to claim as their own, the story they refuse to shift or even check, will be disturbed. At other times they remain friendly but avoid speaking honestly to one another. This can result in conversation that is merely white noise, a cacophony of voices that fail to engage with one another.

Gina says, "Before—you know, before Sam gave me her kidney—we never stopped talking. We'd meet up, and it was like a switch was opened, and we'd just talk and talk. Sometimes it was catching up with things that happened since we last met; but it always went back to things that happened before. 'I used to hate you for that,' I could say, and she'd let on that she knew, that she understood, that she was sorry. That's what she said. She was sorry: I mean, isn't that sweet? She was apologizing because I hated her! Because she knew she'd made me hate her. She remembered how she'd behaved, and now was seeing it my way. She knew she'd been awful, and she knew it must be awful to hate your sister. That kind of thing meant so much to me, that she remembered and understood and was now okay about it.

"Well, now we meet, and at first there's still that urge to talk. I see her face, and the talk-switch opens! But I've realized something now. We talk as much, but it doesn't go anywhere. It's just filler. I really want to talk about how things have been for me. I mean, how it is, having her kidney. How it feels. How it feels now for me. But our take on what happened is so different. Sometimes she seems to be blaming our mother, and that's not right. Or she seems to be blaming me. All I want is for her to see what things were like from my point of view. But she doesn't want to know. So I still am confused about what really was going on."

The break in the sister conversation leaves a gap in her own story. Unable to explain herself to her sister, she feels anxious and incomplete.

Some sisters cling to their negative views of one another. Gill is willing to forgo the pleasure of her sister's company in order to avoid any challenge to her family story. "Frances can be funny and warm. And I start thinking, 'Well, maybe she isn't so bad. And that means that maybe she has a point. And then she says something that makes me angry, and reminds me how angry I've been with her, for a real long time. Having things shift around like that is just too confusing. I don't need this."

Gill "freezes" her view of her "warped and mean" sister. Rather than have her angry view of Frances challenged by talking to Frances, or even just meeting with her and experiencing the good aspects of their sister bond, Laurie decides to let her anger be carved in stone. "There's no point in seeing her. She'll be nice for maybe one minute, and then it will be the same thing. She's mean about money, and she's mean about other people. She's tactless, and she's selfish. I don't need to know more about her."

Frances is well aware of Gill's view of her. "She's said awful things about me to my dad, to my aunt, to my cousins. I have to live with these descriptions. Whenever I see my cousins, I feel I'm trailing these awful stories I know she tells them."

The terrible power wielded by one sister's view of another is demonstrated by two sisters, Margaret Drabble and Antonia Byatt, who have carried out some sister-knot battles on the open field of literature. When Margaret Drabble writes about a young woman with a clever, beautiful, selfish, and duplicitous sister who recently graduated from Cambridge,[3] Antonia Byatt counters by writing about a woman whose sister has written about her, and who thereafter has to "drag this grotesque shadow, our joint creature"[4] around with her throughout her life. The story one sister tells of the other sticks, like a spider's web: The different family narratives, even when transformed into fiction, are an affront. After all, the family history is shared. Each sister has possession of it. But if your story is different, then what status does mine have? Different stories give rise to feelings of conflict because sisters identify with each other. "When we were children, we were not quite separate," reflects Antonia Byatt's character Cassandra. "We shared a common vision, we created a common myth."[5] Thus, each may experience the other's story as something shared, even when she would rather repudiate it.

A BREAK IN THE SYSTEM

OUR VIEWS OF the family inevitably shift when a family member dies. When we mourn someone we love, memories become newly charged with meaning. Our retrospective appreciation of what we have lost is heightened, and we take comfort from remembering and reliving, and from sharing those memories. It is not simply practical necessities surrounding a family death that bring the survivors together. Siblings who have distanced themselves from one another often need to meet again, to discover whether they can, this time, find some common ground.

The impulse of siblings to meet and to have one final showdown in matching family memories and family stories is the theme of Arthur Miller's play *The Price*. Financial arrangements and old emotional scores make a tense drama from a simple meeting between two brothers. Victor and Walter, now well into middle age, challenge one another's life-guiding stories about why each made the early-adult choices he did: why one brother stayed with the father and cared for him and accepted the financial burdens of the family; why the other brother left, went to college and medical school, and fostered his own potential, looking to his own needs. The self-sacrificing son then comes to understand that story he has told himself throughout his life—that his father was in dire financial need, that the only way to keep him from starving was to take a job—was a sham. The price of the furniture and other household objects they saw every day, and, thirty years later, are now selling, would have allowed Victor the freedom to pursue any career. The story he has been telling himself—that he made a necessary sacrifice—is now shattered. The "selfish" brother shows the "self-sacrificing" brother that his sacrifice was unnecessary. The father was manipulating him and destroying him, and the cost of his education was clearly visible in the expensive furniture they saw every day.

The dramatic challenge to Victor's story exposes him as having been easily duped by a selfish father. The change precipitated by a father's death forces recognition of what was always obvious and always denied. Revision of stories can shatter the frame in which one sees oneself. No one can shatter this frame more easily than a sibling who also has a stake in the family story.

Mourning pushes suppressed feelings to the surface. This changes the way siblings relate to one another. Sometimes these clashes arise from the old annoyances, the small irritations and jars that created distance in the first place. But often new tensions arise as a system changes. Former constraints on what can be said are lifted. Changing the view of how the family works has, for some siblings, a dramatic, devastating impact.

When Maria and Dora's mother died, the sisters at first experienced a new comfort. "Together," Maria reflected, "we could assess the damage. When we buried her I felt such a strange peace. Something blissful. I walked beside my sister and for the first time in a long time I felt that childhood togetherness we had when we walked to school, away from our awful home, knowing just what we would and wouldn't say to our friends."

Dora and Maria share their relief: "At least we can't hurt her anymore," they said to each other. Dora explains that her mother had always said that she would have been fine in life, content and productive, if she had not had children to contend with. When their mother dies, Dora is able to talk to Maria openly about the awful feelings she had while acting as a dutiful daughter. She is able to tell her sister how her "good" behavior stemmed from a belief that she had to make amends for the harm she had done to her mother simply by being born. "For all our closeness, Maria and I never really admitted how awful it was, living with our mother's illness. I wanted to see if we could share something, so I wouldn't feel so bad about how bad I felt."

But Maria soon grows uneasy with the peace that is derived from her mother's death. She tells her sister, "You were so good at doing *her* job, so good at housework, so good at organizing all the kids, that Mom felt she had no purpose in life." Dora concludes curtly, "I didn't feel free from the shadow of my mother's blame for long. It was as though my sister was suddenly taking the role my mother had taken. Maria became the accuser." A rush of connection was followed by ferocious clashes.

Dora goes on to note a series of changes in her sister. "Before my mother died, I thought I really knew my sister. She was hard as nails. She had guts. She wasn't afraid to show me who she was. She never pretended. I mean, she never pretended to feel guilty about saying awful things about people. But since mom died, she's become a different person, all high and mighty, and telling me what I could and couldn't say, and I didn't know what she was really thinking."

Dora agrees that the mother's death provided the opportunity for "our coming together, something that felt so right, the tension between us just evaporated. We got drunk, and we all laughed horribly as we imitated her ritual declaration to us in her depressed phase, 'Well, at least I can always die.' When Dora said that, she was Mom to a T; and we all collapsed, appalled because we found it so true to life, and also so funny. It was the first time we could make fun of her hysteria, and, boy, was that liberating. But then I felt awful, and didn't want to see Dora. And I wanted to spend time with Dad. And I couldn't feel comfortable with my father when I was saying such awful things about Mom to my sister."

The sisters, now in midlife, rational and capable in every other sphere of life, are like squabbling children, arguing over symbolic possession of the father, arguing over how to preserve the mother's memory. But the squabbling is that of sisters fighting over a version of the family story that makes sense to them. And neither sister can say to the other, *We see things differently: That's okay.*

Sister talk is wide ranging, but it functions according to rules as to who needs protection and who is owed loyalty. Arguments about a sister's family narrative raise questions about loyalty to parents and blame on parents. When the rules are given a shakeup by a parent's death, sister talk has to settle on new freedoms or new regulations. Maria and Dora have not yet found a new status quo. They come together, argue, and then brood on the other's "crimes," and these offenses are constituted simply by holding opposing views of the family. Maria says, "I go over and over what she said and what I said. I swing between thinking I was really mean and thinking it's all her fault. And then I have to run back to her to find out what *she* thinks. And it starts over again."

* * *

Beth Henley's play *Crimes of the Heart* depicts a group of sisters who successfully maneuver the new family stories that emerge from a family crisis. Three sisters, Lenny, Meg, and Babe, have lived throughout adolescence and early adulthood with the story of their mother's "freakish" and "ghastly" behavior. Questions press on all the sisters as they grow up: Why did she kill herself? Was she insane? Will the daughters inherit their mother's madness? Any why did she kill, alongside herself, the poor innocent family cat? Was this some kind of bizarre cruelty, which her daughters, too, will inherit? These questions, suppressed by shame and distorted by neighborhood gossip, tear into the sisters' lives. When the youngest sister, Babe, is accused of trying to kill her husband, the old family tragedy lights up as a new scandal.

Haunted by the unresolved family story, Babe tries to reenact it. She is saved in part by the farcical weakness of the chandelier on which she tries to hang herself, but her real savior is her sister Meg. As Meg pulls Babe's face from the oven, in which she is now trying to gas herself, Babe returns to consciousness with the gift of understanding their mother's story: Their mother did not kill the cat because she hated it but because she wanted company. The angels she would meet when she died would have "high scary voices" and "little gold pointed fingers that are as sharp as blades and you don't want to meet 'em all alone."[6]

Once the sisters solve, together, the riddle of that family story, they reassure each other that however sad their mother's death, it does not mean that any of them is afflicted with her problems. The difference is that their mother was alone, with only a cat as a companion; the daughters have each other, and it is their sister bonds that will ensure that they survive, even the bad days. Together the sisters solve the riddle of their mother's unhappiness and the family's shame; and, in so doing, they thrive.

Lenny, Meg, and Babe have had the endless fights and persistent resentments common to most sisters; they have belittled one another and envied one another. They have sulked over the fact that one is marked as the grandfather's favorite, and one is the pampered beauty, and one sees herself, in contrast to the other two, as the "loser." They have argued over dresses and birthday chocolates, over slights and put-downs. But when they make themselves whole by piecing together the family puzzle, they cannot even remember what all the fights and all the jealousy have been about.

We are all natural storytellers; we want to understand the basic elements of our experience. We need to be able to match our memories and observations with what other people tell us. The accuracy of family stories is difficult to establish for several reasons. Our memories seem to play tricks, and are changed by different phases of maturity, so that we reprocess as teens what we experienced as children. We sometimes remember what we've been told as much as the event itself, and these two different sources sometimes become confused. One very clear aim of sister talk is to enliven our memories and shape the stories we have been told into stories that are truthful.

10

Success and Insecurity: When One Sister Outshines the Other

T HE FAMILIAR DAYDREAM of being a "star" may be childish, but it marks a profound need. Up front and center stage, we imagine the delight we'd feel if we could claim others' attention and adoration. This common fantasy stems from the innate need to be noticed, a need to be central to others, and a presumption that we are up front and central in our personal environment. This is balanced by the need to respect and admire others we care for, who share this need to be central.

In this chapter I look at the ways sibling ties, and in particular, the sister knot, shape continuing efforts to secure the attention of people whose love we crave. Concern about our status in the eyes of others leads us to compete for attention and recognition of our successes. We also focus on our sisters' successes; however small these are, we see them with a clarity that makes them appear large. What a sister achieves is always interesting for two very different reasons: First, we identify with her, so her successes are partly our own; second, within the world of our family, in which our own status is a lifelong concern, her successes may eclipse ours. As a sister we feel ourselves to be one of a pair, or group, that constitutes a whole; we also see a sister as a competitor on an opposing team.

WHY BEING NOTICED IS SO IMPORTANT

AT BIRTH INFANTS are already well equipped to satisfy their powerful need for parents' attention. They exert a magnetic pull over the people who care for them. At the earliest stage of life their cries are perfected to penetrate and annoy adults. Unable to run to safety alongside others, unable to feed themselves or take steps to keep warm, infants use piercing cries as a strategy for life-sustaining attention. These cries are so distracting that adults who hear them will do just about anything to silence them. Usually they hold, feed, or talk soothingly to the infant; but they can also be driven to fury when their attempts to soothe the infant fail, and can end up taking this anger out on the infant.

Yet infants have excellent strategies to counter people's impatience. Their strategies consist of doing cute things, endlessly, to engage and monitor people's attention. Toddlers, using their new motor skills to crawl or run away from a parent at their own whim, look to parents to assess the safety of their independence. They also challenge adults to remain alert to every movement, since they appear heedless of danger. They ricochet between sharp corners and steep stairs; they stuff poisonous cleansers into their mouths; they climb on every available structure without testing its stability. Children require parents' attention to survive.

It is not surprising, then, that we have psychological mechanisms to ensure that we value attention. We crave attention at the most basic level, but it is not merely physical survival we crave. Recognition is crucial to one's sense of self. A parent's face, from which children assess their approval ratings, represents a mirror. The recognition and delight, the concern, fear, or disapproval displayed in a parent's face, provide a reference point for children as they learn about the pleasures of acceptance and the terrors of disapproval. Not only do we want to be noticed; we also want to be admired.

Parents say they love their children unconditionally. This means that a change of status in a child, even a change of status in a parent's eyes, will not affect a parent's love. Whether a child is a "star" or a "failure," she is loved by her parents. But unconditional love is not enough. We also crave recognition and approval for what we do. Recognition and approval can never be unconditional, because they are based on what a child does and what she achieves.

Throughout childhood we look to others for a confirming answer to questions we can barely articulate. We search for responses to words and actions and skills that tell us who we are. Throughout life, recognition from others helps to define our self and provide assurance that we matter and that we are "special." Lack of recognition disheartens us, makes us feel insignificant and powerless. And our first experiences of gaining recognition and losing status are within the family.

A MORE SUCCESSFUL SISTER

WHEN HILARY DU PRÉ looks back on her life with her sister, Jacqueline, she reflects on her love and admiration for the supreme musician, for the companion with a roguish sense of humor, and for the person whose life was so intricately linked to hers. She also reflects on her terror and grief at being eclipsed by a sister's talent. Jacqueline was the genius in the family, whereas Hilary was merely talented. The difference in their relative positions was not clear from the start. As very young children Hilary and Jackie performed at the same recitals and got the same glowing applause from audiences who loved the beaming, poised little girls as much as the music they played. Some of these recitals took the form of competitions, but the sisters did not mind competing against each other. Each girl would get a medal of some kind, and who got first prize, this time, and who got second prize, was immaterial, for the places would be exchanged at the next event. On one such occasion, however, a shift occurred that made a permanent change in the landscape on which Hilary and her sister stood.

The event began predictably enough. The first sister went to the stage to receive her prize and then skipped happily off the platform. She made her way to the back of the auditorium to wait for the proceedings to end. Standing beyond the back row, she saw her mother's and teacher's ecstatic faces and heard increased applause. Assuming that she was included in this approbation, Hilary glowed happily. But soon she realized that the audience, and her teacher, and her mother had forgotten all about her. The teacher made a speech about "this remarkable child"; the audience rose to its feet and cameras clicked.

Hilary could not process what was happening. She had played well, and her mother was pleased by her playing. She could not understand why she was not standing on the stage beside Jackie, sharing this rapt applause, these smiles, these tears of happiness. "All eyes and all attention were on Jackie," writes Hilary. "We had always done everything together, but now we were separated and I felt frantic. I turned and ran. . . . I was crying and felt bereft and completely forgotten."[1]

The grief and panic Hilary experienced as she saw her sister in the limelight and felt herself forgotten rest on that primitive need to be noticed. Even when we no longer need attention to survive, we have a deep need for attention. And in the grip of the sibling trauma, we fear that a sibling can eclipse us and leave us in darkness.

The threat of being cast out is so closely linked to the threat of being ignored that inattentiveness arouses acute anxiety. Hilary knew she had played well at the concert and she, too, had been given medals; but when her mother and teacher and the audience had eyes only for her sister, her mind raced "in a whirl of loneliness, dismay, failure."[2] At a primitive level our achievements are drained of meaning if they go unrecognized.

The psychologist William James observed, "No more fiendish punishment could be devised, were such a thing physically possible, than that one should be turned loose in society and remain absolutely unnoticed by all the members thereof." James went on to emphasize this point by showing how this profound need is reflected in common phrases. "To cut one dead" means to turn away, to ignore someone; and in James's view it really does feel like a kind of death. The discomfort in being ignored is tantamount to physical pain. Indeed, James says that being ignored arouses "a rage and impotent despair . . . from which the cruellest bodily torture would be a relief."[3]

The need to be noticed and to secure recognition is a basic human need for love. The strong psychological link between status and love has been recently explored by Alain de Botton. In his book *Status Anxiety*, Botton writes, "To be shown love is to feel ourselves the object of concern. Our presence is noted, our name is registered, our views listened to, our failings are treated with indulgence and our needs ministered to."[4] The prototype of this love is the early child-parent bond, before we become aware of "competitors" in our interpersonal world. When we seek fame and riches and other measures of success, we are probably seeking ways to secure the love we thought we had before we conceptualized siblings.

THE BIRTH OF STATUS ANXIETY: A PERSONAL REFLECTION

I SPENT MY early teenage years in a sulk because my sister was the golden girl who got good grades, and was fast-tracking to what my parents thought was the only useful thing—a profession in medicine. She also had poise and could talk to the grown-ups who were frequent guests at our dinner table. She was pretty and well formed, and I felt like nothing next to her. When she sat, prim and proper, discussing courses and her future career and clothes with my mother, I felt an extreme annoyance: Why were people taking her so seriously? Why did she get attention so easily? Why was I so easily maneuvered into the background?

The irritation I expressed was put down to a number of things. Being spoiled, being stubborn, and being a teenager were a few of the causes cited. But I was simply a sibling suffering from acute sibling rivalry. Hatred for my parents surged in me because they appeared to prefer my sister, not because I wanted to rebel against them. I worked hard to define myself as different and superior. I hammered out my own views at every opportunity, and used the common strategies of devaluation and contempt to manage my envy. While I appeared proud to others, I felt I was fighting for breathing space in my world.

It was at that time, too, that I became aware how other girls could threaten my place in the family. One of my many talented and beautiful cousins, for example, could get into a prestigious school, or have an excellent examination result, or prove herself to be an elegant dresser or a particularly caring daughter. I could see that my mother was also rattled by the qualities of her sister's children, and was irritated by her own mother's praise of them. I can recognize this now as a long-playing version of the sister knot, but at the time I simply registered the danger to my status. Anyone who was roughly comparable to me in terms of gender and age, and had the qualities that my parents admired, could make me into "nothing" by eclipsing me on the family stage. Long after we were finished with the roughhousing of sister play and the bickering over toys and "whose turn it was," I was still struggling with the threat of losing status relative to my sister and my cousins, even while I felt that their successes would pull me up, too, and their failures would pull me down.

THE FEAR OF A SISTER OUTSHINING US

WHERE DO I stand in my social world? What is my status relative to someone else? How secure am I in where I stand? What will happen to my position when a sister rises higher in the world? Will I always be admired for who I am?

Even when such questions no longer affect our material or physical well-being, they have an enormous impact. Indeed, our sense of status, where we are relative to the others who matter to us, is now recognized as central to well-being, a crucial factor in our health and longevity.[5] The role of status has been explored from many angles—from our relation to our neighbors, our childhood friends, our colleagues, our parents. Surprisingly, it has not been considered from a sibling perspective. Yet that is where it starts, and where its significance lies.

"There are few relationships as close—or as hierarchical— as the relationship between siblings," notes Deborah Tannen as she analyzes family conversation.[6] Put-downs ("Stupid," "Babyish"), taunts ("Mine's better than yours"), and senseless but relentless competitions ("I got the bigger piece") all mark the everyday need to say *I'm better than you* and *I have more than you* and *I'm luckier than you.* These familiar manuevers among siblings are attempts to mark one's status relative to the other.

The adult sisters in my study reported vivid memories of a sister's triumph, while their own successes seem less clearly delineated. Each member of every sister clan in my study, of whatever age, had memories of a sister event that threatened her with obscurity relative to a sister's high visibility, as marked by some status symbol. Jenny, sixteen, reports that one of her most vivid memories of sistering was a time when she was nine years old, when her "sister got to be taken to see Granny in the hospital, but I wasn't allowed. I thought, Why can Bridget see her and not me? We were always told we were loved the same, and our ages—she was eighteenth months older than me—usually made no difference. It was what we did and who we were that counted. But all of a sudden being older gave her a status that I didn't have. Or, even worse, there was something about her that I didn't know that gave her that edge. Everyone was nodding, 'Yes, Bridget should go see Gran,' and I was thinking, Why? What's going on here?

I still don't understand it, and I still sometimes brood over it. Is she better at talking to Gran? Is she better at talking to everyone? It's hard to explain why it hit me. Maybe it was obvious to everyone else why it was Bridget and not me. But it wasn't obvious to me. When I asked why Bridget got to go and I didn't, no one understood that I was asking a real question. They told me to stop whining. I still feel uneasy when I think about it."

To Bridget, however, this is an insignificant piece of family history. "I think we'd been told that Gran could only have two visitors at a time. Neither Jenny nor I could go on our own, so it had to be a grown-up and a kid. I think people used "the oldest" just as a way of making a decision. I guess they were trying to look fair. Boy, that failed!"

Getting ahead of a sister seemed far less memorable than the experience of falling behind a sister. What Bridget remembers is the silent speed with which Jenny came up behind her, performed with ease the tasks that she had struggled with, always outstripping her in social ease, in sports, and eventually in height. "She was only a year behind me in school. See, she was young for her year, and I was in the middle for mine. I remembered how awful my first day in junior high was, and how down I was, for such a long time. Her first day at school? Well, she just bounced out of the house, not a care in the world, and came home bubbling with her good news about guys she met and girls who wanted to meet up with her. It was her first day in that enormous school, and she'd already made herself a cosy home!

"Then there was the schoolwork. I had to struggle in biology, and then, in the blink of an eye, she was doing the same class. I'd sweat at it, and then she'd breeze by with As. Everyone tried to take it in good spirit. My mom always said, 'Everyone's different. Stop comparing yourself with her.' But it was impossible not to compare. There she was, at the same school, always running so close behind me she kept knocking me over."

Competition is highly charged between sisters, but it does not destroy the bond. Jenny and Bridget enjoy one another's company. They depend on each other for support. They admire each other, and in many ways each is proud of the other. But each experiences the privilege or success of the other as a challenge to her own status. "Maybe one day I'll outgrow this," says Bridget, "but it's more likely to be a matter of getting far enough away, somehow, so I don't feel measured against her." And Jenny says, "I really hate her telling me that I'm ousting her when I come up trumps. It can trash my mood. I deliberately ignore it whenever I can. Sometimes I think, I'm going to sing and dance about this success and I don't care what Bridget thinks. But that carefree mood doesn't last. I know I do care. And it can really ruin good stuff. But even worse, there's this shadow, because I know she's going to get even. I know one day she'll find really important stuff easy. There's something in her lying in wait."

Jenny and Bridget, still teenagers, hope that their uneasy checking-up glances at where one is relative to the other will simply "go away." The sisters are never entirely sure who is ahead and who is behind. In fact their competition is built on the fantasy that one needs to outshine the other in order to be worthy of love. Whatever their parents may do to put this fantasy to rest, the question persists, as sure as a heartbeat: How secure am I in where I want to be relative to her?

THE ROMANTIC TRIANGLE:
LOVE AND STATUS

A YOUNG WOMAN who has already been married for ten years dreams that she is attending a concert for which she purchased tickets in advance. When she arrives she finds that half the seats are empty. The gist of her dream, "I was in too much of a hurry," is related to her discovery that she has heard that a good friend, close to her in age and social standing, a sister figure, has just become engaged: "I could have waited and been much better off," is Freud's guess at the dream's meaning.[7] The woman was not aware of being dissatisfied with her own husband, yet comparison with a twinlike figure sparked the questions, Did I make the right choice? and Did I choose too quickly?

It is often said that parents present role models for future romantic partners. So much has been written about romantic choices in the context of mothers and fathers as models, but very little is written about the ways a sister's romantic attachments and histories affect another sister. During their middle and late teenage years, girls were talking to me about choices in terms of their similarities and differences from a sister. They wanted to impress a sister and to surpass her in her own romantic partner. Adi said that her sister Jessica's ridicule could freeze romance at the core. "I really liked this guy. For a while I really liked him. But when Jessie heard I'd agreed to go out with him, she jumped in with both feet. 'He's a weirdo. He has these ears that move when he chews. No one wants to sit next to him in the cafeteria. How can you even talk to him? No one in my year thinks he's anything but gross.'

"When my sister said that, it really cut my feelings for him dead. I said, 'Oh, no, I don't really want to go out with him,' and I made some excuse to him about why I couldn't go out with him. I really liked him before she said that, and I really didn't like him after that. It was a total reversal."

Was Jessica being mischievous: Was she denigrating Adi's prospective boyfriend as a means of spoiling something for her sister? Was she being protective? Did she genuinely think, He isn't good enough for you? Jessica tells me she can barely remember what she said, but she does remember the boy. "I don't remember saying anything, but I was relieved when Adi didn't go out with him. My friends made fun of him constantly. It would have been real embarrassing if he went on even one date with my sister."

Sisters may say to each other, "Who you choose is your own business." A sister may say, "I wouldn't dream of judging your choice." Nonetheless sisters always assess each other's partners. A sister may wonder, out of curiosity and anxiety, might my sister's partner have chosen me over her? For most of us this query is transient; but there are sisters who put this query to the test. Surely this was the motive behind Jacqueline du Pré's "need" to make love to her brother-in-law: At a time of intense insecurity, when her own marriage was distinctly uneasy, Jackie sought the assurance that she could triumph in the sibling trauma: *If I can take someone away from my sister, then I can prove my superiority and my power.*

Hilary responded to this as a sister: On the one hand she was terrified, doubly betrayed by a husband and a sister; on the other hand she accepted her sister's need for affection and reassurance. The sisterly identification gave Jacqueline a sense of entitlement to her sister's partner, and led Hilary to accept the infidelity.

In romantic love we hope to secure the exclusivity that was denied us in the child-parent bond. As children we have to share the parent we love best with another partner, perhaps another parent, and with a sibling. Taking a lover from a sister could be seen as a symbolic victory: *I have used my charms to take away the love that you had first.* For Hilary du Pré, who had been given hard lessons in the sibling trauma, being displaced was one element of sharing. For the artist Frida Kahlo, the displacement was intolerable: Diego Rivera's infidelities with other women were maddening but tolerable; when Frida discovered him making love to her sister, she left him and cut her long hair.[8] The gesture speaks out: *If as a woman, I can be replaced, then I must "un-sex" myself to regain my sense of self, with a new and very different place in the world.*

In families struck with incest, the daughter who is victim may also feel that she is specially chosen; when a father turns to another daughter, she is relieved but also bereft. "I hated myself because of what he'd done, and then I hated myself for wanting to keep him, when he turned to my sister," Frances whispers to me. The cruelties of incest have many consequences; one is that parent-daughter incest always compounds the sister knot, piling confusions on to already uneasy questions about preference within the family.

REAL SUCCESSES

"I THOUGHT WHEN I turned twenty-one," Kate reflected, "that I'd be a grown-up like my sisters. What struck me was that I was never going to be like them. Rosalind's been given three promotions in the past two years. She just flies through everything. She works in a swish building, has two secretaries and a snazzy office. Diana already has pretty much been promised tenure at her college. Even my little sister, Sue, is a hotshot journalist on the student paper. I mean, she won't have any trouble whizzing through life like the others.

"Until a few years ago I thought that Diana and Rosalind had what they had because they were grown-ups. I thought you grew up, and you got a job you liked, and you earned enough money, and you started climbing even higher. My sisters were so different and so competent, and I was proud of them. I mean, I'm still proud. I'm really proud of them. But where does this leave me? I see my dad looking at me, like he can't understand why I'm putzing around, why I take these stupid dead-end jobs and then give them up, and why whatever I decide to do doesn't go anywhere. I have all the same start-up perks as my sisters. I went to the same high school they did. I went to college like they did. But they're successful and know where they're going, and I'm in a fog. And it makes it worse that they don't have a clue what this means. Diana tries to be helpful, and Rosalind tells me not to worry, and they're so sweet to me, I'm so lucky to have such sisters. But they sure are daunting."

Even when relative worldly success is not so clearly delineated, sisters note differences, and note them with feeling. Miri, thirty-three, even as a confident woman, with sister love intact, is uneasy about her shifting position relative to her sister. She explains that she is different from her sister, but also "very close." "I feel accepted by her, and I think I love her. We talk a lot, and there is true friendship, but there is also, on my part—an unappeasable urge to measure and match. Is her life better than mine? Are her kids better? Do our parents like her girl more than they like mine? I hate this in myself, but there it is. And there's this divided response when she gets low. I am sorry for her, but I also think: Am I a little ahead now? But it's not really that I want to be ahead. It's that I don't want to be behind."

Which sister is ahead of and which sister is behind the other are seldom clear-cut. Jacqueline outshone her sister, Hilary, in music, but perhaps saw Hilary as more fully realized as a daughter, wife, and mother. Sensing this "superiority," Jackie tried to displace her sister on these fronts, too, by seducing Hilary's husband. It is because the measure of success keeps shifting that the competitiveness never comes to a definite finish point. The resolution is not in surpassing a sister, but in overcoming anxiety about who is more successful.

SUCCESS AND SCHADENFREUDE

ENJOYMENT OBTAINED FROM the trouble of others, for which the German language has its own term, *Schadenfreude*, arises from anxiety that another's successes will diminish us. It arises in many contexts. The sudden and unexpected success of a close friend may make us uneasy, however much we normally root for her and support her; when we hear of her disappointment then we may be pleased, not because we are innately nasty but because the success of someone close to us awakens primitive fears. These primitive fears first make their appearance in the sibling trauma.

Miri does not want anything bad to happen to her sister or to her sister's family: "I'd be appalled," she explains, "if something really awful happened. It's the little disappointments that I focus on. When they come—when she's made a bad financial investment, when her kid gets a bad grade—I feel this secret relief." This, she assures me, is "not meanness, even though it must seem mean." What Miri seeks is reassurance that she is not inferior, that her own status is adequate. But she also knows that the relative places are not fixed; being obviously ahead is a little safer, so that when there is movement again, she won't be obviously behind.

Her competitiveness stands alongside closeness. She identifies so closely with her sister, that she assumes, on one level, they must conform to a single standard. Hence the differences between them open up questions as to who is closer or further from some ideal standard. If the sisters are different, is one closer to the person the other should be? This presents a maze in which any difference is threatening, even though each sister needs to be different in order to be special.

The association between "being less successful than a sister" and being "displaced from the place that is most important to me" is where envy breeds. Envy is a kind of grief. It is grief that we cannot secure for ourselves all we need to prove that we are absolutely special, that we are the sole possessors of the qualities and attributes that we value.

The resolution of this grief is piecemeal, often painstaking, and always necessary. It is part of learning about one's own capabilities and limitations. In managing and overcoming envy, we exercise the skill, essential to sanity, of admiring others without suffering attacks of misery. Practicing envy survival also spurs us to be as good as we can, and to gauge the distress of not being good enough. It is part of what makes us endlessly active goal setters, and spikes our fascination with other people's achievements.

SISTER ENVY IN A SOCIAL CONTEXT

IN TODAY'S SOCIETY a plethora of anxiety-inducing questions, for women, are inevitable. Should I shape my life so that my family has priority, or my career? Is it possible to achieve a perfect balance between my need for close personal involvement with others and more public expressions of skill? And, It looks as though *she* has done everything just right. Why can't I be like her?

Lifestyle choices have proliferated for women, but this will not lead to a more flexible and capacious notion of success until we resolve the rigid terror of seeing another woman surpass us. The rigidity stems from the fantasy of an ideal woman, who elicits loving and admiring responses from all the people we care about. "Isn't she wonderful!" we may imagine them saying; and in consequence we suppose that we ourselves will be displaced. We idealize a woman who secures unsurpassable success and is unchallengeable from any angle. This ideal could only be achieved if one was the only member of her generation.

Throughout their lives women reassess gender-related decisions about life balance with reference to a sister or someone who, in their lives, comes to represent a sister. This may be a woman who is like her, someone who appears to her as the woman others (particularly a parent) wanted her to be. These comparative maneuvers are performed on the assumption that a powerful judge is keeping score. This "judge" is a remnant of a child's view of a parent's eye. It is informed and distorted by parents' broad-ranging wishes and ideals, and by cultural norms. In a context in which norms are in flux, the question, Who must I be to be loved? seems unanswerable.

When someone close to us, someone with whom we have long identified, such as a sister, follows what seems to be "the right path," when we are posing inevitable questions about our own choices, the sister knot tightens. As forty-two-year-old Alison reflects, "Why did my sisters find it so easy? Why did things work out so well for them, and get messed up for me? These feelings leave scars. I get so angry, and think and say such awful things. But it makes me ache, just feeling what it's like to be them, and thinking I should be just like them. Or even more: I should be here. She is in my place. She is living my life."

Alison speaks about the frustrations of her acting career, in which she has had little success. In putting her career first, she had forgone a family, but she had not gained what she sought. Her attention keeps returning to her sisters. "They've done so well. They're all doing different things, and they're all interesting things—things that make sense, things that make money! I love seeing them, but when I hear what they're doing, and see their children, and walk into their houses, my legs buckle with envy. That kind of rhythm to their lives . . . it's what's behind it all, the feeling they must have of being safe and established. I can taste it, even though it's miles away from me. . . . That feeling is so awful, that the only way I can comfort myself is by thinking that if it gets worse, or doesn't go away, I can always kill myself. That's a sick kind of comfort, I know. But it is reassuring. . . . You see, the feeling is just so awful."

The disappointment of not succeeding is a "narcissistic wound"—that is, a blow to our primitive optimism that things will be okay for us. Disappointment is not easy for anyone, but we normally get through the low times that follow disappointments with a range of comforts. There are the physical comforts of rest and food and warmth, or the physical buzz of dancing or working out. We distract ourselves with the pleasures of a book or a film or a chat with a friend. More important, we learn how to define ourselves in different ways, outside constraining comparisons with others. We learn the necessary skill of accepting our limitations and enjoying our abilities. We invest in our own proven talents. We demonstrate our effectiveness across a range of social and intimate environments. We establish our own network of personal bonds that reinforce our sense of self, regardless of what others achieve. Thus it is that Juliet Mitchell sees self-respect as emerging from the sibling trauma. Alison, however, describes herself as "locked into a room with the person I wanted to be but now know I won't."

In her extremity she lays bare the structure of envy: "I am nothing because other people have what I want." The challenge for her is to modify those self-assessments activated in the sibling trauma, by which we measure ourselves according to what a sister achieves. It is not until I meet Alison again, six years later,[9] that she is able to enjoy the different lives she and her sisters lead. "My nephews and my niece belong to me, too. I'm proud of that, and I'm so relieved that whole pile of resentments didn't ruin things for me and my sisters. You know, I think back on them now, and wonder what all that was about. Because my sister isn't responsible for my disappointments. And she doesn't take anything away from me."

When we untie the sister knot, we expose the primitive fear of losing one's place in the family. The most devastating realization of the sibling trauma is the discovery that competitive bids have to be placed for the love one needs to survive. We expose the fear of being sidelined by those upon whose love we depend for basic care. Yet we are also primed to love the siblings who threaten our place. We want to stand alongside others and feel secure; but recognition and attention are in flux. The problem, so often seen to be a problem of learning how to share, is really a problem of fearing one cannot share.

Where we love, we tend also to admire; but admiration for a sister brings with it anxiety: Is she more loveable than I am? How do her qualities affect her status in the family? Within the day-to-day bonding of childhood come sudden stabbings of jealousy: "That's mine," "It's my turn," and, "I want to be the leader," and, "It's not fair that she gets new shoes," and "I never get a birthday cake like that." These puffs of anxiety never die out completely. We may no longer squabble and whine as children do, but the unease about status remains: Who deserves more? and Who is loved more? or, Who is noticed more? are questions that we may learn to manage, and ignore, but that rarely disappear without a trace.

There is, however, another very different aspect to a sister's status. The identification among sisters gives rise to pride in a sister's achievements. A sister stands in the limelight, and we, too, feel that our star rises. When I meet Alison for a subsequent interview, she says, "I think about what road I might have taken. I certainly didn't see what I'd be giving up at the time. I didn't see how hard it would be, how risky the whole thing was. But my sisters' families are my families, too, and when I see them with their kids, I think, That's part of me!" And Hilary du Pré, whose memories of her sister mark so many terrors and conflicts in the sister knot, was also her sister's greatest admirer and supporter. Her whirlwind experience of seeing Jacqueline so clearly and completely outstrip her as a musician stood her in good stead. She could be greeted with, "How's that wonderful sister of yours?" without being crushed. The shock of that concert, she writes, "taught me how to enjoy and take part in the overwhelming interest in Jackie."[10] And it also encouraged her to clarify her own abilities and limitations. That vividly rendered experience of the sibling trauma engraved in her the necessary lesson that she must learn to accept and respect herself, even when she knew that her sister was "speeding ahead of me and I couldn't keep up."[11]

11

Sistering: A Lifelong Tie

I N *Blackberry Winter*, Margaret Mead takes a cool look at the sister bond, and notes that childhood squabbles and teenage wariness carry over into adulthood. These shift into rivalries over whose children rank higher in the ever-present and ever-changing hierarchies constructed by siblings. She concludes, however, that *eventually* things turn out okay: "Sisters, while they are growing up, tend to be very rivalrous, and as young mothers, they are given to continual rivalrous comparisons of their several children. But once the children grow up, sisters draw closer together and often, in old age, they become each other's chosen and most happy companions."[1]

My sister and I muse on many things, as any two women

might who exchange a register of references that ramble from infancy to midlife. She catches the shudder I feel when I talk about old age, and knows the range of ghostly anxieties this topic calls up in me. But she, the big sister with the answers, shoos away my dread: "When we're in our nineties, and both widows, we'll live together. We'll read the same books and we'll watch films, and I'll knit and you'll do your stuff and we'll talk and we'll be fine." And, little sister that I am, I'm grateful that she is taking charge. I note as a familiar, comfortable gesture the put-down implied in my "stuff," and enjoy the scenario: Two old women, two sisters, enjoying day-to-day life, keeping up the rhythms of the shared interests they developed in childhood and adolescence. Together we will keep possession of our childhood histories as we negotiate old age.

I no longer feel irritated when I discover that my big sister is right *again*. Her description of what a good old age can be, I learn, is confirmed by research. In a survey of family relationships of the elderly, 75 percent found siblings a primary source of psychological support.[2] And the older the age group, the more important siblings became. Even if they did not see a sibling often, older adults reported great feelings of closeness with siblings.[3] Older people living with siblings were found to have higher morale and greater emotional security. In particular, women living with sisters remained stimulated and challenged in their day-to-day lives.[4] I imagine my older sister telling me to get a grip, make an effort, and stop being such a self-doubting wuss, even at age ninety. She'll make her criticism easier to take because she'll remind me of what I can do. For there are times when I think that no one has greater faith in my abilities or more comprehensive acceptance of my limitations. If I had had more than one sister, I would undoubtedly feel curious about the time the others spent together, would be greedy for news of one from the other, and fret about how the two of them talked about me in my absence. I would want to secure special alliances with each one, and monitor their relative closeness to me and to one another.

The shared world of siblings has a lifelong power. So closely bound is one sister to another that it may never be possible to dissociate oneself psychologically from one's sibling. The relationship, whether welcomed or dreaded, seems inevitable. Its longevity exceeds that of bonds to parents or children.[5] In a sibling we see how closely our pasts hug themselves to our present lives. As Jane Mersky Leder notes, "It doesn't seem to matter how much time has elapsed or how far we've traveled. Our brothers and sisters bring us face to face with our former selves and remind us how intricately bound up we are in each other's lives."[6]

It is hard, now, in middle age, to remember the intensity of the rivalry my sister and I faced, or to remember times when we were less than close. Like most groups of sisters, we went through a phase when we identified intensely with each other, and each watched the other for minute changes in status. As with many sisters, there was a period during which we kept our distance from each other. In very early adulthood, life became so difficult, so barbed with doubts as to the rightness of any choice, that wariness lest the other was making better choices drove a wedge between us.[7] But once we reached our mid-twenties, having survived, somehow, the self-doubts fostered by the education system and the job market, the different paths each took came to represent intriguing possibilities rather than threats to the other. Now my sister's talents and virtues seem to complement mine. She signals what someone who belongs to me can be and achieve. She is an extension of me, not a competitor. So through her, as part of my psychological history as a sister, I have learned what it is to be part of a sisterhood.

At a more basic level we occupied a special space, a family within the family, a world in which what each experienced danced around and bounced off the other. Whether I was suffering a parental scolding or a humiliation in the classroom, I was a sister as much as a single self.

For me, now, it is uncomfortable to focus on the tension within that togetherness, when, as a pair, "either" and "or" shaped our relationship, when what she did and what I did encroached on the other. It was chilling to discover in my research for this book that some sister groups remain frozen in that competitive stance. When later experiences, either within the family or in the broader social environment, bear out the primitive fears awakened in the sibling trauma, then the continuing reruns of ancient competitions infect closeness, and one sister cannot look upon the other without seeing a possible usurper and annihilator. Ann Landers and Abigail Van Buren were twins, born seventeen minutes apart, and each raced for whatever goal the other set her sights on, whether it was playing the violin or marrying a millionaire. Each sister distanced herself from the other, insisting that *she* was the one to triumph.

The two advice columnists cannot salve their wariness of one another. Each lobs her attack on the other's character: While Abby crowed over being the first sister to succeed in the romantic sphere, Ann publicly exposed the dark side of her sister's character: "She's just like a kid who beats a dog until somebody looks, and then she starts petting it."[8] The De Havilland sisters, Olivia and Joan Fontaine, also chose the same career and also remained frozen in competition. Olivia's reluctant reception, at sixteen months of age, of a sister may not be unusual; but this common trauma was compounded by having a sister who also became an actress and an Oscar winner. Each sister remained, throughout adulthood, hypersensitive to the other's success and denigration. Olivia refused to accept her first Oscar (for the aptly titled film *To Each His Own*) when she learned that Joan would be presenting it.[9] Nor could Olivia ever forgive Joan for criticizing her first husband. Even after she divorced the man, her sister's contempt for someone once connected to her remained a grudge-justifying insult.

For some sister pairs, enmity is a matter of pride. The personal or professional status of each continues to feel threatened by that of the other, or the identification between them is so unpleasant, that the childhood squabbles continue. In every case of continuing sister enmity, the real dispute has a triangular form: Will her successes and attributes take away from me the love and admiration I want for myself?

THE COHESIVE TRIANGLE: DEMANDING
SHARED LOYALTIES

THE CARE OF elderly parents opens a new chapter in the sibling saga, with familiar questions taking on a bright new polish. Instead of demanding, Who is loved more? the questions become, Who loves more? and Who cares more?

The kick of these questions is gendered. Not caring as much as another does, not loving enough, are accusations equivalent to the label of "bad woman." Some sisters successfully support each other against the charges, which they know each hears in her own mind, about care and love. "Dorri and I are closer than we've been for a long time," explains Annette. "When Mom started going downhill, I was really tempted not to bring Dorri into it. Dealing with her can be awful. When I call up to tell her something, she gives me all this extra stuff about her life and how I've been really mean to her before. But I finally had to bite the bullet and call, and suddenly we knew how to talk to each other. It takes a load off me to swap news of my mother. We laugh at her; I couldn't do it with anyone else. My kids think I'm terrible when they hear me talking to my sister. But with her I can laugh at what really worries me, and I don't feel I'm being a terrible person.

"My brother's a sweetheart; he's real concerned about Mom, but it never occurs to him how much there is to do. So my sister and I make fun of him, too. He goes down to see her and then forgets to do the yard, or he'll take her out to dinner but forget to make sure she has food in the refrigerator. He says, 'Why are you going down to Mom's again?' and I have to tell him over and over again why someone has to visit at least once a week. My sister says he's as spaced out as Mom."

But sisters do not always work well together in caring for their parents. Felicity and Julia are now helping their parents support each other. Their father cares for their diabetic mother, who is now nearly blind and very weak. Felicity says, "Our dad has always been controlling. But now he is even more difficult to deal with. He calls me five times a day. Sometimes I'm just too busy to do what he wants. Usually he wants some help organizing something. Or he wants to give me the lowdown on Mom. When I don't have any time, I suggest he try phoning Julia. But he says Julia's too busy. 'You know how busy she is. Did you hear the latest on her? A real successful lady, that one.' So I have to help him because I'm not as good as she is? I ask her to step in, do her fair share, but she just tells me I have to understand Dad. *She* doesn't find him difficult. Yeah, here we are, grown women dealing with our pathetic parents, and we're still bickering like children."

In one study of adult siblings, half the families reported conflict over care-giving arrangements.[10] The stresses of taking on new and unpredictable family responsibilities are great, but even while the conflicts made sense within the present context, they can be linked to events that occurred long before caregiving responsibilities became an issue. "Dad's always been more appreciative of you. I do more for him, but he thinks you are doing more," Felicity tells Julia. And Julia says, regretfully, "Felicity blames me for everything Dad does. It's driving a wedge between us. You'd think we were kids again."

Even when a parent dies, the competition for the specially loving or dutiful or caring daughter may continue. Miri and Elizabeth, still in their thirties, are coping with their mother's recent death. "I hated the way Elizabeth bagged the speech at Mom's memorial service. The spotlight was really on her and her grief. I know I've given more pleasure to my mother over the years, me and my children, than Elizabeth has."

The death of their mother has not ended the battles between two successful sister writers as they jostle over their different views, delineated in print, about their mother and about each other. "Why should one love a sister?" Margaret Drabble wonders.[11] The relationship is interesting and complicated and binding, Drabble notes, but does not necessarily—perhaps not even ordinarily—involve love. Drabble's reasoning follows that of Sigmund Freud, who mused, "I do not know why we presuppose that the relation [of children to their brothers and sisters] must be a loving one; for instances of hostility between adult brothers and sisters force themselves upon everyone's experience and we can often establish the fact that the disunity originated in childhood, or has always existed."[12] But the enmity is not now about status in the family; it is about which sister honors the memory of the family more.

The sisters in my study who judged each other to be lacking in family loyalty managed their negative feelings by avoiding each other. "I can't stand seeing her because I don't want to be with someone I feel so close to and who disses the mother I love," said Gill. "Frances should love our mother, but all she does is criticize her. It makes me feel ashamed. Even though it's not me who's being disrespectful, it makes me ashamed." When their mother dies, Gill is stung further by what seem to her unfair legacies: "I keep asking myself: Why did Frances get that summer house? Did Mom really want her to end up with more than me? What was she thinking of? Sometimes I wonder whether Mom loved her more all along. The thought gives me the chills." As Gill goes on to think again, to wonder whether at the time of making the will, some other part of the family estate had been worth more, she marks the continuing question about the quality and quantity of gifts of love.

The rivalries that begin in early childhood do not end there. Recent studies revealed that up to 71 percent of adults report feeling sibling rivalry at some point in their lives, with 45 percent still feeling rivalrous in adulthood.[13] Older adults revealed as much sibling rivalry and conflict as did younger ones. Even after a parent's death, questions about the quality and quantity of a parent's love can be a source of argument. Though most rivalrous siblings seek to repair their relationships by later adulthood and old age, it is clear that rivalry persists into old age.[14] The love and the rivalry endure long after the childhood squabbles are at an end, because siblings inhabit one another's psyche.

At the heart of the sister knot is identification. The sense that Ginny has, of her and her sister Rose being "one another's true selves,"[15] is shaped by the multidimensional understanding that emerges as children grow up together, as girls observe each other within a family, and as women today negotiate a series of choices that impinge on their sense of worth. "She is like me" and "She is part of me" lie at the heart of rivalry ("She will overtake/surpass me") and anxiety ("She may replace/usurp me"); but this identification also gives rise to the love that grows from understanding and empathy. Above all, a girl's and woman's identification with a sister gives each significance to the other. Whatever sisters feel for each other, they are always interested in one another, their lives and their experiences, their level of coping and their level of success. No woman is truly indifferent to a sister's large-scale successes or failures, or indeed, to the small-scale details of her life.

In the sibling bond, hostility does not normally eclipse love, and love is indeed the norm. Sisters have arguments, conflicts, and jealousies, but in the long run they maintain, more than brothers do,[16] close and affectionate relationships. When the relationship is disrupted, sisters show signs of depression, and efforts are made to restore the relationship. Sisters, more than brothers, support each other through the major tasks and events of adulthood: marriage, child rearing, divorce, widowhood, aging, and dying.[17] Even those who went through childhood on almost unbroken terms of enmity with their siblings are ready to stand by them. As Dorri says, "If I died, Annette would take my kids. And I'd trust her with them more than anyone." She then is startled by what she has just said. "I didn't expect that to come out of my mouth. I really didn't expect I'd say that. But what's between us doesn't affect certain things. I know she'd take my kids."

Dorri is stunned by her declaration of trust; but she lights on the bond of care and protection that remains untouched by rivalry: Siblings' genes are carried by one's children, and care for them is as common as is the rivalry that Margaret Mead highlights, over whose children are "better," smarter, more attractive, or more favored by the grandparents they shared. Our deepest bonds are shaped by the needs of those selfish genes; these include sexual attraction, romantic love, the overwhelming force of parental love, and the sibling bond.

SIBLING LOSS AND THE CONTINUING RELATIONSHIP

SISTERING DOES NOT always bring out the best in us, but what we learn from the sister bond is that all close relationships have mixed elements, that envy and resentment are best managed as part of connection rather than as the markers of hate and hatefulness. The wish that a sister die may be common, but one of the most difficult losses to overcome is the death of a sibling.

Shena had just turned forty-one when her older sister Sarah Ann was diagnosed with ovarian cancer. "At first things looked awful, but she had surgery and then she had chemo, and we thought, Well, she'll beat this. She died last June. I feel I'm living both our lives. Everything I do is kind of double. There's me, and now there is Sarah Ann, too. It's hard to say whether she's a great big presence or a great big absence. There's this hole, you know? I see myself getting on with my life, and I'm worried she thinks it's really unfair that I'm still here. Except I guess she isn't here to think anything!

"You know she did a lot of looking after us kids—me and my little brother—when she was still a teenager. And I still depended on her when I was in my twenties. So I wonder whether she resented it. Now I'm still here, and she's not."

When eighteen-year-old Amy spoke of her older sister, who had died three years before, she said, "I feel her inside me. Really, I can tell you where she is. Sort of in my throat? So when I do stuff, I sort of do it double. She's there, always. But I still miss her. I think about her and me. I see how my body's changed. But she hasn't changed. I don't know what that means. Am I older than her now? I still don't get it, how I'm still alive and she isn't."

The remaining sibling has a prevailing sense of being a "survivor" when one sibling dies. The attachment and identification, combined with the guilt, make mourning for a sibling one of the longest-term. The relationship with a sister sets up a lifelong dialogue, and the death of one sibling does not end the survivor's conversation. "It has been said," note the two pioneering psychiatrists who were among the first to document the importance of the sibling bond in the psyche, "that death ends only a life: it does not end a relationship."[18]

FREQUENTLY ASKED QUESTIONS

D URING THE past four years, I have presented a number of lectures and seminars on the sister knot, and of the questions that have been fired at me afterward, the following came up most frequently.

What Can I Do to Protect My Children from the Sibling Trauma?

The "sibling trauma" is an inevitable part of getting to understand the interpersonal world. The realization that others can take our place is not damaging; it is part of learning to live with other people. Without experiencing something like the sibling trauma, children would fail to realize that they have to share the world with other people, that other people can also be loved by those who love them. So it is more worrying to suppose that a child would not confront the sibling trauma. What she learns is crucial to her relationships with peers as well as siblings.

How Can We Overcome the Insecurities That Arise Within the Sibling Trauma?

It is rare that we overcome all anxiety about our place in the world, so I think it helps to understand how basic, and how normal, such insecurities are. We can manage them, however, as we clarify our own abilities and limitations, and as we demonstrate our capacity to make a positive difference to people who matter to us. When we see, in very general terms, what we may be anxious about, we note that there will always be other people who have competing qualities and achievements, but that these will not destroy us or our attachments to others.

Will Understanding the Sister Knot Help Improve Sister Relationships?

Some psychologists believe that the key to change is understanding. I believe, at least, that problems are more bearable when we understand them. When we see glitches in a sister bond as part of our own development, we may be able to put specific clashes into a broader context. It is always helpful to approach a problem from a new perspective. A fresh vision may present us with a new solution.

Do I Have to Resolve My Feelings Toward My Sister to Put to Rest the Anxieties That Arise in the Sister Knot?

Not really. We learn in a variety of contexts that we can

maintain self-respect and earn admiration from others. The family into which we were born may be a welcome source of support throughout life, but we establish other sources of support too. Some people continue to be bothered by old rivalries among their sisters, but have wide-ranging skills in managing questions about competition and self-worth. Sometimes our sisters do not bring out the best in us, but the best nonetheless functions well throughout other areas of our lives.

Why Are You Emphasizing the Sister Knot When You Talk About the Sibling Trauma?

The sister knot is one outcome of the sibling trauma. By following the development of the sibling trauma through the sister knot, we gain a new perspective on many questions raised in female psychology. Many of the themes in the sibling trauma have highly prominent features in the sister knot. They generate new answers to questions as to why the passionate bonds between women friends are characterized by both pleasure and pain, why envy persists, and why the fear of losing love casts a particular shadow over women. These themes are not women's alone, but they are closer to the surface in women's lives, and so looking at how they function among women is the best place to begin framing a new psychology.

Are Boys as Affected by the Sibling Trauma as Girls? Why Do You Focus on Girls?

Both girls and boys experience a sibling trauma, a realization that they are not unique, that someone can replace them in that constellation of personal relationships on which their life depends. Both girls and boys learn how to contain these fears as they secure and develop bonds with parents, as they refine a unique sense of self through contrast and similarity to other family members. They continue to manage their fears of displacement in the schoolroom and the playground, in friendships and at work, as they forge new connections and develop an individual sense of self.

Both girls and boys find safety in connection and feel threatened by loss; but in girls the need for connection and the threat of loss are less deeply buried by cultural demands of independence and toughness. In girls and women, needs for connection and fears of loss tend to be more accessible; so it is by looking at girls and women that we can, at last, gain understanding of their formation.[1]

How Is the Sibling Trauma Expressed Between Sisters and Brothers?

Love and envy between brothers and sisters have many further dimensions of pain, fear, and outrage. The displacement of the sibling trauma here functions on a larger social scale, with multiple reference points. Here there is rage or shame, and a sense of annihilation so deep that it often cannot be spoken. This "defeat" gives rise to protests, from George Eliot to Virginia Woolf, against the burial of a self. The rage and terror of being replaced, and losing one's connections and therefore losing a self, is magnified in a context in which one gender has status over the other. When a brother takes precedence, both in the home and in the wider social world, simply because he is male, the sister has a different challenge.

Here the sibling trauma bites so deeply there is no way out: My brother will be preferred to me, whatever I do, because he is male. Here the sibling trauma joins with a cultural displacement. The family system that sidelines a daughter to put the son at center stage is shaped by a social system that sidelines women to put men center stage. But when gender preference is not an issue, the sister-brother bond may be very comfortable, and less competitive.

How Does a Study of Sisters Change Basic Assumptions About the Psychology of Women?

By looking at the sister knot, we can see how broad-based differences in women's psychology give sistering special features: The empathizing skills in which girls and women are more likely than boys and men to excel, and the personal connections they often give priority to, make sistering easier to see throughout the life span. The close identification between sisters, because they share gender, may also foster greater closeness.

But sistering also highlights aspects of female psychology that have been ignored. In sistering we see that girls grow up learning how to fight with other girls, and that they have daily experience in jostling openly for status, and that they are adept at defending their rights and drawing boundaries between self and other. They share these skills with their brothers, but with very different experiences among friends and in the broader social world, these general human impulses and skills are shaped differently.

The powerful protectiveness in the sister knot challenges the conceptual division between selfishness and altruism.

This love is not "selfless"; the ideals of a selfless love should be redrawn.[2] In the sister knot, too, we can see the inevitable ambivalence we have to negotiate to keep the relationship alive. I believe it is by recognizing the mixed elements in our selves and in our attachments that we can come to an integrated and truthful vision of female bonds in general. The key to sisterhood lies in the understanding of sistering.

Is the Configuration of the Sister Knot Universal?

The only universal statement that holds true in psychology is that no psychological finding is universal. Development, meaning, psychological health, or aberration all occur in a social and cultural context. The sibling trauma and the sister knot are no exception.

In every society, as far as we can imagine, people have to share resources with others. But in contemporary Western societies, especially in what is called "the developed world," prominent values about the importance of being individual and special extend the impact of the sibling trauma. When being unique—and being loved and admired above others—is crucial to a sense of self, then facing another person who is like oneself and who has the capacity to take one's place carries a greater threat than it would in a culture in which the concepts of love and self-worth were not so closely linked to exclusivity.

The sister knot so often takes on the configurations described in this book because girls' and women's relationships develop in a context in which competition and love are seen as incompatible, particularly in female codes of emotional conduct. Their unease at sparring with someone they love changes the shape of the conflict. Brothers, too, feel competitive, but the fact that our society actually *sanctions* the direct expression of this fosters a different configuration of sibling bonds.

Ideals of femininity and masculinity police our behavior and mold our relationships. When cultural expectations are grounded in impossible ideals, the knowledge that we ourselves do not come up to standard, combined with the fantasy that another girl or woman might, heightens the danger that a rival presents. We can expect the sister knot to change as cultural ideals and social resources change.

NOTES

Introduction: Why Sisters?

1 Klein, *Envy and Gratitude.*
2 Mitchell, *Siblings.*
3 Ibid., p. 4
4 The participants lived in two countries, the United Kingdom (Twenty-four: fourteen sisters from the Greater London area and ten from East Anglia) and the United States (eighteen: ten from Chicago, six from New York, and two from Southern California). The range in ethnicity and class is broad and fairly evenly spread across the vast range of so-called working and middle class. The variation in family size and structure should be clear from the sisters' stories: Family structures changed over the course of the sister bond, so labeling a family as headed by a single parent or two parents, whether biological or step, would be misleading.
5 Apter and Josselson, *Best Friends.*
6 Barth, "Introduction," pp. 9–38.
7 Most notably by Gilligan, *In a Different Voice.*
8 See Sulloway, *Born to Rebel,* p. 15.

9 Harris, *The Nurture Assumption*, p. 232.

10 Traeder and Barry, *Girlfriends*.

11 Simmonds, *Odd Girl Out*; Wiseman, *Queen Bees and Wannabes*.

12 Mooney, *I Can't Believe She Did That*.

13 Melanie Mauthner coined the term "sistering."

14 Mauthner, *Sistering* p. 3.

Chapter One: The Power of Complicated Feelings

1 Dunn, *Sisters and Brothers*, p. 17.

2 Cited in ibid., p. 40: Wyndol Furman interviewed a large number of ten to thirteen-year-olds about their relationship with their sibling.

3 Ibid., p. 47

4 Ibid., p. 28.

5 Adler, *What Life Should Mean to You*, p. 115.

6 Sigmund Freud, *Introductory Lectures*, pp. 251–52.

7 Dunn found that usually the aggression and naughtiness are directed, at this early stage, at the mother. *Sisters and Brothers*, p. 19.

8 Ibid., p. 31. Ninety-five percent of the children observed in her study wanted to help with the baby.

9 Mitchell, *Siblings*, p. xv.

Chapter Two: Younger Sisters and Other Variations

1 Willett, *Winner of the National Book Award*, pp. 20–21.

2 See Apter, *Fantasy Literature*, p. 120.

3 Sigmund Freud, *Introductory Lectures*; Fishel, *Sisters*; Dunn, *Sisters and Brothers*, all have this focus.

4 Dunn and Kendrick, *Siblings*, pp. 93–94.

5 Mitchell, *Siblings*, p. 47.

6 Ibid., p. 10.

7 Conley, *The Pecking Order*

8 Ibid., pp. 57–63.

9 Dowling, *The Cinderella Complex*.

10 Bettelheim, *The Uses of Enchantment*.

11 Lévi-Strauss, in Mitchell, *Siblings*, p. ix.

12 Hirsch, "Imagining Sisters."

Chapter Three: The Sister Knot

1 Chodorow, *The Reproduction of Mothering*.

2 Gilligan and Brown, *Meeting at the Crossroads*.

3 Gilligan, *In a Different Voice*.

4 While postnatal depression has been found to have greater long-term impact on boys than on girls, a mother's responsiveness to a newborn seems more likely to disrupt a mother's relationship with an older daughter. See Cooper, Murray, Wilson, and Romaniuk, "Controlled trial," pp. 412–19. See also Dunn and Kendrick, *Siblings*, pp. 200–204.

5 Dunn, *From One Child to Two*, p. 64.

6 Dunn and Kendrick, *Siblings*, pp. 146–47.

7 Mitchell, *Siblings*, p. 3.

8 For an account of blindness to girls and women in established psychological theories see Gilligan, *In a Different Voice*.

9 Dunn, *Sisters and Brothers*, p. 103.

10 Gray, *Women Are from Venus*.

11 Baron-Cohen, *The Essential Difference*.

12 The most significant writers in this field do not make the mistake of thinking that differences are sharp and global. Nancy Chodorow (*The Reproduction of Mothering*) and Carol Gilligan (*In a Different Voice*) emphasize general and subtle differences that overlap between developmental trends in male and female children. But often enough their context-sensitive theories are simplified by others, and it is such simplifications that I aim to correct.

13 Mitchell, *Siblings*, p. 10.

14 Ibid.

15 Quoted in Friday, *Jealousy*, p. 52.

16 Shakespeare, *Othello*, 5.1. 19–20.

17 Cicirelli, "Sibling relationships," pp. 7–20.

18 Sigmund Freud, *The Interpretation of Dreams*, pp. 250–55. Freud

admits that he has known one exception, but "it was easy to interpret this as a confirmation of the rule" (p. 253).

Chapter Four: Shared Minds

1 Bank and Kahn, *The Sibling Bond*, p. 110.
2 Baron-Cohen, *The Essential Difference*, "The female brain is predominantly hard-wired for empathy. The male brain is predominantly hard-wired for understanding and building systems," p. 1.
3 Farmer, *Sisters*, p. 17.
4 Dunn and Kendrik, *Siblings*.
5 Dunn, *The Beginnings of Social Understanding; Sisters and Brothers*.
6 Dunn and Kendrick, *Siblings*, p. 4.
7 Ibid.
8 Ervin-Trip, "Sisters and Brothers," pp. 184–95.
9 Dunn, *Sisters and Brothers*.
10 Stillwell, "Social Relationships," cited in ibid., pp. 43–44.
11 Dunn and Kendrick, *Siblings*, p. 158; Whiting and Whiting, Whiting and Edwards, cited in ibid., p. 158.
12 Stern, *The Interpersonal World of the Infant*.
13 Dunn, *Sisters and Brothers*, p. 6.
14 Friday, *Jealousy*, p. 495.
15 Chodorow, *The Reproduction of Mothering*, p. 67.
16 Gilligan, *In a Different Voice*.
17 Bank and Kahn, *The Sibling Bond*, p. 199.
18 Baron-Cohen, *The Essential Difference*.
19 Apter, *Adult Stories of Sibling Cruelty*.
20 Adcock, "Bluebell Seasons," p. 19.
21 Bank and Kahn, p. 110.
22 Ibid., p. 106–9.
23 Stern, cited in Friday, *Jealousy*, p. 500.
24 Fishel, *Sisters*, p. 21.
25 Bank and Kahn, p. 65.
26 Cicirelli, "Sibling Relationships."
27 Ephron, *Hanging Up*, p. 71–72.

Chapter Five: "Just Like" and "Completely Different"

1 Sulloway, *Born to Rebel*, p. 353.

2 Twins, with the obvious salience of similarity and the need to construct differences, should not be seen as exceptional cases of siblings. They are, as Juliet Mitchell notes, "the extreme instances that highlight the problems, the glories and nightmares of the 'sibling' norm." Mitchell, *Siblings*, p. 224–25.

3 Bank and Kahn, *The Sibling Bond*, p. 12.

4 Schachter and Stone, *Practical Concerns*, cited in Klagsbrun, *Mixed Feelings*, p. 28;

   College students from two- and three-child families were asked to judge whether they were alike or different from their siblings on 13 bipolar personality traits. Judgements of being different from the sibling were regarded as sibling de-identification. "First pairs" (a first born and a second born) showed greater de-identification than "second pairs" (a second born and a third born). Schachter theorized that first pairs should be more rivalrous since they had undiluted competition before the third child arrived; jump pairs would be least rivalrous due to the presence of the intervening sibling. De-identification was viewed as a socially acceptable way of dealing with feelings of rivalry by developing areas of the self that do not compete with the sibling's strong points.

5 Dunn, *Brothers and Sisters*, p. 112.

6 Dunn and Kendrick, *Siblings*, p. 146; Dunn, *Sisters and Brothers*, p. 26.

7 Klagsbrun, *Mixed Feelings*.

8 Apter, *You Don't Really Know Me*.

9 Bank and Kahn, *The Sibling Bond*, p. 42ff.

10 *Diary of Anne Frank*, p. 278.

11 du Pré and du Pré, *A Genius in the Family*.

12 Bank and Kahn, *The Sibling Bond*, p. 144.

13 See chapter 7, "Sisters and Friends."

14 Dunn, *Sisters and Brothers*, p. 124.

15 Ibid.

16 Dunn and Plomin, *Separate Lives*, p. 125.

17 Harris, *The Nurture Assumption*.

18 Tannen, *I Only Say This Because I Love You*, p. 249.

19 Wasserstein, *The Sisters Rosensweig*, p. 95 (2.2).

20 Mitchell, *Siblings*, p. 225.

Chapter Six: Protection and Resentment

1 Cash and Evans, "Brood Reduction," pp. 413–18.

2 Gargett, *The Black Eagle*.

3 Gilmore, Dodrill, and Linley, "Reproduction and Development of the Sand Tiger Shark," pp. 201–25.

4 Mock, *More than Kin*, p. 3.

5 Ibid. So common is it, throughout species, for parents to try to keep the peace among siblings, that the indifference the black eagle parent shows toward the attacks of one chick and the distress of the other has flummoxed naturalists. It is supposed that in this species the parents' acceptance of their offsprings' ferocity and suffering functions like some kind of insurance policy. The parents bet more on the stronger, and turn attention to the weaker chick only if the stronger dies. Or they wait to see if the weaker chick is sufficiently strong to survive the older. Then, as the first-hatched chick grows, it needs less care, each mouthful of food becomes less crucial to its survival; and at this point the parent can transfer investment to the younger chick. See also Pinker, *How the Mind Works*, p. 441.

6 Sulloway, *Born to Rebel*.

7 Prochaska and Prochaska, "Children's Views of the Causes and 'Cures,'" pp. 427–33.

8 Dunn and Munn, "Sibling Quarrels and Maternal Intervention," pp. 583–95.

9 Faber and Mazlish, *Siblings Without Rivalry*, p. 14.

10 Kilner, Madden, and Hauber, "Brood parasitic cowbird nestlings," pp. 877–79.

11 Mock, "More than Kin," p. 3.

12 Dawkins, *The Selfish Gene*.

13 Mock, "More than Kin," p. 53.

14 Pinker, *How the Mind Works.*

15 Ibid., p. 44.

16 Some full siblings share more genes than others. Parents share precisely half of their genes with their offspring: They pass on either one or the other of each of their twenty-three pairs of chromosomes to a child. Siblings are 50 percent similar on average: For each chromosome pair, siblings have a fifty-fifty chance of receiving the same chromosome from each parent. It is likely that the common range of genetic similarity is from 40 to 60 percent. Some twins are identical; and theoretically, nontwin sibs could also be identical; and theoretically it is possible that sibs receive none of the same chromosomes.

17 Mock, "More than Kin," p. 22. When the cost to us in acting, on the one hand, and the likely benefit to the siblings, on the other, do not cancel one another out, then there are broad grounds for anticipating altruistic behavior toward a sibling. The calculation is called Hamilton's Rule and is named after the British biologist W. D. Hamilton. When the mix of relatedness, benefit to recipient, and cost to the donor is greater than zero, altruism can spread; when the risk to the donor, combined with relatedness to the donor and benefit to the recipient, is less than zero, then one might expect nasty behavior even among close kin.

18 Pinker, *How the Mind Works*, p. 431.

19 Weisner and Gallimore, "My Brother's Keeper," pp. 169–90.

20 Minturn and Lambert, *Mothers of Six Cultures.*

21 Kosonen, "Siblings as Providers of Support," pp. 267–79.

22 Apter, *Secret Paths*, p. 186.

23 Edelman, *Motherless Daughters.*

24 Ibid., p. 136

25 Sandler, "Social Support Resources," pp. 41–52.

26 Kosonen, "Siblings as Providers of Support."

27 Freud and Dann, "Experiment in Group Upbringing."

28 Bank, "Remembering and Reinterpreting Sibling Bonds," p. 145.

29 The position of a stepparent is, from the point of view of the selfish gene, far more adversarial than any rivalrous sibling. The stepparent has chosen a mate with regard to her or his own genetic longevity, and any family resources diverted to stepchildren have no benefit to

her or his genes. The arguments against this view are, first, that many stepparents genuinely love their children, and adopting parents do not show significantly more aggression toward children than biological parents. The fact that so many stepparents genuinely love and care for stepchildren is a sign of goodwill and good nature; the fact that adoptive parents behave toward their adopted children just as biological parents do is not an objection to this argument: Parents who adopt know they want a family, and are committed to these children. See Pinker, 1997.

30 Cited in Dunn, *Sisters and Brothers*, p. 118–19.

31 Banks and Kahn, *The Sibling Bond*, p. 269.

32 Taylor, *The Tending Instinct*, cited in Marmot, *The Status Syndrome*, p. 144.

33 Walker, *The Color Purple*, p. 170.

Chapter Seven: Sister and Friends

1 In her study of married women friends, Oliker, "Best Friends and Marriage," found that a quarter of the twenty-one women she spoke to named their sister, rather than their mother or a friend, as their best friend.

2 Rubin, *Just Friends*.

3 O'Connor, *Friendships Between Women*, cited in Mauthner, *Sistering*.

4 Whereas closeness with other relatives—in particular with a mother—also involved friendship, these relationships were more likely to be characterized by practical help, or patterns of comforting regression (such as going home to Mom for pampering). Mauthner, *Sistering*, p. 23.

5 Apter and Josselson, *Best Friends*, p. 21.

6 Orbach and Eichenbaum, *Bittersweet*, pp. 17–18.

7 Minuchin, *Families and Family Therapy*, p. 59.

8 Dunn, *Sisters and Brothers*, p. 113.

9 Coates, *Women Talk*; Tannen, *I Only Say This Because I Love You*.

10 Griffiths, *Adolescent Girls and Their Friends*.

11 Apter and Josselson, *Best Friends*.

12 Lever, "Sex Differences," pp. 478–87.

13 Dunn, *Sisters and Brothers*, p. 103.

14 Harris, *The Nurture Assumption*, p. 167.

15 Thirty percent of sisters, compared to 21 percent of brothers and 17 percent of opposite-sex siblings. Klagsbrun, *Mixed Feelings*, p. 381.

16 For example, see Wiseman, *Queen Bees and Wannabes.*

17 Barash, *Sisters: Devoted or Divided*, p. 192.

18 Mooney, *I Can't Believe She Did That.*

19 Mitchell, *Siblings*, p. 225.

20 Apter and Josselson, *Best Friends.*

21 Ibid., p. 146.

22 Quotes in Farmer, *Sisters*, p. 98.

Chapter Eight: Group Dynamics Among Sisters

1 Lerner, *The Dance of Intimacy.*

2 Lever, "Sex Differences in the Games Children Play," pp. 478–87; Pogrebin, *Among Friends*; Sharabany et al., "Girlfriend, Boyfriend," pp. 800–808.

3 Bank and Kahn, *The Sibling Bond*, p. 50ff.

4 Edelman, *Motherless Daughters.*

5 Smiley, *A Thousand Acres*, p. 332.

Chapter Nine: The Power of Sister Stories

1 Dalal, *The Sisters.*

2 Cited by David Brooks, "Courage in Cancerland," *New York Times*, Nov. 6, 2005. See also Williams, *The Woman at the Washington Zoo.*

3 Drabble, *A Summer Birdcage.*

4 Byatt, *The Game*, pp. 273–74.

5 Farmer, *Sisters*, p. 266.

6 Henley, *Crimes of the Heart.*

Chapter Ten: Success and Insecurity

1 Du Pré and du Pré, *A Genius in the Family*, p. 52.

2 Ibid., p. 53.

3 James, *Principles of Psychology*, pp. 187–90.

4 Botton, *Status Anxiety*, p. 11.

5 Marmot, *The Status Syndrome*.

6 Tannen, *I Only Say This Because I Love You*, p. 248.

7 Freud, *Introductory Lectures on Psycho-Analysis*, pp. 102–4.

8 Walter, "Feel my pain," p. 16.

9 I first interviewed Alison in 1994, and her story is written in *Secret Paths: Women in the New Midlife*.

10 Du Pré, *A Genius in the Family*, p. 53.

11 Ibid.

Chapter Eleven: Sistering

1 Mead, *Blackberry Winter*.

2 Cicirelli, "Sibling Relationships Over the Life Course," p. 115.

3 Ibid. Sixty-five percent reported feeling close or very close, and they also reported being confidants of one another in middle age and old age. (See also Connidis and Davies, "Confidants and Companions," p. 55.)

4 Ibid., p. 63.

5 Sanders, *Sibling Relationships*; also Bank and Kahn, *The Sibling Bond*; Sanders quotes Ross and Milgram, "Important Variables," p. 1–2.

6 Leder, *Brothers and Sisters*.

7 Bedford, "Changing Affect," cited in Cicirelli, "Sibling Relationships Over the Life Course," p. 60, postulated an hourglass effect in sibling relationships in which sibling closeness and interaction decreased in early adulthood and gradually increased from then on.

8 Hitchens, "O Brother, Where Art Thou?" p. 62.

9 Fontaine, *No Bed of Roses*.

10 Matthews and Rosner, "Shared Filial Responsibility," cited in Cicirelli, "Sibling Relationships Over the Life Course," p. 132.

11 Craig, "Margaret Drabble and Antonia Byatt," p. 271.

12 Cited in Dunn, *Sisters and Brothers*, p. 135.

13 Cicirelli, "Sibling Relationships Over the Life Course," p. 56.

14 Bedford, "Changing Affect"; Ross and Milgram, "Important Variables," cited in ibid.

Notes

15 Smiley, *A Thousand Acres.*

16 Cicirelli, "Sibling Relationships Over the Life Course," p. 73.

17 Ibid., p. 74.

18 Bank and Kahn, *The Sibling Bond,* p. 271.

Frequently Asked Questions

1 Gilligan, *The Birth of Pleasure.*

2 For a very different method of arguing a similar point, see ibid.

BIBLIOGRAPHY

Adcock, Fleur. "Bluebell Seasons," in *Sisters: An Anthology*, edited by Penelope Farmer. London: Allen Lane, 1999.

Adler, Alfred. *What Life Should Mean to You*. Edited by Alan Porter. London: Allen Unwin, 1932.

Apter, Terri. "Adult Stories of Sibling Cruelty." Paper presented at a meeting of the London Psychological Society, Tavistock Square, June 5, 2005.

————. *You Don't Really Know Me!* New York: W. W. Norton, 2004

————. *Secret Paths: Women in the New Midlife*. New York: W. W. Norton, 1995.

————. *Altered Loves*. New York: Fawcett-Columbine, 1991.

————. *Fantasy Literature: An Approach to Reality*. London: Macmillan; New York: New York University Press, 1982.

Apter, Terri, and Ruthellen Josselson. *Best Friends: The Pleasures and Perils of Girls' and Women's Friendships*. Crown: New York, 1998.

Bank, Stephen. "Remembering and Reinterpreting Sibling Bonds." In *Children's Sibling Relationships: Developmental and Clinical Issues*, edited by F. Boer and J. Dunn, 139–51. Hillsdale, NJ: Lawrence Erlbaum Associates, 1992.

Bank, Stephen, and Michael Kahn. *The Sibling Bond*. New York: Basic Books, 1982.

Barash, Susan Shapiro. *Sisters: Devoted or Divided*. Bridgewater, NJ: Replica Books, 1994.

Baron-Cohen, Simon. *The Essential Difference: Men, Women and the Extreme Male Brain*. London: Penguin, 2003.

Barth, Fredrik. "Introduction." In *Ethnic Groups and Boundaries*, edited by Fredrik Barth. Boston: Little, Brown, 1969.

Bedford, V. H. "Changing Affect Towards Siblings and the Transition to Old Age." Proceedings of the Second International conference on the Future of Adult Life, Leeuwenhorst, the Netherlands, July 1990.

Bettelheim, Bruno. *The Uses of Enchantment*. New York: Vintage Books, 1989.

Bialosky, Jill. *House Under Snow*. New York: Harcourt, 2002.

Botton, Alain de. *Status Anxiety*. London: Hamish Hamilton/Penguin Books, 2004.

Bowlby, John. *Attachment and Loss*. Vols. 1, 3. London: Hogarth Press/Institute of Psycho-Analysis, 1969, 1980.

Byatt, A. S. *The Game*. New York: Vintage Books, 1992.

Campbell, Anne. *Men, Women and Aggression*. New York: Basic Books, 1993.

Cash, K., and R. M. Evans. "Brood Reduction in the American White Pelican." *Behavioral Ecology and Sociobiology* 18 (1986): 413–18.

Chodorow, Nancy. *The Reproduction of Mothering*. Berkeley: University of California Press, 1978.

Cicirelli, Victor. "Sibling Relationships Over the Life Course." Paper presented at the Forty-Ninth Annual Scientific meeting of the Gerontological Society of America, Atlanta, GA, November 1994.

———. "Sibling Relationships in Cross-Cultural Perspective." *Journal of Marriage and the Family* 56 (1994): 7–20.

———. "Relationship of Siblings to the Elderly Person's Feelings and Concerns." *Journal of Gerontology* 32 (1977): 317–22.

Coates, Jennifer. *Women Talk: Conversation Between Women Friends*. Oxford, England: Basil Blackwell, 1996.

Conley, Dalton. *The Pecking Order: Which Siblings Succeed and Why*. New York: Pantheon Books, 2004.

Connidis, I. A., and L. Davies. "Confidants and Companions in Later Life: The Place of Family and Friends. *Journal of Gerontology: Social Sciences* 45 (1990): 141–49.

Cooper, Peter J., Lynne Murray, Anji Wilson, and Helena Romaniuk. "Controlled Trial of the Short- and Long-Term Effect of Psychological Treatment of Post-Partum Depression: 1. Impact on Maternal Mood." *British Journal of Psychiatry* 182 (2003): 412–19.

Craig, Amanda. "Margaret Drabble and Antonia Byatt." In *Sisters: An Anthology*. London: Allen Lane/Penguin Press, 1999.

Dalal, Nergis. *The Sisters*. Hind Pocket Books, Delhi, 1973.

Dawkins, Richard. *The Selfish Gene*. 2nd Ed. Oxford: Oxford University Press, 1989.

Dilke, Annabel. *The Inheritance*. London: Simon & Schuster UK Ltd., 2004.

Dowling, Colette. *Perfect Women: Hidden Fears of Inadequacy and the Drive to Perform*. New York: HarperCollins, 1989.

———. *The Cinderella Complex*. New York: Summit Books, 1981.

Drabble, Margaret. *A Summer Bird-Cage*. London: Weidenfeld & Nicolson, 1965.

Dunn, Judy. *The Beginnings of Social Understanding*. Oxford: Basil Blackwell, 1988

———. *From One Child to Two*. New York: Ballantine Books, 1995.

———. "Sibling Relationships in Early Childhood. *Child Development* 54 (1983) 787–811.

———. *Sisters and Brothers: The Developing Child*. Cambridge, MA: Harvard University Press, 1985.

Dunn, J., and C. Kendrick. *Siblings: Love, Envy and Understanding*. Cambridge, MA: Harvard University Press, 1982.

Dunn, J., and P. Munn. "Sibling Quarrels and Maternal Intervention: Individual Differences in Understanding and Aggression. *Journal of Child Psychology and Psychiatry and Allied Disciplines* 27, no. 5 (1986): 583–95.

Dunn, Judy, and Robert Plomin. *Separate Lives: Why Siblings Are So Different*. New York: Basic Books, 1990.

Eckert, Penelope. "Cooperative Competition in Adolescent 'Girl Talk.' " *Discourse Processes* 13 (1990):1.

Eichbaum, Luise, and Susie Orbach. *Between Women: Love, Envy and Competition in Women's Friendships*. New York: Penguin Books, 1989.

Edelman, Hope. *Motherless Daughters*. New York: Addison Wesley, 1994.

Eliot, George. *The Mill on the Floss*. New York: Bantam Classics, 1987.

Ephron, Delia. *Hanging Up*. London: Fourth Estate, 1997.

Erikson, Erik. *Childhood and Society*. London: Hogarth Press, 1965.

Evans, Diane. *26a*. London: Chatto and Windus, 2005.

Ervin-Trip, Susan. "Sisters and Brothers." In *Sibling Interaction Across Cultures*, edited by P. G. Zukow. New York: Springer-Verlag, 1989.

Faber, Adele, and Elaine Mazlish. *Siblings Without Rivalry*. London: Sidgwick and Jackson, 1988.

Farmer, Penelope, ed. *Sisters: An Anthology*. London: Allen Lane/Penguin Press, 1999.

Fels, Anna. *Necessary Dreams: Ambition in Women's Changing Lives*. New York: Pantheon, 2004.

Fishel, Elizabeth. *Sisters: Shared Histories, Lifelong Ties*. New York: William Morrow, 1979.

Fontaine, Joan. *No Bed of Roses*. London: W. H. Allen, 1978.

Frank, Anne. *Anne Frank: The Diary of a Young Girl: The Critical Edition*. Prepared by the Netherlands for State Institute for War Documentation. London: Viking, 1989.

Freud, Anna, and Sophie Dann. "An Experiment in Group Upbringing." In *Psychoanalytic Study of the Child*. London: Imago, 1951.

Freud, Sigmund. *The Interpretation of Dreams*. (1900–1901). Vol. 4 of *Standard Edition of the Complete Psychological Works of Sigmund Freud*. Edited and translated by James Strachey. London: Hogarth Press and the Institute of Psycho-Analysis, 1953.

———. *Introductory Lectures on Psycho-analysis*. Translated by Joan Reviere. London: George Allen and Unwin, 1922.

Friday, Nancy. *Jealousy*. London: Collins, 1986.

Gargett, Valerie. *The Black Eagle*. San Francisco: Acorn Books, 1990.

Gilligan, Carol. *The Birth of Pleasure*. New York: Knopf, 2002.

———. *In a Different Voice: Psychological Theory and Women's Development*. Cambridge, MA: Harvard University Press, 1982.

Gilligan, Carol, and Lyn Mickel Brown. *Meeting at the Crossroads*. Cambridge, MA: Harvard University Press, 1992.

Gilligan, James. *Violence.* New York: Vintage, 1997.

Gilmore, R. G., J. W. Dodrill, and P. A. Linley. "Reproduction and Development of the Sand Tiger Shark, *Odontopsis taurus* (Rafinesque)." *Fishery Bulletin* 81 (1983): 201–25.

Goldhill, Simon. "Antigone and the Politics of Sisterhood." 2005.

Goldstein, Rebecca. *The Dark Sister.* New York: Viking Penguin, 1991.

Goodwin, Marjorie Harness. *He-Said-She-Said: Talk as Social Organization Among Black Children.* Bloomington: Indiana University Press, 1991.

Gray, John. *Men Are from Mars, Women Are from Venus.* New York: HarperCollins, 1992.

Griffiths, Vivienne. *Adolescent Girls and Their Friends.* Aldershot, England: Avebury, 1995.

Harris, Judith Rich. *The Nurture Assumption: Why Children Turn Out the Way They Do.* New York: Free Press, 1998.

Hirsch, Pam. "The Fantasy of Having a Sister." Paper presented at the Interdisciplinary workshop on sibling relationships, University of Essex. March 28, 2000.

Hitchens, Christopher. "O Brother, Where Art thou?" *Vanity Fair,* June 2005, p. 62.

Horner, Matina. "Toward an Understanding of Achievement-Related Conflicts in Women." *Journal of Social Issues.* 28 (1972): 157–76.

Jack, Dana Crowly. *Silencing the Self: Women and Depression.* Cambridge, MA: Harvard University Press, 1991.

James, William. *Principles of Psychology.* Reprint, Chicago: Encyclopædia Britannica, 1952.

Kilner, Rebecca, Joah Madden, and Mark Hauber. "Brood Parasitic Cowbirds Use Host Young to Procure Food." *Science* 305 (2004): 877–79.

Klagsbrun, Francine. *Mixed Feelings: Love, Hate, Rivalry and Reconciliation Among Brothers and Sisters.* New York: Bantam Books, 1992.

Klein, Melanie. *Envy and Gratitude.* In *The Writings of Melanie Klein.* London: Hogarth Press, 1957; reprint, Institute of Psycho-Analysis, 1975.

Kosonen, M. "Siblings as Providers of Support and Care During Middle Childhood: Children's Perceptions." *Children and Society* 10 (1996): 267–79.

Lamb, Michael. "The Development of Sibling Relationships in Infancy:

A Short-Term Longitudinal Study." *Child Development* 49 (1978): 1189–96.

Lamb, Michael, and Brian Sutton-Smith, eds. *Sibling Relationships: Their Nature and Significance Across the Lifespan*. Hillsdale, NJ: Erlbaum, 1982.

Lawrence, D. H. *Women in Love*. Everyman's Library edition. New York: Random House, 1992.

Leder, Jane Mersky. *Brothers and Sisters: How They Shape Our Lives*. New York: Ballantine, 1991.

Lerner, Harriet Goldhor. *The Dance of Intimacy*. New York: Harper & Row, 1989.

Lever, Janet. "Sex Differences in the Games Children Play." *Social Problems* 23 (1976): 478–87.

Lévi-Strauss, C. *Structural Anthropology*. New York: Basic Books, 1963.

Marmot, Michael. *The Status Syndrome: How Your Social Standing Directly Affects Your Health and Life Expectancy*. London: Bloomsbury, 2004.

Matthews, S. H., and T. T. Rosner. "Shared Filial Responsibility: The Family as Primary Caregiver." *Journal of Marriage and the Family* 50 (1988): 185–95.

Mauthner, Melanie. *Sistering: Powering and Change in Female Relationships*. Baskingstoke, England: Palgrave Macmillan, 2002.

McAdams, Dan. "Personal Needs and Personal Relationships." In *Handbook of Personal Relationships*. Edited by Steve Duck et al. Chilchester, England: Wiley, 1988.

Mead, Margaret. *Blackberry Winter: My Earlier Years*. New York: William Morrow, 1972.

Michael, Judith. *A Tangled Web*. New York: Pocket Books, 1995.

———. *Deceptions*. New York: Pocket Books, 1994.

Millman, Marcia. *The Perfect Sister: What Draws Us Together, What Drives Us Apart*. New York: Harcourt, Inc., 2004.

Minturn, L., and W. Lambert. *Mothers of Six Cultures*. New York: John Wiley, 1964.

Minuchin, S. *Families and Family Therapy*. London: Tavistock Publications, 1974.

Mitchell, Juliet. *Siblings: Sex and Violence*. Cambridge, England: Polity, 2003.

————. *Mad Men and Medusas: Reclaiming Hysteria and the Effects of Sibling Relations on the Human Condition*. London: Allen Lane/Penguin Press, 2000.

Mock, Douglas. *More than Kin and Less than Kind: The Evolution of Family Conflict*. Cambridge MA: Belknap Press of Harvard University Press, 2004.

Mooney, Nan. *I Can't Believe She Did That: Why Women Betray Other Women at Work*. St. Martin's Press: New York, 2005.

O'Connor, Pat. *Friendships Between Women: A Critical Review*. New York: Guildford Press, 1992.

Oliker, Stacey. *Best Friends and Marriage: Exchange Among Women*. Berkeley: University of California Press, 1989.

Papadopoulos, Renos, and John Byng-Hall, eds. "Towards a Coherent Story of Illness and Loss." Chap. 7 in *Multiple Voices: Narrative in Systemic Family Psychotherapy*. pp. 103–24. London: Gerald Duckworth and Co., 1997.

Pinker, Steven. *How the Mind Works*. New York: W. W. Norton, 1997.

Pogrebin, Letty. *Among Friends: Who We Like, Why We Like Them, and What We Can Do About Them*. New York: McGraw-Hill, 1986.

Prochaska, J., and J. Prochaska. "Children's Views of the Causes and 'Cures' of Sibling Rivalry." *Child Welfare* 64, no. 4 (1985): 427–33.

Rimm, Sylvia, with Sara Rimm-Kaufman and Ilonna Rimm. See Jane Win, *The Rimm Reports on How 1,000 Girls Became Successful Women*. New York: Crown, 1999.

Ross, H. G., and J. I. Milgram. "Important Variables in Adult Sibling Relationships: A Qualitative Study." In *Sibling Relationships: Their Nature and Significance Across the Lifespan*. Edited by Michael Lamb and Brian Sutton-Smith. pp. 225–49. Hillsdale, NJ: Erlbaum, 1982.

Rubin, Lillian. *Just Friends: The Role of Friendship in Our Lives*. New York: Harper & Row, 1985.

Sanders, Robert. *Sibling Relationships: Theory and Issues for Practice*. Basingstoke, England: Macmillan, 2004.

Sandler, I. "Social Support Resources, Stress and Maladjustment of Poor

Children." *American Journal of Community Psychology* 8 (1980): 41–52.

Schachter, Frances Fuchs, and Richard Stone, eds. *Practical Concerns About Siblings: Bridging the Research-Practice Gap.* New York: Haworth Press, 1987.

Schwartz, Christina. *Drowning Ruth.* New York: Doubleday, 2000.

Shakespeare, William. *Othello.* Folger Shakespeare Library; New York: Washington Square Press, 2004.

Sharabany, Ruth, et al. "Girlfriend, Boyfriend: Age and Sex Differences in Intimate Friendship." *Developmental Psychology* 5 (1981): 800–808.

Sheldon, Amy. "Conflict Talk: Sociolinguistic Challenges to Self-Assertion and How Young Girls Meet Them. *Merril Palmer Quarterly* 38 (1992): 95–117.

Simmonds, Rachel. *Odd Girl Out: The Hidden Culture of Aggression in Girls.* New York: Harcourt, Inc., 2002.

Smiley, Jane. *A Thousand Acres.* New York: Knopf, 1991.

Stern, Daniel. *The Interpersonal World of the Infant: A View from Psychoanalysis and Developmental Psychology.* New York: Basic Books, 1985.

Stillwell, Robin. "Social Relationships in Primary School Children as Seen by Children, Mothers and Teachers." PhD diss. University of Cambridge, 1984.

Sulloway, Frank. *Born to Rebel: Birth Order, Family Dynamics, and Creative Lives.* New York: Vintage, 1997.

Tannen, Deborah. *I Only Say This Because I Love You.* New York: Random House. 2001

———. *Talking From Nine to Five: Women and Men at Work.* New York: William Morrow, 1994.

———. *You Just Don't Understand.* New York: William Morrow, 1990.

Tannenbaum, Leora. *Catfight: Rivalries Among Women.* New York: Seven Stories Press, 2002.

Tartt, Donna. *The Little Friend.* London: Bloomsbury, 2002.

Taylor, Shelley. *The Tending Instinct.* New York: Henry Holt and Company, 2002.

Traeder, Tamara, and Carmen Renee Berry. *Girlfriends.* Berkeley: Wildcat Canyon Press, 1995.

Walker, Alice. *The Color Purple*. New York: Harcourt, 1992, reprint edition, p. 170.

Walter, Natasha. "Feel My Pain." *Guardian Review*, May 21, 2005, p. 16.

Wasserstein, Wendy. *The Sisters Rosensweig*. New York: Harcourt Brace and Company, 1993.

Wiseman, Rosalind. *Queen Bees and Wannabes*. New York: Crown Publishers, 2002.

Weisner, T., and R. Gallimore. "My Brother's Keeper: Child and Sibling Caretaking." *Current Anthropology* 18, no. 2 (1977): 169–90.

Whiting, B., and J. W. M Whiting. *Children of Six Cultures*. Cambridge, MA: Harvard University Press, 1975.

Whiting, B., and E. Pope-Edwards. "The Effects of Sex and Modernity on Behavior of Mothers and Children." Report to the Ford Foundation, 1977.

Willett, Jincy. *Winner of the National Book Award: A Novel of Fame, Honor and Really Bad Weather*. New York: St. Martin's, 2003.

Williams, Marjorie. *The Woman in the Washington Zoo: Writings on Politics, Family, and Fate*. New York: Public Affairs, 2005.

INDEX

Index

Index

Index

Index

first-born, 15–25, 27, 48, 76–77, 131–32
frequently asked questions about, 272–77
genetic factors for, 99–100, 129, 131, 141–44,
   172, 174–75, 269–70, 284n–85n
grief and, 11, 15–16, 90, 111–13, 230–36, 254,
   267, 270–71
group dynamics of, 203–18
guilt and, 4, 10, 42, 51–58, 132, 155, 170, 171,
   271
ideal, 192–95, 197–98, 201
identification with, 4–5, 43, 50–51, 55–60,
   63–120, 134, 144–48, 151, 170–71, 182,
   200, 216, 217–18, 237–40, 253–54,
   258–59, 268–71, 282n
imitation of, 43, 69, 75–76, 107–8, 111–13
incest and, 250–51
insecurity of, 237–59
intelligence of, 123–26, 128, 158
jealousy of, 4, 9, 16–20, 21, 24, 28–29, 34, 38,
   41–42, 48–51, 58, 75, 77, 92–93, 111–13,
   150, 159, 187–89, 192, 195–97, 199, 202,
   210–11, 218, 240–44, 253–59
labels for, 123–29, 135–36
as lifelong relationship, 11, 125, 153–55,
   260–71, 287n
love between, 3, 21, 22–24, 46–48, 55–56, 97,
   121–23, 147, 158–61, 170–71, 173,
   176–202, 207–8, 252, 267, 269–71
manipulation and, 12, 17, 44, 75–76, 80, 81–83,
   103–4, 115, 129, 156–57, 169, 201–2, 209,
   222–23, 226–27, 231–32, 266–67
maturity of, 104, 111–13
memories of, 27, 51–56, 68, 81–83, 86–90,
   118–19, 148, 219–36, 245–46, 261, 267
middle, 31–33, 97, 168–69, 212
in midlife, 125, 153–55, 234, 262–63, 287n
moral values of, 22, 31–32, 83–84
as mothers, 36, 60–62, 71, 108–9, 173–75,
   269–70
mothers' relationship with, 13, 33, 86, 91, 94,
   98, 113–16, 121–22, 124, 125, 128, 129,
   151, 166–68, 191, 203–6, 212, 213,
   219–20, 225, 226–27, 232–36, 265–68
mutual support of, 4–6, 9, 12, 15, 23, 55–58,
   60–62, 65–68, 75–76, 80–81, 94–97,
   137–75, 197–202, 207–9, 211, 214,
   215–18, 249, 269–70, 272–73, 276–77
narratives of, 10, 28, 33, 102–3, 120–23,
   126–27, 148, 157–58, 219–36, 245–46
older, 4–7, 8, 9–10, 11, 15–25, 27, 48, 53–55,
   60–62, 64–68, 76–77, 81–83, 92–94, 97,
   104, 106–7, 127–29, 131–32, 146–58,
   164–71, 209, 212–13, 214, 216–17,
   245–47, 260–63, 270–71
pairs of, 203–9, 238, 263–64, 282n
parents' relationship with, 127–31, 203–6,
   265–70
as peers, 7, 9, 11, 103, 179, 180, 184, 272–73

personalities of, 100–120, 129–30, 146–48,
   164–65
physical boundaries set by, 106–7
private language of, 64, 86–90, 176, 180
psychological development of, 8–14, 21–25,
   35, 40–51, 52, 59, 79, 92–93, 99–120, 127,
   133–34, 148, 173–75, 179–80, 270–71,
   273, 276–77
quarrels of, 18–20, 21, 28, 38, 51–55, 84, 85,
   90–94, 116, 140–41, 183–84, 190, 211,
   212–13, 244, 258, 260
research on, 7, 8, 11–14, 21, 23, 25, 31, 42,
   47–48, 71, 72, 77–78, 130, 257, 272–77
resentment of, 7, 9, 10, 23, 44–46, 53–55, 56,
   137–75, 254–59
rivalry of, 6–7, 10–11, 18–24, 27, 41–42, 43,
   95–97, 106–23, 137–75, 178, 179,
   198–202, 204, 209–10, 211, 237–74, 276
in school, 6, 13, 53–55, 87–88, 100, 111–13,
   132, 148–51, 155–56, 168, 176–77, 206,
   224, 231, 246–47, 263, 275
self-identity and, 4–7, 8, 10, 12, 13–25, 27,
   31–32, 38, 41, 43, 44, 46–51, 55–124,
   134–36, 144–48, 151, 170–71, 181–82,
   187–89, 200, 216, 217–18, 224–25,
   231–32, 237–40, 253–54, 258–59, 263,
   268–76, 277, 282n
sexuality and, 93, 120–23, 186, 211, 216–17,
   250–52, 270
shame of, 28–29, 50, 53–55, 59, 100, 111–13,
   148–52, 195–96, 211, 218, 235–36, 263,
   267, 275
social context of, 10, 25, 50–51, 53–55, 56,
   99–100, 102–3, 172, 174, 198–202,
   244–45, 254–59, 263
status of, 7, 31–32, 44, 45, 50–51, 237–59,
   267–68, 276
step-, 33–35, 132
stress of, 140–41, 171–73, 203–6
successful, 10–11, 43, 237–59, 263–64
surrogate, 248, 255
twin, 26–27, 59–60, 102, 119, 182, 263–64, 284
younger, 6–7, 8, 15–32, 53–55, 60–62, 64–68,
   81–83, 92–94, 97, 104, 106–7, 127–29,
   132, 146–58, 164–71, 206, 209, 212–13,
   214, 216–17, 245–47, 260–63, 270–71
Sisters (Fishel), 86
Sisters Rosensweig, The (Wasserstein), 134–35
sleepwalkers, 52
Smiley, Jane, 215–18
social context, 10, 41–46, 50–51, 65, 68–69, 76,
   158, 171, 172, 183–85, 186, 275–77
socialization, 68–69, 184–85
social workers, 156
solidarity, 44, 80–81, 198, 201
sons, 87, 88, 141–42
"sororal alert," 170–71
status, 7, 31–32, 44, 45, 50–51, 237–59, 267–68, 276